THE GREEK–TURKISH CONFLICT IN THE 1990s

Του Γιάννη και της
Γούλης με πολύ
αγάπη
Δ.Κ
18.3.91

The Greek–Turkish Conflict in the 1990s

Domestic and External Influences

Edited by

Dimitri Constas

Professor of International Relations,
Director of the Institute of International Relations,
Panteios University, Greece

M
MACMILLAN

PUBLISHED WITH THE ASSISTANCE
OF THE FRIEDRICH NAUMANN
FOUNDATION, BONN

© Dimitri Constas 1991

All rights reserved. No reproduction, copy or transmission of this publication may be made without written permission.

No paragraph of this publication may be reproduced, copied or transmitted save with written permission or in accordance with the provisions of the Copyright, Designs and Patents Act 1988, or under the terms of any licence permitting limited copying issued by the Copyright Licensing Agency, 33–4 Alfred Place, London WC1E 7DP.

Any person who does any unauthorised act in relation to this publication may be liable to criminal prosecution and civil claims for damages.

First published 1991

Published by
MACMILLAN ACADEMIC AND PROFESSIONAL LTD
Houndmills, Basingstoke, Hampshire RG21 2XS
and London
Companies and representatives
throughout the world

Printed in Great Britain by
WBC Ltd, Bridgend

British Library Cataloguing in Publication Data
The Greek–Turkish conflict in the 1990s:
domestic and external influences.
1. Greece. Foreign relations with Turkey
2. Turkey. Foreign relations with Greece
I. Constas, Dimitri
327.4950561
ISBN 0–333–53927–3

To Xanthi

Contents

List of Tables ix

Acknowledgements x

List of Abbreviations xi

Notes on the Contributors xii

1 Introduction
 Dimitri Constas 1

2 Greek–Turkish Relations in the Post-1974 Period
 Richard Clogg 12

PART I DOMESTIC INFLUENCES ON FOREIGN POLICY

3 Turkey and the 'Davos Process': Experiences and Prospects
 Mehmet Ali Birand 27

4 Greek Political Party Attitudes towards Turkey: 1974–89
 Van Coufoudakis 40

5 Turkey's Relations with Greece: Motives and Interests
 Heinz Kramer 57

6 Linkage Politics Theory and the Greek–Turkish *Rapprochement*
 Geoffrey Pridham 73

Contents

PART II DOMESTIC PERCEPTIONS OF CHALLENGES TO NATIONAL SECURITY

7 Greece's Strategic Doctrine: In Search of Autonomy and Deterrence
   Athanasios Platias   91

8 The Strategic Matrix of the SEM: A Turkish Perspective
   Duygu Sezer   109

PART III SYSTEMIC INFLUENCES ON AN INTRA-ALLIANCE CONFLICT

9 Systemic Influences on a Weak, Aligned State in the Post-1974 Era
   Dimitri Constas   129

10 Greece, Turkey and the Improvement of US–Soviet Relations
   Matthew Evangelista   140

PART IV THIRD PARTIES IN GREEK–TURKISH DISPUTES

11 Third-party Involvement in Greek–Turkish Disputes
   Ronald Meinardus   157

12 US Policy towards Greece and Turkey since 1974
   Helen Laipson   164

13 Soviet Relations with Greece and Turkey: A Systems Perspective
   Robert Cutler   183

14 The EC Factor in the Greece–Turkey–Cyprus Triangle
   Constantine Stephanou and Charalambos Tsardanides   207

Appendices   231

Index   269

List of Tables

1 Defence expenditures as percentage of gross domestic product 121
2 Equipment expenditures as percentage of total defence expenditure 121
3 Deployment of key military equipment by Greece and Turkey 121

Acknowledgements

I wish to express my appreciation to the Friedrich Naumann Foundation of the Federal Republic of Germany for generous financial support, both of the Athens Conference and the publication of this volume. Thanks are also due to Gary Larsen, my research assistant at the Wilson Center for Scholars, Washington, DC, for his contribution to the compilation of the tables included in the Appendices, and my colleague Christos Rozakis for his valuable comments.

Institute of International Relations D.C.
Panteios University, Athens

List of Abbreviations

ABM	anti-ballistic-missile systems
AKEL	Reform Party of the Working People (Cyprus)
CFE	conventional forces in Europe
CSCE	Conference on Security and Co-operation in Europe
DECA	Defence and Economic Co-operation Agreement
EPC	European Political Co-operation (European Community)
FIR	Flight Information Region
ICAO	International Civil Aviation Organisation
ICJ	International Court of Justice
INF	intermediate nuclear forces
IR	international relations
LANDSOUTHEAST	Allied Land Forces Southern Europe (NATO)
NATO	North Atlantic Treaty Organisation
NOTAM	Notice to Airmen
PASOK	Panhellenic Socialist Movement (Greece)
RPP	Republican People's Party (Turkey)
SACEUR	Supreme Allied Commander Europe (NATO)
SDI	Strategic Defense Initiative
SEM	south-east Mediterranean
SEVENATAF	7th Allied Tactical Airforce (NATO)
SIXATAF	6th Allied Tactical Air Force (NATO)
TRNC	Turkish Republic of Northern Cyprus (a self-proclaimed 'state' in Cyprus territory under Turkish military occupation, recognised only by Turkey)
UNCLOS	United Nations Convention on the Law of the Sea
UNIFICYP	United Nations Forces in Cyprus

Notes on the Contributors

Mehmet Ali Birand, one of Turkey's most respected foreign-policy commentators, is the head of the Brussels and Moscow bureaux of the Turkish daily *Milliyet* and producer of *The 32nd Day*, a monthly international news programme on Turkish television. Most of his major books, such as *30 Hot Days* (1975), *Blood Money* (1977), *Turkey and the EEC* (1979), *12 September 04.00 hours* (1983) and *Yes Sir!* (1985), deal with different aspects of Turkey's defence and foreign policies and have been translated into English, Greek and German. He has won 40 prizes for his books, articles and television programmes.

Richard Clogg is an Associate Fellow of St Antony's College, Oxford. He is the author of *A Short History of Modern Greece* (2nd edition London, 1986), *Parties and Elections in Greece: The Search for Legitimacy* (London, 1987) and *Politics and the Academy: Arnold Toynbee and the Koraes Chair* (London, 1986). He has also edited a number of volumes of conference papers and has published numerous articles on aspects of modern Greek history and politics.

Dimitri Constas holds an MA degree from Carleton University, Ottawa, and AM, MALD and Ph.D degrees from the Fletcher School of Law and Diplomacy, Tufts University, Boston, Mass. He is Professor and Director of the Institute of International Relations, Panteios University of Social and Political Sciences, Athens, as well as the President of the Hellenic Society of International Law and International Relations. He was a Robert Schuman, Fulbright and Wilson Fellow at the Woodrow Wilson International Center for Scholars, Washington, DC, and a Visiting Professor at the Department of Political Science, University of British Columbia, Vancouver. He has written or edited several books in the Greek language, and his articles have appeared in books and journals published in Canada, Cyprus, West Germany, Holland and the United States.

Van Coufoudakis is Professor of Political Science and is currently serving as Associate Vice-Chancellor for Academic Affairs at Indiana University–Purdue University at Fort Wayne. He received his Ph.D in political science and his MPA degree from the University of Michigan. He also holds a BA degree from the American University of Beirut. He has written extensively on post-Second World War American foreign policy, and the politics, foreign and defence policies of Greece, Turkey and Cyprus. His work has appeared in books and professional journals published in the United States, England, Belgium, Italy, Greece and Cyprus.

Robert Cutler is a member of the Department of Political Science at Laval University, Quebec, Canada. Trained at the Massachusetts Institute of Technology and the University of Michigan, he has been Research Fellow and Exchange Scholar at universities in the United States, France, Switzerland and the USSR. His work on Soviet foreign policy has been published by *International Affairs*, *Soviet Studies*, *World Politics* and other journals and he has also written on political psychology and nineteenth-century Russian anarchism.

Matthew Evangelista is Assistant Professor of Political Science at the University of Michigan, Ann Arbor. He was educated at Harvard and Cornell Universities and the Pushkin Institute in Moscow and has held fellowships at the Brookings Institution and Stanford University. He is the author of *Innovation and the Arms Race: How the United States and the Soviet Union Develop New Military Technologies* (1988) and numerous articles in journals such as *International Security*, *World Politics* and *International Organisation*.

Heinz Kramer is a member of the research group on 'West European Politics' of Stiftung Wissenschaft und Politik, Ebenhausen, Federal Republic of Germany. He studied economics and political science at the University of Hamburg and the University of Saarbrücken. He holds degrees in economics from the University of Saarbrücken. His main fields of research are political aspects of EC integration process, and relations between Turkey and the EC.

Helen Laipson has been at the Congressional Research Service of the Library of Congress since 1970. Her work has focused on the Arab–Israeli conflict, North Africa, and the Eastern Mediterranean. Prior to joining the CRS, she worked as a Turkish and Greek affairs analyst in the Department of State's Bureau of Intelligence and Research, and from 1986 to 1987 she was detailed to the Policy Planning Staff at the Department of State. She has a BA degree from

Cornell University and an MA from Johns Hopkins School of Advanced International Studies.

Ronald Meinardus studied political science and modern history at the University of Hamburg. His books include *Die Afrikapolitik der Republic Südafrika* (1981) and *Die Türkei-Politik Griechenlands* (1985) and he has contributed to German scientific journals on the Cyprus issue, Greek–Turkish affairs and Greek domestic policy.

Athanasios Platias is an Assistant Professor of Strategic Studies at Panteios University, Athens. He holds a Ph.D from the Department of Government, Cornell University (1986). He has been a Ford Foundation Fellow at the Center for Science and International Affairs, Harvard University, a Research Fellow at the Peace Studies Program, Cornell University and a SSRC–MacArthur Fellow in International Peace and Security at MIT's Program in Science, Technology and International Security.

Geoffrey Pridham is a Reader in European Politics and Director of the Center for Mediterranean Studies, University of Bristol. His publications include *Transnational Party Cooperation and European Integration* (1981); *The New Mediterranean Democracies: Regime Transition in Spain, Greece and Portugal* (editor, 1984); *Coalitional Behavior in Theory and Practices: An Inductive Model for Western Europe* (editor, 1986); *Political Parties and Coalitional Behavior in Italy* (1988); *Securing Democracy: Political Parties and Regime Consolidation in Southern Europe* (editor, 1990); and *Encouraging Democracy: The International Context of Democratic Transition in Southern Europe* (editor, forthcoming).

Duygu Sezer is Professor of International Relations at Bilkent University, Ankara. She was a Visiting Professor at the School of International Affairs, Columbia University. Her publications include *Turkey's Security Policies* and various articles in learned journals.

Constantine Stephanou studied law and international relations and earned his Ph.D degree at the University of Thessaloniki. He is Assistant Professor of International Institutions at Panteios University, Athens, and Visiting Professor at the Universities of Nice and Grenoble. He is also Director of the Greek Centre of European Studies and Research, and General Secretary of the Hellenic University Association of European Studies. He has written and edited numerous books and articles on EC affairs.

Charalambos Tsardanides was educated at the University of Athens, Department of Political Science, and at the University of London, London School of Economics and Political Science, where he earned his Ph.D. He is currently Assistant Professor of International Relations at Panteios University, Athens and a Research Associate at the Foundation of Mediterranean Studies, Athens. He is the author of *The Politics of the EC–Cyprus Association Agreement: 1972–1983* (1988).

1 Introduction
DIMITRI CONSTAS

The Greek–Turkish rivalry reappeared in the arena of interstate politics in the middle 1950s, after a thirty-year interlude, as a result of the Cyprus problem. The creation, in 1960, of the Republic of Cyprus, following negotiations that established three guarantor powers (the United Kingdom, Greece and Turkey) of Cyprus's independence, did not prove a lasting solution. For almost fifteen years, prudent national leadership and/or foreign – American – 'vigilance' prevented escalation of the problem of Cyprus's ethnic conflict and strategic alignment into a war between two NATO allies. But in the summer of 1974 both restraints were absent and the disaster occurred: the Turkish military, reacting to a *coup d'état* staged by officers of the Greek dictatorial regime against President Makarios of Cyprus, invaded the island and occupied close to 40 per cent of its territory. Their continued presence there, as well as the unilateral declaration of the TRNC have evolved into a major issue of conflict between Greece and Turkey.

These events completely altered established modes of interaction in bilateral relations between the two countries. The use of force for the advancement of national objectives at the expense of the other side, and the creation of a *fait accompli* by such means, left an indelible mark on perceptions and behaviour patterns. As side-effects of the 1974 crisis other issues involving conflicting claims of sovereignty over the continental shelf, sea and air regions of the Aegean or functions entrusted to either state by NATO emerged, for the first time, as serious items of dispute and created tension with no parallel in the recent history of the two actors.

In the years after 1974, the Greek–Turkish conflict followed its own course in a relatively stable international environment and was only marginally affected by the advent to power, in both countries, of governments with divergent political philosophies. Periods of high tension, like those of 1974, 1976, 1983 and 1987, were succeeded by interludes of relative stability and *détente*. Today, sixteen years after the events of 1974, the views of the political élites of the two countries remain far apart as regards the items to be included in the agenda of negotiations, the methods for the settlement of the disputes and, of course, substantive solutions of the problems involved.

Compared to other interstate disputes, the Greek–Turkish case has rarely become the focus of world public opinion. There have been two principal exceptions to this rule, both occurring within the last four years. In March 1987 a crisis over oil exploration rights in the Aegean brought the two countries close to war. This was followed by an equally dramatic *rapprochement*, culminating in the meeting of premiers Papandreou and Ozal in Davos, Switzerland in January 1988 and the latter's official visit to Athens five months later. Throughout this period Greek and Turkish jets kept engaging, on an almost weekly basis, in 'dogfights' over disputed parts of the Aegean and the prospect of an outbreak of hostilities remains plausible even today.

Tension in bilateral relations is just one aspect of the dispute. Over the years, Greek–Turkish differences spilled over and disrupted the functions of a number of international organisations, global but especially regional, NATO and the European Community being the most representative cases in point. These problems, however, remain the domain of the foreign policy élites in the countries and institutions concerned, rarely attracting the attention of the broad public outside Greece and Turkey. One reason, among others, accounting for this is the approach adopted by Greek Cypriots, with the consent of Greek governments, to find solutions to the Cyprus problem through international organisations and avoid violent means of gaining the attention of world public opinion such as the use of international terrorism typical of the Arab–Israeli conflict.

The fact that the Greek–Turkish conflict seldom takes forms visible to a wider audience is just one explanation for the limited coverage it receives from the international mass media. A second explanation may be ascribed to the broadly shared perception that this is a 'manageable' conflict and, therefore, susceptible to collective (NATO) or hegemonic (US) involvement.

This latter explanation could also account for the minimal interest the dispute has roused among the international relations community of scholars outside the two countries.[1] The dominant view is that IR theory has little to gain from the analysis of a 'special case', intra-bloc conflict, bearing few resemblances to other international disputes. It is this particular perception that has alienated IR generalists and rendered the rivalry into a preoccupation of, exclusively, area specialists. At the same time, the vigour with which both countries have launched their 'public relations' campaigns – with primary targets the US Congress, the European Parliament and the Consultative Assembly of the Council of Europe – and the often heated debates among their supporters have reinforced this trend.

Another feature of the manner in which scholars have treated this conflict is the excessive emphasis they have placed on the predominance of the international environment among the factors influencing Greek and Turkish decision-makers. This stems in part from the fact that in most of the literature the subject is analysed at the regional and, occasionally, the international system levels, focusing on each country's strategic displacement as assessed by the United States or other NATO partners, estimates of damage caused by the dispute to the West, the role of the two rivals in regional politics and their ability to draw support for their policies from the United States, western Europe or the Middle East. Greece, as the weaker of the two, is more likely to be presented at the mercy of fluctuations in power configurations in her external environment. Such perceptions are coupled with an equally strong conviction that domestic influences on foreign policy formulation are either insignificant or too intricate and Byzantine to merit separate, in-depth analysis.

The quest for theory and a more elaborate treatment of domestic factors influencing bilateral interaction has inspired the structure and, to a degree, the content of this volume. Most contributors were participants in a unique event: a three-day Conference on Greek–Turkish Relations organised by the Institute of International Relations, Panteios University, Athens (3–5 March 1989), the first such university-sponsored meeting open to the public to take place in either country. Three others – Robert Cutler, Van Coufoudakis and Helen Laipson – were invited, at a later stage, to make contributions on aspects of the conflict that were not sufficiently explored in the conference.

Richard Clogg provides an insight into the historical background of the current relationship between the two countries and defines the main dispute areas as they evolved after the Cyprus crisis. He predicts no major breakthrough in the deadlock since it appears that in the past the two countries have moved to settle their differences only at times of imminent, common external threat.

The review of the domestic environments begins with **Ali Birand** who discusses the attitudes of Turkey's major political parties toward the bilateral differences with Greece, placing special emphasis on the leader of the Motherland Party, Turgut Ozal – the then prime minister and now president of the Republic – and his personal battle for the transformation of the long-established perceptions and policies in this area. Although most of Birand's analysis focuses on the political leadership, he recognises as major obstacles to the implementation of such 'personalist' policies, the opposition by foreign policy élites and collectively shared images. Birand, like Clogg, sees no imminent breakthrough, not on the grounds of lack of external pressure, but because of Turkish domestic political instability.

Van Coufoudakis compares the foreign policy of Greece's two major parties: the conservative New Democracy and the socialist PASOK. He argues that despite differences in style, both parties demonstrated, after coming to power, remarkable continuity in handling core foreign policy questions. (This consensus in foreign policy towards Turkey was even more evident with the ecumenical government of conservatives, socialists and communists of November 1989 to April 1990.) This is particularly striking in the case of PASOK whose radical platform, as an opposition party, posed formidable ideological restraints to foreign policy making. Most spectacular among several adjustments to PASOK's original positions was the decision taken, in the aftermath of the March 1987 crisis, to engage in high-level negotiations with Turkey while the latter's troops remained in Cyprus. He concludes that the post-1974 cycle of confrontation–negotiation–confrontation is likely to continue given the number and significance of issues dividing the two countries.

Heinz Kramer examines the evolution of Turkey's policies towards Greece in the context of her broader foreign-policy orientation, placing on an equal footing psychological-perceptual and 'real world'-operative factors. He argues that given the prevalent national consensus on the fundamental principles guiding Turkish foreign policy, any government in Ankara engaging in meaningful negotiations with Greece would run serious risks unless it could prove that concessions on sensitive issues were balanced by substantial trade-offs.

Geoffrey Pridham addresses the post-1987 Greek–Turkish *rapprochement* from the theoretical perspective of linkage politics, stressing the interaction between the international environment and the domestic political scene. He underlines that the eventual slow down of the *rapprochement* process was the result of domestic constraints that undermined the initiatives of the principal decision-makers in the two countries. Such constraints were more evident on the Greek side since 'Davos' implied a spectacular turn of policy, although constraints placed on Ozal by the diplomatic and military apparatus considerably reduced his diplomatic manoeuvrabilitiy.

The next two contributions explore – from a national perspective – challenges to security emanating from the 'other side', the regional or the global context. **Athanasios Platias** focuses on the national level. He discusses Greece's strategic doctrine and specifies the main elements of the 'Turkish threat' as well as other factors accentuating Greece's insecurity. He subsequently defines four different types of deterrence associated with Greek security doctrine and, apart from military remedies, he analyses political strategies that could attain foreign policy objectives by 'reducing the risk of war' rather than 'increasing the cost of attack'.

Duygu Sezer investigates the Turkish view of the strategic milieu of the south-east Mediterranean at three levels: East–West, regional and local. She argues that dramatic developments in the first two levels should not distract attention from the fact that, in a final analysis, it is the nature and pattern of interaction between Greece, Turkey and Cyprus – that is, the local level – 'that makes, in a more immediate sense a direct imprint on the SEM strategic scene'. Despite criticisms, the Davos meeting set in motion a conciliatory process that should be given a chance to address the issues. In her conclusions she makes the point that the ultimate challenge for local actors in the SEM would be 'to resist pressures to take advantage of the new found freedom offered by the erosion of alliance discipline and loyalty'.

The rest of the book looks at the conflict from an international/external perspective and is divided into two parts. The first examines the effect of changes in the international system on the external balancing capabilities of the two rivals and in extending opportunities for confidence-building measures. In his contribution, **Dimitri Constas** examines the international system as a potential source of strength to a state that is 'weak', 'aligned' and 'threatened by an ally', that is, an international actor resembling Greece. He suggests that the fluctuations of tension in times of bipolarity will have only a marginal effect on that type of state whose chances of drawing from within or outside the alliance resources to redress an intra-bloc power assymetry remain meagre under both tension and *détente*. However, the outlook becomes less gloomy once the problem is removed from the context of political/military bipolarity and economic, technological, raw material and other aspects of national power are taken into account.

Matthew Evangelista contends that neither IR theory nor past experience of US–Soviet relations supports the thesis that reduction of global tensions will benefit a conflict of the Greek–Turkish variety. But he discerns an opportunity to that effect in the adoption, by the two rivals, of armed forces restructuring measures currently discussed or already agreed upon at the East–West level. He argues that the reduction of offensive capabilities and the reorientation of Greek and Turkish armed forces toward territorial defence would give a boost to domestic proponents of *détente* by minimising threat perceptions and enemy images.

The second section reviews the policies of the two superpowers and the European Community toward the Greek–Turkish dispute. **Ronald Meinardus** examines the tactics used by both countries in eliciting US, NATO and EC support for their positions on the Cyprus problem and their bilateral differences. He claims that increasing EC influence in the SEM would inevitably foster a more energetic Community role that he hopes will prove more constructive than the role played heretofore by the United States and NATO.

Helen Laipson analyses US policies toward the Greece–Turkey–Cyprus triangle both thematically and chronologically by pointing out broader trends in American foreign and domestic policies that have contributed to specific actions. By examining where policy toward Greece and Turkey fits such general trends she tries to anticipate the impact on US policies of the current dramatic changes in East–West relations. She suggests that the expected downgrading of the strategic value for the West of Greece and Turkey would be a challenge for their supporters in Congress and the administration 'to conceptualise the US stake in these two countries with a new vocabulary'.

Robert Cutler looks into the history of Greek–Turkish relations with the Soviet Union and Imperial Russia under different international systems as evolved since 1713 and generates a set of propositions associating specific changes in the international environment with changes in state behaviour. He then 'tests' these propositions against the background of post-1974 politics among these actors, drawing indications for future patterns of interaction. His final conclusions underline the greater importance of Turkish territory for the Soviet Union compared with that of Greece. He suggests, however, a modification of this general projection in order to take into account that Turkish–Soviet differences could be managed but not resolved and that in time 'Soviet policy in the region will increase its attention to Greece'.

Finally, **Constantine Stephanou** and **Charalambos Tsardanides** treat separately EC policies toward the Cyprus problem and bilateral Greek–Turkish dispute items. They give little credit to Greece's role in the Community for the deterioration of the EC–Turkey relationship, which they attribute to the generals' coup of September 1980, and subsequently to the immediate recognition by Turkey of the establishment, in 1983, of the TRNC. Unwieldy obstacles of an economic and social nature have eroded support for Turkey's application for admission, which was submitted in 1987. But the Greek factor could become important once other barriers to closer Turkish ties with the Community are removed.

Two tables have been placed in the Appendices: a chronology of major events connected with Greek–Turkish relations and the Cyprus problem (1974–88) and an agenda of Greek–Turkish disputes. They were both compiled by the editor who alone is responsible for the selection and accuracy of the data presented therein. The reader is encouraged to peruse these tables as they provide a concise event and issue panorama of the conflict essential to understanding the more specialised readings in the volume.

The majority of the authors express guarded optimism as regards the effects of the 'Davos experiment' upon the psychological environment of both countries' foreign policy élites and general public opinion. However, subsequent developments have shown that the softening of enemy and threat stereotypes cannot have a lasting impact unless other conditions are met. The record (see Appendix 1) establishes some correlation between 'political stability', meaning primarily the exercise of power by strong, enduring governments in *both* countries and the launching of bold *rapprochement* initiatives. This is particularly pertinent for Turkey where – unlike, pre-1989, Greece – governments were often formed by coalitions of political parties with divergent political–ideological orientations, which, weakened by fragile majorities in parliament, were unable to deviate from bureaucracy and army dogma as regards Greece.

Domestic government stability alone is not sufficient however. An equally essential factor is leadership receptive to external inputs in the formulation of foreign policy objectives and able to overcome party and bureaucratic sclerosis hindering their implementation. The consent given by the Turkish generals in 1980 to the re-entry of Greece into NATO and the various unorthodox steps taken by Papandreou and Ozal are cases in point.

The importance of external incentives in stimulating flexible approaches to bilateral disputes is a function of both the rigidity of domestic values and perceptions as well as of size, geographical position and dependencies from abroad. Turkey, the stronger of the two rivals, is at the same time the less vulnerable to external influences/pressures and the one more at ease with the existing status quo in the major conflict area, namely Cyprus.

One should note at this point that the distinction 'domestic/external' is blurred when it comes to both countries' interaction with their compatriots in that island given the dual capacity of Greek and Turkish Cypriots as 'unofficial' participants in the foreign policy formulation apparatus and principal objectives of that policy. This is crucial with regard to the Turkish Cypriots, whose leader, R. Denktash, an ardent supporter of the status quo in the island, has managed to acquire considerable autonomy within Turkey's political scene despite 'the leverage that the latter derives from its military presence and economic subsidies'.[2]

In times of rapid change, accurate prediction of the evolution and interaction of these three sets of variables – 'domestic government stability', 'powerful and innovative principal decision-makers' in both countries plus 'constructive external influences' – is fraught with difficulty. Nevertheless, in the light of current developments in Greece, the future of single-party governments and charismatic leadership is questionable, while in Turkey, Ozal's ascent to the presidency left the arena of everyday politics open to politicians of lesser stature and more traditional operational codes. On the other hand, the fact that the two protagonists in the Davos experiment remain important actors in domestic politics and apparent public satisfaction with the more relaxed state of bilateral affairs in the post-Davos era could deter destabilizing moves emanating from that level.

The latter assumption brings to the forefront the international environment and its disruptive or constructive potential. To identify concrete effects on the Greek–Turkish conflict of an international system undergoing rapid and drastic transformation is an intriguing but rather futile undertaking. One can only trace in the current state of world affairs the beginning of certain trends whose consolidation could make more or less conflictual the present patterns of interaction between the two neighbouring countries.

One such trend is, as Richard Clogg suggests, the further erosion of perceptions of a common external threat, a result of 'the remarkable transformation that has taken place in East–West relations'. Unlike the past, where the fading of such perceptions was a result of improved relations with the Soviet Union that enhanced each country's external balancing capabilities and intra-alliance freedom of action, this time the erosion originates from a broadly shared view that prospects for Soviet aggression in the SEM, or elsewhere in the world, are very remote indeed, and that the Western alliance should adjust its policies and strategies accordingly. Should such views be substantiated, incentives for alliance or hegemonic interference to prevent deliberate or accidental outbreak of hostilities will decrease. Unilateral intervention by one or more concerned great powers can hardly be deemed a substitute.

It appears that the upsurge of nationalist tension and territorial conflicts is the price for the decline of bipolarity and cold war politics in Europe and the world. The Greek–Turkish conflict, once viewed as a rare remnant of the territorial disputes of the past, is now overshadowed by a chain of eruptions of nationalism within state frontiers, in most cases those of members of the Eastern Bloc, threatening to spill over into the arena of interstate politics. Soviet Transcaucasia and the Balkans are the latest additions to the list of turbulent regions of the world.

Amidst this international and regional environment, Greece and Turkey could find few common interests to substitute for their fading NATO allegiance and collective security goals. The Balkans, where decades of bipolarity and authoritarian domestic regimes had frozen ethnic minority questions, has now become the main field of interaction for Greece, Turkey and their neighbours. Greece, concerned over its Muslim minority in the northern part of the country, close to the Greek–Turkish border, would have grounds to withstand domestic nationalist pressure to put forward territorial claims against, for example, southern Albania (northern Epirus) to protect the religious and linguistic freedoms of the Greek community there and, in general, to become enmeshed in frontier delimitation questions. Turkey, on the other hand, whose minority trouble-spots are located in the Kurdish regions, far away from the Balkans, has no such inhibitions and could well emerge as a revisionist force in that area. Turkey, by endorsing in the future demands by ethnic Turks in Greece and

Bulgaria for autonomy or self-determination, could pacify domestic religious or Pan-Turkish forces or extract concessions on bilateral issues from the countries concerned.³

Finally, as the recent Opinion of the Commission of the EC on the question of Turkish membership shows, the needs of the post-1992 single European market, the spectacular changes occurring in eastern Europe and the new era in East–West relations might reduce European interest in closer association, in the near future, with that country. It is premature, at this stage, to discern in current EC attitudes the elements of a long-lasting policy. Assuming, however, that this is indeed the case, the repercussions on the Greek–Turkish conflict will be negative. The prospect of closer Community ties, besides presenting the political leadership of Turkey with incentives for reconciliation with Greece, at the same time strengthens the forces of modernisation and secularism and encourages political stability, that is those prerequisites for foreign policy-making enjoying public support and keeping within the established norms of international behaviour.

In short, only two assumptions could shed some light of optimism on to the otherwise gloomy picture projected by the situation in the domestic and external environments of the Greek–Turkish conflict. First, there is no alternative for Turkey but to continue efforts for closer ties with a European Community that is assuming the status of a major pole of world economic and political power. Secondly, the current apparent decline of EC interest in Turkey and the European south could be reversed once the rhythm of change and convergence with eastern Europe slows down. Data supporting the first of the two assumptions are more readily available than for the second. In any case, to keep alive the hope for the future has a value of its own matching that of measurable evidence.

NOTES

1. The last single volume on the subject, in the English language, was produced six years ago: J. Alford (ed.), *Greece and Turkey: Adversity in Alliance* (Aldershot: Gower House, 1984).
2. Richard N. Haas, 'Cyprus: Moving Beyond Solution?', *The Washington Quarterly*, vol. 10, no. 2 (Spring 1987) pp. 183–190, 187. Denktash concerned over the prospect of being bypassed in the context of the

'Davos process', made his presence felt when it counted. So on 15 April 1988, a few weeks prior to Ozal's visit to Athens, he announced that in the future he will require the presentation and stamping of passports as a condition for entering his 'state': J. Randal, 'The Cyprus Issue to Test Athens–Ankara Détente', *The Washington Post*, 5 July 1988, p. A12. On Denktash's views on the Cyprus problem, see his book *The Cyprus Triangle* (London: Allen & Unwin, 1982).
3. In late 1989, Denktash, with the apparent consent of Ankara, admitted to 'TRNC' a few families of Muslim refugees from Bulgaria and threatened a massive transfer of others unless a visit by Cypriot President Vassiliou to Sofia was cancelled and Greece moderated its pro-Bulgarian position in western fora. Of course, the latter demand was not met but an excuse was found to postpone the Vassiliou visit.

2 Greek–Turkish Relations in the Post-1974 Period
RICHARD CLOGG

Before I begin my presentation on the evolution of Greek–Turkish relations since 1974 I should like to make one general observation. One sometimes encounters, among diplomats and policy-makers, who look at the Greek–Turkish conflict from the outside, patronising attitudes of the 'Greeks and Turks are condemned by geography to be good neighbours' variety, coupled with an implicit assumption that all that is needed for a resolution of the conflict is for the application of common sense, goodwill and a proper understanding of common interests. But situations of ethnic conflict are far too complex for such simplistic notions as I, coming from the United Kingdom, am all too aware, given the intractable nature of the conflict in Northern Ireland. So I trust that whatever I say can be absolved from the charge of being patronising. It is perhaps because I am by training an historian that I am very aware that when geography and history come into conflict, history tends to prevail.

Because the burden of the past weighs so heavily over the current conflict it is essential, however briefly, to sketch in something of the prehistory of the confrontation between Greece and Turkey at the time of the Turkish invasion of Cyprus in the summer of 1974 with which my presentation formally commences.[1] It is, of course, a truism to say that Greece's very existence as an independent state arose out of a war of national liberation against the Ottoman Turks, while the Turkish republic had its genesis in the Greek–Turkish war of 1919–22. Just as the Greeks celebrate their (partial) liberation from the Turks on 25 March, the day that is held to mark the outbreak of the Greek war of independence, so on 30 August each year the Turks mark Mustafa Kemal Ataturk's victory over the Greeks in 1922 during Turkey's war of independence. The protracted process, lasting over a century, by which Greece achieved her present boundaries inevitably involved conflict with the Turks, while the crushing defeat of the Greek campaign in Asia Minor and the ensuing exchange of populations in 1923–4 necessarily presaged a poor climate in relations between the two countries.

Within a remarkably short time, however, the statesmanship of Eleftherios Venizelos brought about, through the Ankara Convention of 1930, a dramatic improvement in relations between the two countries, but this *rapprochement* was achieved only by considerable concessions on the Greek side. Moreover, actions such as the Varlik Vergisi, the confiscatory tax imposed by the Turkish authorities in 1942 and purportedly directed against war profiteers, but which bore quite disproportionately heavily on minorities, added to the remembrance of past wrongs, real or imagined, suffered by the Greeks at the hands of the Turks.[2] The immediate post-war period, however, was something of a golden age from the point of view of the Greek minority in Turkey, while the emergence of the Cold War, with both countries under threat, or perceiving themselves to be, from the Soviet Union and/or its satellites, led to close political co-operation between the two countries, to the entry of both into the NATO alliance in 1952 and to the formation of the short-lived Balkan Pact of 1953. The Greek prime minister of the day, Nikolaos Plastiras, even floated the idea of a Greek–Turkish union. But, as demands for the *enosis*, or union, of Cyprus with Greece during the 1950s became ever more insistent, this brief honeymoon in Greek–Turkish relations ended abruptly with the anti-Greek riots of 1955 in Istanbul. A short-lived climate of relative *détente* between the two countries was ushered in by the Zurich and London agreements of 1959, which prepared the way for the independence of Cyprus, when, by all the criteria of national self-determination, the outcome should have been *enosis*.

In parenthesis, I should like to draw attention to a fact hitherto unknown to me, namely that the Greek government in the late 1950s was prepared to consider the possibility of an exchange of populations between the Greek minority of Istanbul and the Turkish minority on Cyprus. The proposal foundered, however, over Turkish insistence that only an exchange involving the Greeks of Turkey and the Turks of western Thrace could be considered.[3]

The uneasy *détente* of the early 1960s was soon to collapse in 1963, with the breakdown of the 1960 Cyprus constitution, rightly described by one British authority as a 'tragic and occasionally an almost ludicrous document',[4] and the outbreak of inter-communal fighting on the island. Turkish military intervention in Cyprus in 1964 was only narrowly averted by a stern injunction on the part of President Johnson against the use of American-supplied weapons for such a purpose. From this time onwards, both Greek and Turkish defence policies for the first time in the post-war period took account of the possibility of outright war between the two countries, while the situation of the Greek minority in Turkey sharply deteriorated. (From a population of some 90 000 in 1955, the Greek community in Istanbul – together with Imvroz and Tenedos – declined to approximately 3000 in 1989.)[5] The possibility of such an armed confrontation became perilously close a few months after the military junta seized power in Greece in 1967 and was only resolved by a humiliating climb-down by the junta, involving the withdrawal of the large numbers of Greek troops infiltrated on the island in excess of the 950 permitted by the 1960 settlement. It was not to be long, however, before Colonel Papadopoulos, the leader of the Greek junta, was to be declaring himself in favour of a Greek–Turkish federation.[6]

If Greek–Turkish relations recovered quickly from the *débâcle* of November 1967, relations between Athens and Nicosia steadily worsened as President Makarios resisted the strident demands emerging from the junta that Greece be recognised as the 'national centre' of Hellenism. Strictly bilateral relations between Greece and Turkey, moreover, were to deteriorate sharply in 1973. The conjunction of the world-wide energy crisis and the discovery of oil in commercially exploitable quantities off the island of Thasos prompted the Turkish government, in November 1973, to issue licences to the state-owned Turkiye Petrolleri Anonim Ortakligi to conduct exploratory soundings in the vicinity of the islands of Lemnos, Mytilini and Chios, in international waters but in a region that Greece regarded as constituting part of her continental shelf. The Turkish plans envisaged the establishment of exploratory drilling rigs, which would be surrounded by a 500-metre safety zone maintained by Turkish naval vessels.

In February 1974, the Greek government, still of course under military control, although Colonel Papadopoulos had been ousted from power the previous November by Brigadier Ioannidis, made a formal protest to Ankara, stressing that the areas marked out for exploration by Turkey formed part of the Greek continental shelf under the terms of the 1958 Geneva Convention to which Greece was a signatory but Turkey was not. In reply, Turkey replied that the areas in dispute formed part of the natural extension of the Anatolian Peninsula and rejected the Greek claim that the islands generated their own continental shelves. The situation deteriorated further when, on 29 May 1974, the Turkish survey ship *Candarli*, escorted by Turkish warships, initiated a programme of seismological surveys. A few days later, on 12 June, Turkey formally declared that any extension of Greek territorial waters from six miles to the more normal twelve would constitute a *casus belli*.

The growing crisis in the Aegean was soon to be overshadowed, of course, by the Turkish invasion of Cyprus which, as both sides mobilised, brought the two countries to the brink of war. It is worth remembering here that the Turkish prime minister, Bulent Ecevit, before launching the invasion, sought joint Turkish/UK intervention, for the United Kingdom was, with Turkey and Greece, a guarantor of the 1960 settlement. It is at least possible that, had the United Kingdom agreed to this proposal, then the eventual outcome might have been different. The chaos of the Greek mobilisation and the stark exposure of her international isolation precipitated the downfall of the military dictatorship and its replacement by a civilian government headed by Constantine Karamanlis. Karamanlis soon made it clear that he did not envisage war as affording any kind of way out of the Greek–Turkish impasse. But relations between the two countries remained in a critical state and, since that time, a whole complex of factors, of which Cyprus is but one, have bedevilled relations between the two countries. The continental shelf dispute pre-dated the July 1974 crisis. To this complicated issue and the problem of Cyprus were added further apples of discord.[7]

The first of these concerned air traffic control in the Aegean area. Under a 1952 decision of the International Civil Aviation Organisation, virtually the whole of the airspace of the Aegean had been placed under the control of the Athens FIR, the eastern extremity of which followed Greece's land and sea frontiers with Turkey. But, a few days after the invasion of Cyprus, Ankara challenged the status quo by issuing NOTAM 714, the effect of which was to require all flights to report to Turkish air traffic control on crossing the Aegean median line, a measure that would manifestly have affected flights to the Greek islands. Greece retaliated by issuing NOTAM 1157, which declared the entire Athens FIR to be a danger area. Direct flights between the two countries were thus suspended. Turkey subsequently declined to accept Greece's 1931 declaration that her national airspace extended to ten miles. Since 1974, Greek protests at infringements by Turkish military aircraft of the zone between the six-mile limit of her territorial seas and her ten-mile airspace have been a recurrent feature of Greek–Turkish relations.

The second source of contention concerned the rearmament of Greece's Aegean islands in the wake of the Turkish occupation of northern Cyprus. Turkey maintains that the treaties of Lausanne and Paris of 1923 and 1947 provide for the demilitarisation of the islands. To this Greece replies that the provisions of the Montreux Convention of 1936 override the relevant clauses of the Treaty of Lausanne, notwithstanding the fact that no treaty provisions could negate a country's basic right under international law to defend its own borders.

The whole complex of differences, known collectively as the Aegean dispute, brought into question the treatment by each country of its respective national minorities, the Greek minority in Istanbul and the islands of Imvros and Tenedos straddling the approaches to the Dardanelles, and the Muslim, predominantly Turkish, minority in Greece. Each side has charged the other with infringing minority rights and during the period under review the Greek minority in Turkey has dwindled to the point of extinction. A particular bone of contention from the Greek point of view has been a Turkish law restricting the rights of Greek nationals expelled from Turkey in 1964 in the wake of the 1963–4 Cyprus crisis to dispose of their property, a law that has been rescinded following the Davos agreement of January 1988.

Although the immediate crisis in 1974 was to be defused, relations between Greece and Turkey remained tense and the real risk that the Aegean dispute might flare up into armed conflict was apparent in the crisis of the summer of 1976 when Turkey once again carried out seismological surveys in disputed waters. In February 1976, Ecevit, who had consistently taken a more intransigent line over the Aegean than had his right-wing opponents, just as Andreas Papandreou had adopted a markedly tougher tone than his conservative opponents in Greece, announced that surveys would resume in the region of Thasos. The Greek government repeatedly warned against such a move. The Turkish government in turn made it clear that it would not tolerate any forcible interference with the mission of its survey ship *Sismik 1*.

When, in early August 1976, the *Sismik* began to carry out explorations between the islands of Lemnos and Mytilini, Papandreou, not yet, of course, the leader of the official opposition, called for the sinking of the ship. Constantine Karamanlis's conservative New Democracy government, following the rejection by Turkey of two notes of protest, on 9 August requested a meeting of the UN Security Council, claiming that Turkey's repeated violation of Greece's sovereign rights over the Aegean continental shelf had created an imminent danger to peace. Simultaneously Greece appealed to the

ICJ in The Hague for an interim judgement restraining Turkey from carrying out further explorations in disputed waters until the extent of the two countries' continental shelves had been defined. The response of neither organisation was very helpful from the Greek viewpoint. The Security Council urged restraint on both parties and invited them to consider the contribution that might be made by the ICJ. The ICJ, in its turn, was scarcely more positive, noting that the Security Council had called for bilateral negotiations, and declaring itself incompetent to pronounce judgement on the Aegean continental shelf issue. But the pronouncements of both bodies did take some of the heat out of what had been an extremely tense confrontation. The climate in bilateral relations was further improved following meetings between the Greek and Turkish foreign ministers, which resulted in meetings in Paris and Berne in November 1976 to discuss questions of flight control and the delimitation of the two countries' respective continental shelves. It was agreed to open a 'hot line' between the tactical air force headquarters in Larisa in Greece and Eskişehir in Turkey. By the Berne declaration of November 1976 both sides undertook to refrain from actions that might impede a resolution of bilateral differences through peaceful means.

These negotiations were followed in March 1978 by a summit meeting in Montreux between the two prime ministers, Karamanlis and Ecevit. Although a climate of mutual confidence was said to have been established, little was accomplished in practical terms, although Karamanlis subsequently repeated his offer of a non-aggression treaty with Turkey. The summit, in turn, led to regular but inconclusive meetings between the secretaries-general of the two foreign ministries.

In 1980, however, there appeared to be significant signs of movement. In February, Turkey, without prior notification, rescinded NOTAM 714, a move that effectively restored the pre-1974 status quo for civil aviation in the Aegean FIR. On 5 October 1980, shortly after its 12 September coup, the Turkish military junta stated its belief that all outstanding differences between the two countries could be settled 'in a just manner through bilateral talks held with goodwill and constructively'. As a token of this apparent new climate of goodwill, the Turkish military government withdrew the insistence of its civilian predecessors that the reincorporation of Greece into the military command structure of the NATO alliance, from which she had withdrawn in 1974 in the wake of the Turkish invasion of

Cyprus, should be dependent on the negotiation of new operational control responsibilities in the Aegean region for the armed forces of the two countries.

The following year, 1981, was a momentous one for Greece, for not only did she join the European Community as the tenth member but a radical PASOK socialist government was elected, with a mandate for domestic reform and for breaking the cycle of dependency perceived to have characterised the country's foreign policy since independence. What was particularly significant from the point of view of Greek–Turkish relations was that the new prime minister, Andreas Papandreou, had been a fierce critic of his right-wing predecessors, accusing them of being prepared to negotiate away Greece's sovereign rights in the Aegean. His basic line had been that negotiations with Turkey were basically pointless because there was nothing to negotiate. However, although he had softened his line on a number of foreign policy issues, for example over membership of the European Community and NATO, there had been no relaxation of his intransigent line towards Turkey. This was manifested in his immediate, but unsuccessful, demand on coming to power for a NATO guarantee of Greece's eastern borders.

In the summer of the following year, 1982, both sides agreed to desist from polemics and provocative actions preparatory to a meeting of foreign ministers with a view to reopening the dialogue over their Aegean differences. Following repeated Greek allegations of Turkish infringements of Greek airspace, however, the meeting was cancelled and Papandreou took the unusual step of personally handing out a memorandum detailing the Turkish infringements at a meeting of the NATO ministerial council in December. Papandreou's visit to Cyprus in February 1982, the first ever by a ruling Greek prime minister, was matched by the visit of the Turkish prime minister, Bulent Ulusu, to Turkish-controlled northern Cyprus. The proposed meeting of foreign ministers did eventually take place in April 1983, with Yannis Haralampopoulos reaching agreement with his Turkish opposite number, Ilter Turkmen, that both sides should refrain from provocative action. The following September, however, Greece boycotted the NATO exercise 'Display Determination 83' in protest at Turkish insistence that the island of Lemnos should be demilitarised. Two months later, relations deteriorated sharply following the unilateral declaration on 15 November by the Turkish Cypriot Assembly of an independent TRNC and its immediate recognition by the military National Security Council then wielding power in Turkey in the interregnum between parliamentary elections and the formation of a government headed by Turgut Ozal. Papandreou refused to consider participation in tripartite talks with the other guarantors of the 1960 constitutional settelement in Cyprus – the United Kingdom and Turkey – arguing that negotiations were out of the question as long as the Turkish army was in occupation of northern Cyprus.

At the beginning of his term of office, Ozal announced a token withdrawal of Turkish troops from northern Cyprus and lifted visa requirements for Greek visitors. But relations again sharply deteriorated in March of 1984 following allegations that Turkish destroyers on exercise had fired salvoes in the direction of a Greek destroyer observing the exercises from Greek territorial waters. Greek armed forces were placed on alert and the Greek ambassador was recalled to Athens for consultations. This particular crisis, although serious while it lasted, soon blew over but relations reached a new low when in December 1984 Papandreou announced the adoption by Greece of a new defence doctrine, according to which the main threat to Greece was perceived as coming not from the Warsaw Pact but from Greece's NATO ally Turkey.

Papandreou did meet with his Turkish counterpart, Ozal, in February 1986 but polemics between the two countries continued unabated. Specifically Greece objected to the revival of Turkey's frozen association agreement with the TRNC, arguing that internal repression, the continued Turkish occupation of northern Cyprus and Turkey's aggressive attitude towards Greece ruled out such a possibility. Greece sought the lifting of the 1964 decree discriminating against Greek property-owners in Turkey, together with exemption from an EC commitment to allow the free movement of Turkish workers within the Community.

The existing poor climate was further exacerbated by a frontier incident in December 1986 involving Greek and Turkish border patrols on the Evros river. This resulted in the deaths of two Turkish soldiers and one Greek. This was followed, three months later, in March 1987 by the most serious crisis in Greek–Turkish relations since the *Sismik* incident of the summer of 1976. Like the previous crisis this hinged on proposed oil explorations in disputed waters and likewise involved the survey ship *Sismik*. The Turkish government granted further exploration and exploitation licences to the state-owned Turkish Petroleum Corporation in international waters near the Greek island of Samothrace. At the same time Turkey accused

Greece of having violated the Berne Protocol of November 1976, whereby both sides undertook to avoid provocative actions, by proposals to nationalise the foreign-owned consortium that had been given the concession to exploit the existing Thasos (Prinos) oilfield.

When, on 28 March, the Turkish survey ship *Sismik*, under naval escort, set sail for the Aegean, Greek and Turkish forces were placed on alert and Papandreou declared that all necessary measures would be taken to safeguard Greece's sovereign rights. Holding NATO, and, in particular, the United States, to be responsible for the crisis, Papandreou ordered the suspension of communications facilities at the American base at Nea Makri and promptly dispatched his foreign minister, Karolos Papoulias, to Sofia to brief the Bulgarian leader, Tudor Jivkov. In a calculated snub, the ambassadors of Warsaw Pact countries in Athens were briefed on the crisis in advance of their NATO counterparts. The threat of outright hostilities was averted only when Ozal declared that the *Sismik* would operate only in Turkish territorial seas, while Greece likewise declared that no drilling would take place in disputed waters. Although Greece continued to protest at Turkish violations of its airspace and again refused to participate in NATO's annual 'Display Determination' exercises in the Aegean, towards the end of 1987 there were indications of a more conciliatory note in Greek–Turkish relations, with both leaders talking of the possibility of a face-to-face meeting.

That possibility soon materialised at a meeting of the World Economic Forum at Davos in Switzerland at the end of January 1988. On 31 January Papandreou and Ozal issued a joint statement which emphasised the need to avoid the kind of confrontation that, in March 1987, had brought the two countries to the verge of war. The Davos agreement was subsequently referred to by the PASOK government as the 'symphonia mi-polemou': the 'no-war agreement'. With a view to creating a much-improved climate in bilateral relations the two leaders agreed to establish a 'hot line' between Athens and Ankara, undertook to meet at least once a year and to visit each other's countries. They called for an intensification of contacts at all levels, with particular emphasis on the encouragement of tourism and cultural exchanges. To this end, two joint committees were established to discuss the development of closer political and economic relations.[8] (Trade relations between the two countries were certainly at a very low ebb.) These political and economic committees met twice in 1988 and their sub-committees more frequently.

In an early gesture of goodwill, the Turkish government rescinded the 1964 decree restricting the property rights of Greek nationals in Turkey. In return, Greece lifted her objections to the reactivation of the 1964 Association Agreement between Turkey and the European Community, which had been 'frozen' since the 1980 Turkish military coup. Reciprocal visits by, among others, the Greek and Turkish foreign ministers were followed by an official visit, the first such visit by a Turkish prime minister for thirty-six years, by Ozal to Athens. Papandreou had not reciprocated Ozal's visit by the time of his defeat in the elections of June 1989. This delay was ascribed to the prime minister's health problems and to a heavy schedule arising from Greece's presidency of the European Community during the second half of 1988. Following Davos, Turkey lifted visa requirements for Greek nationals. This resulted in truly enormous increase in visits by Greek nationals to Turkey, with recorded visits being up by some 170 per cent to an astonishing 360 000.

This was certainly one index of an improved climate in relations but it was not long before some of the old strains were to come to the surface. Greece made repeated protests at Turkish violations of Greek airspace and towards the end of 1988 there were distinct signs that the 'spirit of Davos' had lost momentum. In November, the Turkish foreign ministry spokesman, Inal Batu, contested the statement of the Greek government spokesman, Sotiris Kostopoulos, that the only dispute outstanding between the two countries was the delineation of the two countries' respective continental shelves in the Aegean. Batu insisted that the extent of Greece's airspace, the militarisation of the Aegean islands and the status of the Turkish minority in western Thrace were also at issue.

Within NATO, Greece and Turkey vetoed each other's 'country chapters' at the NATO Defence Review Committee and each country raised objections to NATO infrastructural spending in the other. Greece once again boycotted the annual NATO 'Display Determination' manoeuvres in October. More recently there has been disagreement over responsibility for search-and-rescue operations in the eastern Mediterranean, with Turkey claiming responsibility for the area east of the median line, and Greece maintaining that her search-and-rescue responsibilities extended to the whole of the Athens FIR. There were further disagreements at the CSCE held in Vienna, with Greece objecting to Turkey's attempt to exclude the port of Mersin, the nearest large port to Cyprus on the Turkish mainland, from reductions in conventional forces. Both countries, however, despite their continuing differences, continued to refer positively to 'the spirit of Davos'.

Some eighteen months after the Davos agreement, then, it is still too early to say whether it will initiate the sea change in Greek–Turkish relations that its protagonists clearly hoped for. Many of the old sources of friction (and indeed some new ones) continue to rumble not far from the surface, and both Papandreou and Ozal early in 1989 thought it necessary to reaffirm their commitment to the 'spirit of Davos'. In Greece and Turkey 1989 saw important elections, and it was clear that in both countries public opinion did not necessarily share the commitment of the two leaders to *rapprochement*. The need of both prime ministers to be particularly sensitive to their respective electorates in an election year clearly to some degree inhibited their freedom of manoeuvre.

Realistically, then, the omens at the end of the decade of the 1980s for a major breakthrough in the climate of relations between the two countries, paralleling that achieved by Eleftherios Venizelos through the Ankara Convention of 1930, cannot be considered very good. In historical perspective it is worth noting that the two best periods in their mutual relations since the end of the Greek–Turkish war in 1922, namely the late 1930s and the late 1940s and early 1950s, were both periods in which Greece and Turkey shared the same perceptions of external threat. As we enter the decade of the 1990s, with the remarkable transformation that has taken place in East–West relations, no such shared external threat is in sight. Still, as Winston Churchill once put it, 'jaw, jaw' must be preferable to 'war, war'.

NOTES

1. The best overview of Greek–Turkish relations in historical perspective is the collective work by Alexis Alexandris, Thanos Veremis, Panos Kazakos, Vangelis Kouphoudakis, Christos L. Rozakis and Giorgos Tsitsopoulos. *Oi Ellinotourkikes Skheseis, 1923–1987* (Athens, 1988). A useful study which incorporates recent developments is Heinz-Jürgen Axt and Heinz Kramer, *Griechisch–Türkische Beziehungen: von der Konfrontation zur Annäherung? Die jüngste Entwicklung vor dem Hintergrund des Ägaiskonflikts* (Ebenhausen, 1989). See also Ronald Meinardus, *Die Türkei-Politik Griechenlands* (Frankfurt, 1985) and 'Die griechisch-türkischen Beziehungen in den achtziger Jahren', *Beiträge für Konfliktforschung*, vol. xviii (1988) pp. 83–98. Still useful are Christos Rozakis *To Aigaio kai i ellinotourkiki krisi* (Athens, 1979) and Christos Z. Sazani

dis, *Oi Ellinotourkikes skheseis stin pentaetia, 1973–1978*, vol. i (Thessaloniki, 1979). Now somewhat dated is Richard Clogg, 'Troubled Alliance: Greece and Turkey', in Richard Clogg (ed.), *Greece in the 1980s* (London, 1983) pp. 123–43.
2. On the Varlik Vergisi, see Faik Okte, *The Tragedy of the Turkish Capital Tax* (London, 1987) trans. Geoffrey Cox. See also Edward C. Clark, 'The Turkish Varlik Vergisi Reconsidered', *Middle Eastern Studies*, vol. viii (1972) pp. 205–16.
3. Alexandris *et al.*, *Oi Ellinotourkikes Scheseis, 1923–1987*, p. 507.
4. S. A. de Smith, *The New Commonwealth and its Constitutions* (London, 1964) p. 282.
5. For an authoritative study of the fate of the Greek minority in Turkey, see Alexis Alexandris, *The Greek Minority in Turkey, 1918–1956 and Greco–Turkish Relations* (Athens, 1983). No equivalent large-scale study for the Turkish minority in western Thrace appears to exist, but for a Turkish perspective see Umit Haluk Bayulken, 'Turkish Minorities in Greece', *The Turkish Yearbook of International Relations*, vol. iv (1963) pp. 145–64 and for a Greek perspective see K. G. Andreadis, *The Muslim Minority in Western Thrace* (Thessaloniki, 1956). For a survey of recent developments see Ronald Meinardus, 'Die Griechisch–Turkische Minderheitenfrage', *Orient*, vol. xxvi (1985) pp. 4861. See also Baskin Oran, 'La minorité Turco–Musulmane de la Thrace Occidentale (Grèce)', in Semih Vaner (ed.), *Le différend Gréco–Turc* (Paris, 1988) pp. 145–61.
6. Dimitris Kitsikis, *Istoria tou Ellinotourkikou chorou apo ton E. Venizelo ston G. Papadopoulo (1928–73)*, pp. 304–5.
7. Andrea Wilson, *The Aegean Dispute*, Adelphi Papers no. 195 (London: International Institute of Strategic Studies, 1979–80) is a notably balanced analysis of this complex dispute. For recent developments over the Cyprus issue, see Robert McDonald, *The Problem of Cyprus* (London: International Institute for Strategic Studies, 1988–9).
8. Some consternation was occasioned when it was learnt that one of the members of the Turkish economic committee was a Greek from Istanbul, *To Vima*, 11 September 1988.

Part I

Domestic Influences on Foreign Policy

3 Turkey and the 'Davos Process': Experiences and Prospects*
MEHMET ALI BIRAND

Over the past several years, on different occasions, Turkey and Greece have been on the brink of war following a series of severe crises. A major breakthrough in Greek–Turkish relations was the Davos process. Looking at how and why the Davos process was first initiated, one immediately comes across the 'Ozal factor'.

A careful analysis of Greek–Turkish relations reveals that the relatively calm and friendly periods that the two countries have witnessed have been the result of external pressure rather than bilateral efforts. And even then, the basic policy held by the two countries remained stubbornly the same; the methods employed to solve the crisis were usually palliative.

The Turkish Prime Minister Turgut Ozal introduced, for the first time, a policy aimed at changing the public opinion and the rigid subconscious ideas of the 'establishment' and the methods of approach, while at the same time trying to understand 'the other side'. He decided to destroy the deeply rooted anti-Greek sentiments in his country, thereby undoing the taboos set aside by the Greek–Turkish disputes. Greece was now confronted with a whole new set of ideas as Ozal made his courageous attempt to review the problem under a whole new light.

In order to understand the Davos process, it is necessary to examine in greater depth the most essential element of the process, namely the 'Ozal factor'.

---

* When not specifically stated, the bulk of this paper has been based on numerous interviews by the author with Prime Minister Ozal; Foreign Minister Yilmaz; Special Advisor to the Prime Minister, Mr Duna; Ambassador to the EC Mr Sanberk; Mr Demirel and Mr Inonou. These interviews were held between January and May 1989.

AT THE BEGINNING

The Motherland Party won the December 1983 Turkish national elections by an overwhelming margin, despite the fact that the military supported another party. Interestingly enough, the only person in the party with a domestic and international appeal was Turgut Ozal. Following the general elections, in 1984, when Ozal was elected prime minister, he was the only, and undisputable, leader of his party. His uniqueness arose from his ability to discuss complex political and economic issues with a relaxed and open manner. And his style of speech was easy-going, using sentences that were not too sophisticated. Throughout the campaign, contrary to what the public were used to, he spoke the 'truth' – without any hesitation and without being allusive or secretive. As he phrased it, he did not have to account to anyone, nor did he owe anything to anybody.

By destroying the prevailing taboo on discussion of economic and political issues, the public immediately warmed to this liberal leader who promised little, but that which could be accomplished. While being able to spot bureaucratic mistakes, at last there was a leader who could pinpoint the bottleneck of the economy. Following a rigid military administration, Ozal quickly won the hearts of the Turkish people.

Ozal's credibility proved itself not only throughout the Turkish nation but worldwide as well. Throughout economic and financial circles overseas he quickly won the support of the IMF and the World Bank. Seldom has there been a prime minister who has been able to capture such strong foreign support immediately on his appointment.

Turgut Ozal's first priority was to pull Turkey out of its tight financial fix. In order to do this he had to use all means to create a climate that would put the Turkish economy on its feet.

Turkey was at that time confronted by a very inflexible Europe; a United States that paid only lip-service to its nominal role of ally; a traditional rival in the shape of the Soviet Union; a new enemy, Bulgaria, the country now looked on as responsible for all terrorist activities; Syria, Iran and Iraq as friends of necessity; and lastly Greece. Whether it was for human rights and democracy, or political and economic reasons, the ring of pressure placed around Turkey over the last few years brought foreign relations with Turkey to its most sensitive position ever. Ozal's second priority was to break this ring and start an era of dialogue as a solution to all problems. And since 1985, relations with all neighbours, even though basic differences in views exist, have straightened out: an understanding has been reached with Syria, some of the knots with Iran and Iraq have been untangled, a solution to all technical problems with the Soviet Union found, dialogue resumed with Bulgaria, tension with Europe relaxed. And when it came down to relations with Greece, this was of specific value for Ozal.

Up until 1981, Greek–Turkish relations, though never having reached a solution in any specific area, continued under an air of 'dialogue'. After the Turkish military intervention and PASOK coming to power in Greece, relations changed at once. Papandreou, seeing clearly the negative impression created in Europe by the Turkish military government, changed Greece's political approach by taking the following actions. (1) He raised the issue of a possible 'Turkish threat' in NATO and relevant institutions. (2) He became the standard bearer in the European Parliament, which took the lead along with Western sympathisers in condemning Turkey's oblivious attitude towards human rights and democracy. (3) He played an important role in bringing down Turkey's relations with the European Community to their lowest level. (4) He placed pressure on the American Congress through the Greek lobby with regards to military aid to Turkey. (5) He readily accepted and granted basic facilities to dissidents as well as Kurdish and Armenian activists. (6) Finally, using the presence of a military government as an excuse, he cut all dialogue with Turkey. He said he would resume dialogue only under two conditions: Turkish soldiers were to be pulled out of Cyprus; Turkey was to accept Greek rights to the Aegean.

When Ozal first came to power in 1984, following democratic elections, Papandreou still did not change his policy. He claimed that the general elections were fraudulent and conducted under pressure and that the Motherland government and Ozal were under orders from the military. He regarded the new Turkish government as one that would not defy the military.

Turgut Ozal considered[1] Greek–Turkish relations to hold top priority in Turkey's foreign policy. In this respect, he was no different from former Turkish leaders and firmly believed that both countries were bound to co-operate with one another. This would be the only way any major achievements could be won.

The tension in relations created two major disadvantages: the need to increase arms, which would be a heavy drain on the economy because of the spending involved; and the fact that the superpowers would be given an unnecessary amount of freedom to do what they pleased in their relations with Ankara and Athens.

Ozal differed from other Turkish prime ministers in several important aspects. The methods of approach and roles used up until now had changed. Ozal believed that the only solution would be to use a new impetus in order to pull relations with Greece away from a system of fossilised bureaucracy and a rigid establishment. He believed, whether rightly or wrongly, that the Greeks feared the Turks. It was important that the same Greek society be set at ease through the Turkish initiatives. It was up to Turkey to convince Greece that a 'threat' did not exist. Rather than trying to solve old problems through the customary official channels, he believed that it would be far easier to discard any ill feelings between the two societies by setting up new fields of co-operation in areas ranging from tourism to commerce. He discarded the old idea that 'whatever we do the Greeks will never approach us' and started his own offensive. Despite the criticism from the press and the fact that Greece did nothing to change its policy, Ozal continued his campaign. He believed that in the end, seeing that Turkish intentions were sound and that the Turkish people were approaching this matter in all seriousness, the Greek prime minister would resume dialogue between the two countries.

Another point that made Ozal different from other Turkish leaders was that he did not keep Greek–Turkish relations stagnant within the framework of 'military security' and since he had no experience on these issues, he held no preconceived ideas.

During this process, when the whole Turkish press and the establishment saw Papandreou as an unbalanced leader, Ozal regarded him as an *homme d'état*, took him completely seriously, and believed that if any progress were to be made it would be through him.

THE CAMPAIGN

The first step was seen only as the beginning of a dialogue followed by a personal relationship with Papandreou to create an atmosphere of trust. While planning step-by-step procedures towards an answer, Ozal took the following precautions:

1. As a one-sided measure, he lifted the visa requirements for Greek citizens.
2. He took steps to increase commerce and used businessmen on both sides to accomplish this.

3. He changed the former policy taken in 1964 concerning the ownership of property by Greek citizens in Istanbul.
4. He increased calls for negotiations.
5. He prepared himself to sign a series of agreements including the one on non-aggression (1978 Greek proposal).
6. He stopped the government from making adverse statements towards the Greeks and changed the tone of his own statements to the press.

The Greek government, in the first instance, did not appreciate Turkey's approach. From time to time it said openly in its statements that Turkey was still run by the military and the government could not take the initiative on its own; not only did Ozal have bad intentions but he had certain plans of his own in the back of his mind. Particularly in the European Parliament (on Armenian, Kurdish and human rights/democratic issues), Greek parliamentarians continually supported decisions or draft decisions against Turkey. Back in Ankara the opinion was that Ozal's policy of 'extending the olive branch' was turning out to be unsuccessful.

Ozal began to be provocative by pointing out that Greece's refusal to accept a dialogue between the two countries would in turn have a negative effect on international planning. Ozal, especially in his bilateral talks with Western countries and in his statements to the Western press, stressed further and further his policy of the olive branch and the fact that he could not understand why Athens refused to have anything to do with any sort of dialogue. Western reaction became more and more partial towards Ozal. It seemed as if Greece was to pay the price if two important members of the Western alliance's south flank were not to talk. Papandreou's position (especially on various events including the shooting down of a Korean airliner by the Soviet Union) added to the negative atmosphere; the West then started to increase its pressure on Athens.

It was against this background that the first Davos experiment started in 1985 and plans towards a Davos meeting began. Through unofficial channels, efforts were made to arrange for the two prime ministers to have breakfast together. Papandreou backed out at the last minute. One of the reasons for this was because of the news appearing prematurely in the press and speculation arising as a result. Another reason (according to Ankara) was that the Greek prime minister did not believe that the circumstances were right for such an event.

Since the olive branch policy provided no solution, Ankara was forced to believe that its one-sided efforts were useless and began to change its approach. It was at this time that the March 1986 crisis on drilling rights in disputed areas broke out in the Aegean.

Turkey tried to get the Greek government to withdraw the drilling rights that it had given to a private company. Turkey's intense efforts had no effect and the company could not be stopped. If the operation were to go through, Turkey's continental shelf policies would be breached *de facto*.

Ankara had two options, namely to stop the drilling through military means, which meant the possibility of war; or, like Greece, to start drilling in the contested area. The Turkish general staff and the government together supported the second option. The Turkish ship *Sismik 1* set out to the contested area under the protection of Turkish warships.

When the crisis exploded, Ozal was recovering from open-heart surgery in Houston and about to return to Turkey via London. Greece had decided to drill in the Aegean at a time when the Turkish prime minister was not in the country. Nevertheless Turkey took a clear decision as to what to do and though the prime minister was not directly involved with the developments, he was informed as to what steps were to be taken.

The crisis reached its height when warships of both countries approached one another. Greece now thought that the two nations were on the verge of war. But in the midst of all this, Turgut Ozal made a statement from London. In his broken English he said one sentence that changed everything: 'If they don't touch our ship, we don't touch their ship.' These few words revealed to the world and especially the Greeks that Ozal was a man of peace who did not want war, despite the efforts of his military. As the crisis was defused, Ozal was seen in a new light by Papandreou and Greece.

This incident is also a typical example of how two countries could be on the brink of war as the result of a lack of dialogue. After this incident, messages were sent back and forth between both countries, leading in the end to the Davos meeting.

DAVOS 1988

Before the Davos meeting, there was absolutely no idea as to what the results would be on the Turkish bureaucracy. In fact, there were widespread and highly publicised fears that the process would just fizzle out.

The prime minister, too, was not sure what he would encounter. His only security was his conviction that if he was left face to face with Papandreou he would be able to convince him.

The meeting between the two prime ministers in Davos created a totally unexpected atmosphere. Ozal's approach proved that both sides had been the slaves of their own establishment and now was the time to break up the fossilised, rigid ideas and create a new set of relations.

Up until then the fear of war had been the driving force in relations between Turkey and Greece. There were rigid and unyielding moulds which both bureaucracies believed in. Ozal believed that a new set of relations would break the moulds and overcome the stubborness of the bureaucracy and the fossilised attitudes of the establishment.

When Ozal said that he wanted new relations and co-operation between the two countries, he particularly meant an increase in economic activities. According to Ozal, if trade between the two countries rose from 60 million to 2 billion dollars, it would be far easier to deal with mutual problems and with the bureaucracy.

Together with Papandreou, he wanted to wage war against the barriers of bureaucracy. His proposal was that both leaders should show political determination, which would overcome any obstacle.

In the first phase there would be only a dialogue; resolving mutual problems would be left to a later date, and two committees were to be set up. The Economic Committee would look towards mutual benefits, agreements between banks, economic meetings and so on. The Political Committee would in the first instance drew up a 'list of problems'. Both sides would retain their mutual positions and as an air of trust was created, measured steps would be taken towards a basic solution.

Within this framework (according to the Turkish side) the Cyprus problem would temporarily be set aside and if necessary the two prime ministers would later intervene when the timing was right. This, according to Ozal, was the 'spirit of Davos'.

Following Davos, for the first time, there seemed to be some excitement in the Turkish bureaucracy. The impression was that the problems were no longer in the hands of endless committee meetings at technical levels; here was the beginning of a process that was to solve issues at the highest levels. But which of the issues, and how they were to be solved, was not yet known.

Ozal, seeing that his olive branch policy had begun to bear fruit, gained courage and softened his official stand on several key issues. He did not repeat the usual official line that the problem of the continental shelf could not be dealt by the Court of Justice at the Hague but only by bilateral talks. He expanded even further the commercial channels with Greece, even though these were a disadvantage to Turkey. He started to decrease the number of military flights so as to reduce tension regarding the argument over whether Greek airspace extended for six or ten miles.

Although certain circles within the Turkish establishment remained sceptical, the optimists held the upper hand.

BRUSSELS 1988

In Ankara's view, the second summit in Brussels, held in February 1988, gave the first signs that some of the achievements of the Davos process were beginning to fade. According to Ozal, the bureaucracies were making a comeback by seeing everything through the conservative angle of 'national interest'.

Before the summit, according to information received from Athens and comments from the press, part of the bureaucracy in Athens and the opposition were actually putting pressure on Papandreou and were objecting to the fact that Cyprus was left out of the talks.

The Turkish bureaucracy, on the other hand, recalled the consequences of the famous Rogers' Agreement, which was drawn up to bring Greece back under the wing of NATO. The Rogers' Agreement, which was put into effect in 1980 and vetoed as Papandreou came into power, gave Ankara the impression that the 'Greeks would first accept and later reject it', thus practically wiping out the little trust that the Turks had in the Greeks.

The Brussels summit ended with the creation of an economic and political committee.

During the negotiations of the final communiqué in Brussels, the Greek prime minister gave the impression that his bureaucracy seemed to have forgotten the Davos spirit and was now fighting back. This negative atmosphere prevailed until Ozal's visit to Athens in June 1988. Meanwhile, meetings between the Greek–Turkish military delegations on 'confidence-building measures' (where manoeuvres were to take place, time, advance notice and so on) remained unresolved. The disagreements presented by both sides with regards to the manoeuvres proved one thing: that since an agreement had not been reached on any one of the basic principles during the Ozal–Papandreou talks, the experts could not reach an agreement in practical terms.

It now seemed that the Davos process was being undermined by the slithering sands of Ozal's visit to Athens. The Turkish prime minister's trip to Athens was the result of both leaders using their political determination in order to overcome the negative atmosphere created by the opposition in Greece. But because of Greek public opinion and the demonstrations of the Turkish dissidents and Greek Cypriots in Athens, the visit did not live up to its original expectations. Due to the extraordinary security precautions, not only did the Turkish bureaucrats feel isolated but Ozal, too, felt the visit did not give a fresh impetus to the Davos breakthrough. This would have been the perfect opportunity to destroy, even if only symbolically, all of the existing taboos. But because the public was not ready for this, all efforts were in vain.

Even on the last day, during a courtesy call to the Greek president, Ozal was confronted by harsh words that in the end forced him to raise the tone of his own voice. However, when Ozal left the Greek prime minister, a very good atmosphere prevailed.

During the trip to Athens, Turkish public opinion said that not only did the visit end without any results, but the main aim of trying to soften the attitude of both sides had failed as well. The Greek public had expected certain gestures from the Turkish prime minister with regards to Cyprus and were thus disillusioned.

From Ankara's point of view, it can be said that the Davos process seems to be over. Both leaders have tried and failed to override the old values of their own establishments. The excitement that was at its height in the aftermath of Davos began to wither away as the months passed.

Papandreou's health problems followed by internal political problems also had an effect on developments. In the same way, Ozal's internal problems and the fact that he was not sensitive enough to allow the Davos process to go through the necessary incubation period took its toll as well.

I would like in particular to underline the fact that both parties are responsible for what has happened today. It is not the mistake of only one side.

When examining the reasons as to why the philosophy behind the

Davos spirit, which was to create a new set of relations and a whole new set of mutual benefits between Turkey and Greece, did not succeed, the first thing that could be said is that no one had the vision of the prime ministers; neither the Turkish nor the Greek public could understand precisely what was happening, otherwise, surely, the results would have been different. Neither leader was able to explain to his people or to the press just what they planned on doing and the philosophy behind their plans.

There is a good chance that they were not able to form their own philosophy because they did not know exactly what they wanted to achieve. That is why they could not give a proper explanation to their own bureaucracy, even to the point of not being able to give proper orders. What is more interesting is that they authorised that same bureaucracy which had opened war against their philosophy to carry out the 'spirit of Davos'. They could not create a new and proper mechanism to carry these reforms through.

Though they knew the volatile and emotional approach of the public, both Ozal and Papandreou, for some reason, took the expectations of the public lightly. They did not or could not realise that without running a good public relations campaign they would not get the results they expected. They seemed unable, to take the necessary precautions, even for only 'cosmetic' reasons, to soften the atmosphere. They could not find the means to put into practice the philosophy lying in the back of their minds.

PROSPECTS

Recent developments in both countries do not give much hope for a revival of the 'spirit of Davos' as the political weight and influence of the two main architects of Davos have fundamentally changed.

Ozal's accession to the presidency[2] has changed the political balance in Turkey. He will not be in full control of his party, nor will he be able to pursue an active policy as he did in the past to promote his ideas *vis-à-vis* Turkish public opinion. Abandoned by its natural leader and godfather, a power struggle is expected in the Motherland Party in preparation for the general elections of 1992. The Motherland Party will face difficulties in generating new policies and a period of instability is expected to follow. Furthermore, bereft of Ozal's forcefulness, no new leader will be able to convince the party or push the bureaucracy as was done in the past. Ozal's role as a steadying influence and policy-maker will be marginal at best.

Recent polls show that the Motherland Party is not expected to obtain a majority in the elections of 1992 if economic problems are not resolved and if a new charismatic leader does not manifest himself. The general consensus is that from 1992 Turkey will be governed either by Erdal Inonu's Social Democrat People's Party or by a coalition involving Suleyman Demirel's True Path Party.

The approach of Inonu and Demirel to Greek–Turkish problems is very different from Ozal's pragmatic approach. Both opt for traditional, conservative policies instead of taking the initiative and adopting fresh, bold approaches.

In the party programme of the SHP, Greek–Turkish problems are treated in the general context of foreign policy:

> Article 52 – Our foreign policy is based on ensuring the security of the country, contributing to world peace, promoting external relations in the context of the general principles of the UN Charter, securing a balance of interest and equal rights in bilateral relations, promoting economic and social relations in particular with our near neighbours.

It can safely be said that the SHP's policies on Cyprus and Greece would be no different from the policies adopted in the 1960s by the now-banned RPP. Instead of generating new ideas, Inonu and his party have consistently shown that they would much prefer following traditional policies:[3] i.e., that Turkey and Greece should solve their bilateral problems, especially the Aegean problem, on a just and equitable basis; and that the Cyprus problem and Greek–Turkish bilateral problems should be treated separately – both problems should be solved on their own merit.

Based on his declaration during the Ozal–Papandreou summit, Inonu would seem to favour well-planned negotiations whose outcome would be thought through in advance.

Unlike Ozal, Inonu is an over-cautious leader. Ozal could very easily leave by the wayside expected or suggested policies in order to attain his aim. He believed that the leaders of the two countries could solve many problems by mutual trust and understanding. This kind of approach cannot be expected from Inonu who favours a step-by-step approach. If he comes to power, relations would take more time to establish, but the outcome would be more predictable.

On the other hand, Demirel has for the first time very clearly stated what he hopes from Greek–Turkish relations and his views on Cyprus. During his opening speech to the True Path Party Congress on 15 May 1988, he stated:

There are many bilateral problems between Greece and ourselves. We favour a resolution based on their own merit keeping in mind Turkey's interests. . . . We favour a peaceful resolution to these problems. But in so doing we should not make concessions in an area which is unrelated to this problem. . . . Cyprus is a separate issue. We are definitely against taking economic considerations is view [i.e. Turkey's full membership of the EC] while dealing with this problem. We will not accept linkage with other issues.

If we examine Demirel's policies during his on-and-off premierships since 1965, we can see that he placed the greatest emphasis on the Aegean continental shelf problem. His acceptance of taking the issue to the Court of Justice in The Hague through a delicately calculated mechanism during the 1976 summit with Premier Karamanlis in Brussels is the most vivid example of his political reasoning. Apart from this particular issue, Demirel, like Inonu, has favoured a traditionalist approach based on tried-and-trusted foreign ministry methods.

CONCLUSION

In the next few years one should not expect breakthroughs in Greek–Turkish relations. Looming difficulties in domestic policies will probably make it even more hard for both governments to make essential changes in their traditional approaches. However, there is still some hope of 'fallouts' from Davos.

Davos has introduced a new element in Greek–Turkish relations. It put an end to an era of confrontation and paved the way for an era of *détente*. Instead of volatile and nationalistic speeches by the leaders, an effort was made to understand the other's viewpoint and a more conciliatory stance was adopted.

This policy not only benefited Ozal in the eyes of Turkish public opinion, but was also adopted by the press, the bureaucracy and by policy-makers. It is virtually unthinkable that one would go back to the 'brink of war' tensions of the past years. On the contrary, Turkish public opinion seems to have accepted the fact that it will be very difficult to resolve Greek–Turkish problems, but instead of creating new ones, one can at least accept the status quo.

NOTES

1. Interview with Prime Minister Ozal, 5 January 1989.
2. Ozal was elected President of the Turkish Republic on 31 October 1989 by the Motherland Party deputies. The opposition boycotted the election.
3. Based on press conferences, press briefings and television statements given on 14 January 1987, 10 March 1987, 22 June 1988, 25 January 1989, 4 March 1989, 12 April 1989, 24 May 1989.

4 Greek Political Party Attitudes towards Turkey: 1974–89

VAN COUFOUDAKIS

'I feel very happy to be the first Turkish prime minister to pay an official visit to your beautiful country after an interval of thirty six years . . . our two nations . . . genuinely desire to live in an atmosphere of peace, friendship and cooperation.' With this statement, Turkish Prime Minister Turgut Ozal commenced his visit to Athens on 13 June 1988. This visit climaxed a process of direct contacts between the Greek and the Turkish prime ministers that began in the aftermath of the March 1987 confrontation over the Aegean continental shelf, and personal meetings held at Davos, Switzerland (30–1 January 1988) and Brussels (3–4 March 1988). What has been the impact of these developments on Greek–Turkish relations and on Greek foreign policy? How have these developments affected the issues that have dominated Greek foreign policy since 1974? These are some of the questions that this essay will attempt to address.

THE BACKGROUND

Space does not permit a detailed analysis of the issues that have affected Greek–Turkish relations in the inter-war period, and in the years prior to 1974. I have addressed some of these questions elsewhere.[1] Briefly stated (1) the 1923 Lausanne Treaty established the legal status quo in the region after a decade of warfare in the Balkans and Asia Minor. This legal status was further defined by the treaties of Montreux (1936) and Paris (1947); (2) since 1923, Greek–Turkish relations have passed through many difficult phases, but have also enjoyed periods of *détente* such as that in the 1930s under the leadership of Venizelos and Atatürk, and from the Truman Doctrine (1947) to the early 1950s; (3) post-World War Two Greek–Turkish relations were built on common security concerns. However, such concerns did not provide a strong foundation, one that could withstand discord over issues of vital interest to these countries. (4) The Cyprus issue since 1954 has tested Greek–Turkish relations and contributed to their progressive deterioration; affected security cooperation within NATO and among the two countries and the United States; and set the stage for the decimation of the protected Greek minority of Istanbul–Imbros–Tenedos, and for the persecution of the Eastern Orthodox Patriarchate. The United Kingdom also introduced Turkey in 1955 as a party of equal interest in the Cyprus dispute, thus enabling Turkey to control the evolution of the dispute since then. Finally, because Cyprus affected other Greek foreign policy priorities, tensions developed between Athens and Nicosia that led to the secret Greek–Turkish dialogue over Cyprus, and ultimately to the Greek-sponsored coup against the government of Cyprus, and to the 1974 Turkish invasion of the island republic.

ISSUES IN DISPUTE SINCE 1973 AND GREEK ASSESSMENTS OF TURKISH OBJECTIVES AND TACTICS

A number of issues have affected Greek–Turkish relations since 1973. Details of these issues have been presented elsewhere.[2] The present disputes consist of a composite of related and mutually reinforcing issues, some of which are new in origin, as in the case of the continental shelf, while others have been around for decades, as in the case of the minorities and Cyprus. These issues include the delimitation of the Aegean continental shelf; the Turkish invasion and continuing occupation of nearly 40 per cent of Cyprus; the control of the airspace over the Aegean; the right of Greece to extend its territorial waters to twelve miles; the militarization of the Greek Aegean islands off the Turkish coast, and conflicting interpretations of the treaties of Lausanne (1923), Montreux (1936) and Paris (1947) as to the extent of demilitarisation required on these islands; minority questions and allegations of discrimination and persecution by both Greece and Turkey; the implementation of Greece's NATO reintegration agreement, and its provisions on areas of operational responsibility and command structures; the attempt by Turkey to set up search-and-rescue areas in the Aegean; the maintenance of the military balance between Greece and Turkey, including but not limited to the 7:10 ratio of American military assistance to the two countries, the development of a domestic defence industry and so on; Turkey's quest for membership of the European Community and the issue of human rights violations by Turkey against its own public, the Greek minority of Istanbul and in Cyprus; and finally the support extended by Greece to Turkish dissidents and political exiles, especially during the 1980–3 military dictatorship in Turkey.

Following the restoration of democracy in 1974, successive Greek governments attempted to pursue an independent Greek foreign policy in order to protect vital Greek interests. Decades of dependence and external manipulation of Greek domestic politics; the toleration and support by Greece's allies of the military junta that ruled Greece from 1967 to 1974; and the perception that the United States and NATO supported or tolerated Turkey's revisionist objectives in the Aegean and Cyprus, contributed to the development of a far-reaching foreign policy consensus[3] among those who influence opinion across the political spectrum. This consensus was based on the following principles: (1) Greece must pursue an independent and multi-dimensional foreign policy; (2) the major threat facing Greek security is from the east, through Turkey, and not from the north, through the Soviet Union and its Balkan satellites; and (3) in view of the Western attitudes on the Greek–Turkish dispute and Cyprus, a fundamental divergence exists among the interests of Greece and those of her allies that actually threatens vital Greek interests.

This foreign policy consensus, when applied on a practical policy level, created problems for all post-1974 Greek governments. There were tactical as well as ideological differences in the policies of the New Democracy conservatives and the PASOK socialists. However, on the core issues[4] of Greek foreign and security policy, pragmatism and continuity have prevailed.

The consensus that Turkey is pursuing revisionist objectives in the Aegean and Cyprus, creating a vital threat to Greece, has come about for many reasons.[5] Firstly, Turkey's claims in the Aegean would, in effect, enclave most major Greek islands. These islands are an important economic, demographic and security extension of the Greek mainland. Secondly, Turkish suggestions for shared sovereignty and resource utilisation in the Aegean are seen as only the beginning of long-term demands, given Turkey's future population needs. Thirdly, Turkey's possession of the second largest fleet of landing craft among NATO countries, deployed mostly in Aegean ports. Turkey also established in 1975 the 'Fourth Army', known also as the Aegean Army. It is deployed in bases on the west coast of Asia Minor, and is not under NATO command. It is perceived as a major threat to the exposed Greek islands. Fourthly, Turkey is seen as aspiring to become a regional influence supported by the major Western powers that view Turkey as strategically more important than Greece. Fifthly, by seeking revisions in the command structure and operational areas of NATO during Greece's reintegration negotiations, Turkey sought to link its revisionist objectives with NATO's policy and create precedents for similar solutions of bilateral differences. Finally, Turkish demands and pressures for a bilateral definition of a regime governing the Aegean and its resources are seen as intended to exempt the region from the provisions of international conventions on the law of the sea.

Thus, the consensus that developed in Greece over Turkey's revisionism centred on Turkey's aim to overthrow the status quo created by the treaties of Lausanne (1923), Montreux (1936) and Paris (1947), and to partition and annex the occupied areas of Cyprus. Greece also feared that Turkish policy was the result of long-term planning, and was based on long-range objectives. Further, by proposing negotiations for a package deal on all Greek–Turkish differences, Turkey sought to achieve more of its objectives even in areas where it had no legitimate rights. Greece suspected Turkey's constant calls for negotiations on other grounds as well. Turkey attempted to display its peaceful intentions to the international community in order to achieve goals such as the lifting of the US arms embargo in 1975–8, or to make Greece look 'intransigent' if she refused to negotiate over her sovereign rights. By promoting negotiations over judicial solutions to issues such as the continental shelf, Turkey gave preference to a political solution over which it could utilise 'might is right' tactics, rather than risk an unfavourable court decision due to her weak legal position. Finally, the constant violations of Greek airspace, territorial waters and continental shelf were intended to test the readiness of Greek defences in the Aegean. They also emphasised Turkey's determined rejection of Greece's views, and indicated how far Turkey was willing to go to assert its newly established claims.

GREEK–TURKISH RELATIONS, 1974–81

The post-junta Greek governments were faced with limited choices in developing their policy towards Turkey for both domestic and international reasons. No democratic Greek government could accept compromises questioning Greek sovereignty and/or enclaving the

Greek Aegean islands and expect to survive. In accepting negotiations in areas where legitimate issues existed, as in the case of the delimitation of the continental shelf, no Greek government could appear to negotiate under duress, or create the perception that Greece's emphasis on *détente* was a sign of weakness. Moreover, the United States and NATO urged Greece to pursue a negotiated settlement of these differences with Turkey in the interests of stability and cohesion in NATO's south-eastern flank. Successive conservative Greek governments, while pursuing a foreign policy based on the principle of 'we belong to the West', recognised that because of strategic considerations neither NATO nor the United States were neutral in Greek–Turkish disputes. This in turn weakened the credibility of the post-1974 New Democracy governments, questioned the foundations of the entire post-war Greek foreign policy, and strengthened PASOK's credibility and popularity by providing proof for some of its key foreign policy positions.[6] Consequently, the negotiations for the reintegration of Greece to the military command of NATO were complicated not only by domestic political concerns, but also because of the possibility that acceptance of NATO formulas on command and control areas in the Aegean subverted Greek sovereignty and national security.

The New Democracy's policy of negotiations with Turkey over the various disputes was undermined by constant Turkish provocations in the Aegean and Cyprus.[7] Thus, the parliamentary opposition accused the government of negotiating under duress and allied pressure.

Moreover, even if ideologically and politically feasible, Greece could not count on Soviet support on these issues because the other superpower's policy, like that of the United States, was also motivated by regional strategic considerations. As a result, Soviet policy was either generally favourable to Turkey, or adequately vague so as not to antagonise that country. Finally, Greek policy excluded the use of force, unless absolutely necessary to defend Greek territory, and/or even Cyprus, from any further Turkish action. Prime Minister Karamanlis repeatedly proclaimed that his country had no hostile intentions or claims against Turkey. Speaking in the Greek parliament on 10 April 1976, he offered to conclude a non-aggression pact between the two countries,[8] and called on Turkey to agree to submit the issue of the delimitation of the continental shelf to the ICJ. Turkey rejected both proposals and instead pressed for negotiations on all outstanding issues. Turkey also attempted to establish *de facto* claims by unilateral grants of exploration licences in the Aegean and the dispatch of research vessels under Turkish navy escorts in contested areas. This brought the two countries close to armed conflict in the summer of 1976.

Karamanlis's commitment to seek a negotiated settlement of legitimate Greek–Turkish differences resulted in an intermittent dialogue between the two governments at various levels.[9] Even though this dialogue provided a valuable means of communication and of clarifying misperceptions, Greece rejected American suggestions for a 'Camp David' approach to Greek–Turkish differences, as it would legitimise many Turkish claims and Turkey's preference for a solution through political negotiations, rather than adjudication and/or arbitration. Despite the fact that Karamanlis was under pressure from public opinion and the parliamentary opposition to respond militarily against serious Turkish provocations, such as in the summer of 1976, he resorted to the UN Security Council and the ICJ, seeking measures to prevent a threat to peace and protect Greek legitimate rights.[10] These measures were supplemented by high levels of military readiness and military spending on force modernisation and equipment acquisition.

Finally, the New Democracy governments unsuccessfully sought revisions to the DECA with the United States paralleling those signed between the United States and Turkey on 27 March 1976. With the help of the Greek-American lobby a 7:10 ratio in the US military assistance programmes to Greece and Turkey was established; and the Greek government embarked on nearly three years of negotiations for the reintegration of Greece in NATO's military wing.

Looking back at the conduct of Greek–Turkish relations by the two New Democracy governments, one can conclude that they pursued the policy of a status quo power within narrowly defined international parameters and policy assumptions dating back to the early post-war period. Karamanlis's policy was also a highly personal policy, frequently bypassing the experts in the appropriate cabinet ministries. Greek policy priorities were also frequently in conflict, as in the case of Greece's application for membership of the European Community, which in the early stages ran into difficulty due to Greek–Turkish differences and the Cyprus problem.[11]

GREEK–TURKISH RELATIONS, 1981–7

The policies of Karamanlis and Rallis on Greek–Turkish relations set the foundations and the basic direction of the policies the PASOK party was to follow when it came to power in October 1981.

Most of the major issues affecting Greek–Turkish relations had already been defined by the time PASOK was formed in the autumn of 1974. These problems, along with the attitudes and actions of the superpowers towards these issues, and the policies of the New Democracy, enhanced PASOK's prestige and nationalistic policy by confirming the party's positions on international relations. PASOK assessed Turkey's long-term objectives towards Greece as expansionist, aiming at the partition of the Aegean, and/or some other formula under which sovereignty could be shared by the two countries. Turkey pursued these objectives with the tolerance and the support of the United States, if not also the complicity of the Soviet Union. Moreover, the United States and NATO proved unwilling to offer any guarantees to Greece against Turkey's military threat. Instead, they pressed Greece to be responsive to Turkey's demands. This is why PASOK has been explicit on the fact that Greece asks nothing of Turkey but friendship, but that this friendship will not be at the expense of 'an inch of Greek soil'.

Despite PASOK's ideological pronouncements, pragmatism[12] has characterised the formulation and conduct of Greek foreign policy on the core foreign and security policy issues. There is also significant continuity on core issue policies with that of its conservative predecessors, often differentiated by a clearer articulation of position and occasional assertions of independence.

PASOK's handling of Greek–Turkish relations has involved a careful balancing of ideological positions and pragmatic policy requirements. These policy trends have included:[13] (1) the reaffirmation of Greece's commitment to peaceful coexistence with Turkey, but not at the expense of Greek sovereign rights. (2) The avoidance of a unilateral extension of Greek territorial waters to twelve miles, although PASOK maintains that Greece has the right to do so under current international law. (3) Restrained but firm responses to all violations of Greek airspace and territorial water through diplomatic protests to Turkey, the United States and NATO, and the interception of Turkish air and naval craft. (4) The refusal to participate in any joint NATO exercises, questioning existing command and control areas and establishing prejudicial precedents for the resolution of other Greek–Turkish differences. For the same reasons, portions of the 'Rogers' Agreement', under which Greece rejoined NATO's military wing remain unimplemented. However, despite pre-electoral positions, the Papandreou government did not withdraw from NATO as this would have enhanced Turkey's strategic significance for the United States and NATO. The Papandreou government also successfully completed in July 1983 the negotiations originally undertaken by the New Democracy governments for a new five-year DECA with the United States. However, Papandreou was unsuccessful in obtaining guarantees from the United States and NATO against Turkey's threat. American and European technology was also acquired for the modernisation of the Greek armed forces and defence industry. Negotiations for a renewal of the DECA with the United States are currently continuing.

(5) The resumption of the Greek–Turkish dialogue at various levels, within the previously mentioned parameters – that is negotiations free from the threat of force and from any provocation, and only on issues involving other than sovereign rights. However, no summit meeting had been scheduled between Papandreou and his Turkish counterpart prior to 1988, although both sides had indicated that such a summit might be possible with the proper preparation. This intermittent, but inconclusive dialogue led to a short-lived 'moratorium' agreed upon on 22 July 1982, intended to establish a climate conducive to negotiations. Under its terms, both sides were to abstain from provocative actions and statements. However, both parties maintained that their positions on the issues were unaffected by the moratorium, and Greece vigorously presented Turkey's military threat in various international fora, and sought allied guarantees against it. This moratorium was suspended in November 1982, following the cancellation of a NATO exercise excluding the island of Lemnos, and violations of Greek airspace by Turkish aircraft.

The continued occupation of northern Cyprus by Turkey, and Turkey's claims and actions in the Aegean, led to the development of an important Greek position on further negotiations with Turkey. On numerous occasions Papandreou stated that no dialogue could occur as long as there were Turkish occupation troops in Cyprus, and Turkey promoted claims in the Aegean that, if accepted, would result in its partition: 'a dialogue meant give and take, and in our case is only to give. We do not have any claims, and therefore there can be nothing positive for Greece from such a dialogue.'[15] This position would come to haunt Papandreou in the aftermath of his decision to meet Prime Minister Ozal at Davos at the end of January 1988.

(6) The internationalisation of the Cyprus issue. The PASOK government has actively presented the problem of Cyprus as one of occupation and invasion, and not as a Greco-Turkish problem. In meetings of the European Community, NATO and the United

Nations, has sought the implementation of UN resolutions on Cyprus, and has called for the demilitarisation of Cyprus and the expansion of the UNFICYP with the additional costs to be borne by Greece. In February 1983, Papandreou became the first Greek prime minister to visit Cyprus. Despite occasional disagreements with the Cyprus government over the handling of the problem, PASOK has kept its pre-electoral promise of making Cyprus a priority of Greek foreign policy. The Greek activism over Cyprus entered a new phase following the unilateral declaration of independence by the Turkish Cypriots on 15 November 1983. With certainty and speed, Greece condemned this unilateral action, sought and supported multilateral and bilateral measures calling for the non-recognition of the Turkish–Cypriot 'state' and for the reversal of the UDI, threatened to break diplomatic relations with any state recognising the Turkish–Cypriot 'state', and advocated the adoption of practical measures to reverse the Turkish and Turkish–Cypriot actions. However, the Greek government, for practical reasons, did not withdraw its ambassador from Ankara. It only suspended the limited negotiations on economic and tourist co-operation that were under way at the time of the Turkish–Cypriot action. The Greek government also refused to engage in trilateral negotiations among the guarantor powers over the problem of Cyprus, showing preference instead for contacts only through the UK government and the United Nations.

Papandreou had also given verbal support to the Soviet suggestion for holding an international conference on Cyprus. Finally, Papandreou's views on Cyprus were also shaped by the belief that Turkey threatened Hellenism at large, not just Greece, and the United States and NATO were not only responsible for the junta in Greece and its actions in Cyprus, but also for encouraging and tolerating Turkish policy in the Aegean and Cyprus. Thus, Papandreou was emphatic in warning Turkey that any further adventurism on her part in Cyprus would mean war.

The Greek prime minister supported the refusal by the president of Cyprus, Kyprianou, to sign a preliminary draft agreement presented to the leaders of the two Cypriot communities by UN Secretary-General Perez de Cuellar at a New York summit in January 1985, in view of the issues left unresolved and open to future negotiation. Similarly the PASOK government extended its full support to President Kyprianou, and assisted him in developing a consensus position among all Greek–Cypriot political party leaders in response to the proposals presented by de Cuellar in March 1986 to the two sides. In the process Papandreou was accused by the United States and

Turkey of using Cyprus as part of his anti-Turkish policy, and of being the source of Cypriot intransigence in the intercommunal negotiations, a charge naturally rejected by the Greek government.

Thus, PASOK policy towards Turkey prior to 1988 evolved along the lines of ideology tempered by pragmatic considerations, as long as the environment in which this policy was carried out was not dramatically disturbed. That disturbance occurred late in March 1987, when, following the decision of Greece's Northern Aegean Petroleum Company to drill for oil ten miles east of the island of Thasos, Turkey dispatched the oceanographic research vessel *Sismik 1* to carry out seismic research on the continental shelf claimed by Greece. The vessel was escorted by Turkish navy warships. In a dramatic national address, following a meeting of the cabinet's national security council, Papandreou explained his readiness to protect by force if necessary Greece's sovereign rights; put NATO and the United States on notice that they would be responsible for any developments in the region; declared that he was ready to close for the duration of the emergency certain US electronic facilities in Greece; placed the Greek armed forces in a total state of readiness; and sent the Greek foreign minister, K. Papoulias, to Sofia for consultations with the Bulgarian government.

Papandreou's determined response and allied quiet diplomacy defused this latest crisis between Greece and Turkey. Historical hindsight shows that this confrontation[16] became the turning-point of Greek–Turkish relations since 1974. The risks involved in that confrontation pointed to the need for communication between the leaders of the two countries, communication that had been interrupted since November 1983. Following the March 1987 crisis, and for the remainder of that year, Papandreou and Ozal exchanged several written communications, which still remain secret. As a result of these communications the two leaders, in a surprise announcement, decided to meet on 30–1 January 1988, in Davos, Switzerland, for face-to-face discussions. These discussions continued at the NATO meeting in Brussels on 3–4 March 1988, and culminated in Ozal's visit to Greece on 13 June 1988, the first such visit to Greece in thirty-six years.[17]

GREEK–TURKISH RELATIONS SINCE DAVOS

The Greco-Turkish *rapprochement* that emerged from Davos, and the subsequent meetings, has been attributed by both sides to the 'sobering experience' of the March 1987 crisis over the Aegean continental shelf. This crisis pointed to the need for a continuous dialogue, and for confidence-building measures, in order to create a climate conducive for the resolution of their mutual problems. However, additional motives have contributed to this *rapprochement*. For both sides, these summit meetings represented the practical implementation of their calls for peaceful coexistence and negotiation of their differences. It was also a test of the sincerity of these proposals. In addition, Turkey's motives may have also included the elimination of one of the obstacles to increased US military and economic assistance, and of a major political obstacle to her EC membership application; the growing problems of the Turkish economy and the strains caused by the Kurdish question; and, finally, the need to consolidate civilian rule.

Papandreou in turn could claim vindication of his determined policies on Greek–Turkish relations. In addition, he may have wished to disprove Western and Turkish allegations as to his intransigence and of using Greek–Turkish issues for domestic purposes. He also aspired to reduce Greece's heavy military outlays at a time of economic austerity.[18]

These developments occurred amidst positive changes at the international level following the re-emergence of superpower *détente* with its positive impact on regional problems, such as Afghanistan, the Iran–Iraq war and so on. Moreover in Cyprus, despite the unwillingness of the United States to discuss this problem with the Soviet Union, the convergence of the views of the two superpowers on the nature of a federal solution enhanced the UN Secretary-General's ability to convince the two sides to accept new negotiating procedures which he presented to them late in May 1988. The election of George Vassiliou to the presidency of Cyprus in February 1988 also contributed to the improved prospects for a solution to the Cyprus problem, as he brought a new commitment to the search for a solution. The Greco-Turkish *rapprochement* was expected to have a positive effect on the Cyprus problem, by encouraging the submission of more flexible negotiating proposals by the Turkish Cypriots. In turn, positive movement on Cyprus could eliminate one major source of Greek suspicion as to Turkey's motives, and could contribute to building confidence between the two states.

Despite the fact that the Davos and the subsequent meetings constituted a reversal of PASOK's prior policy on negotiations with Turkey without the withdrawal of the Turkish troops from Cyprus,

Papandreou defended his policy on the grounds that this did not change Greek policy on the Greek–Turkish issues; it did not change Greek military strategy versus Turkey; it did not involve bargaining over sovereign issues; nor did it involve the shelving of Cyprus. Even though references to Cyprus were absent from the communiqués issued in the aftermath of these meetings, this was justified by the fact that as Cyprus is an independent state, a member of the United Nations, a solution to its problems was to be found within the framework of UN resolutions and not between Greece and Turkey.

Following Ozal's visit to Athens and the acceptance by the government of Cyprus of de Cuellar's good offices, Papandreou was able to express optimism regarding a solution of the Cyprus problem. However, he also cautioned Turkey that no substantial progress could occur either on Greek–Turkish relations or in Cyprus without the withdrawal of Turkish troops from the island. Finally, the 'no war' pledge that came out of the Davos meeting was the reiteration of the principle advocated by Karamanlis in 1976 and Papandreou in 1981. Such a pledge became possible now because Greece kept the balance of power at a heavy financial cost, and had stood firm in the face of earlier Turkish provocations. This pledge was a necessary step in building a climate of confidence, something expected to take between three and five years, while attempting to manage problems open to resolution.

These developments in Greek–Turkish relations were greeted with surprise and criticism by the opposition political parties in Greece, and with a certain degree of anxiety, but also cautious optimism, in Cyprus. In the latter case, Papandreou repeatedly attempted to assure the newly elected president of Cyprus of the continuity of Greek policy on Cyprus. In summit meetings in Athens the two leaders discussed and co-ordinated policy, especially in the context of the developments in Greek–Turkish relations and the UN Secretary-General's new initiatives. However, Papandreou's about-face on Turkey created a reversal in the positions of Cypriot political parties *vis-à-vis* Greek policy. Cypriot parties critical of Papandreou's earlier hard-line policy, such as the conservative/right-wing Democratic Rally and the Communist-AKEL party, now supported his initiatives. The centrist Democratic party of former President Kyprianou and the Socialist-EDEK party in turn became critical of Papandreou's actions. These parties did not object to Greco-Turkish *détente*. They were concerned about its impact on Cyprus and the manner in which this policy change came about.

Similar in many ways was the situation in Greece. The leadership of the conservative New Democracy party, even though in agreement with the fundamentals of Greek policy towards Turkey, had always been more flexible on the issue of a Greek–Turkish dialogue. However, its leader, C. Mitsotakis, attacked Papandreou's initiatives in a manner reminiscent of PASOK's critique of Greek foreign policy while it was the main parliamentary opposition party. Mitsotakis's critique was not an indication of a breakdown of the foreign policy consensus that had emerged in Greek–Turkish relations since 1974. The criticism was based on the manner by which these policy shifts came about, and of possible compromises of earlier Greek positions that may have been made in order to bring about these meetings. The opposition claimed that these compromises were evident in the wording of the communiqués issued at the conclusion of these summit meetings. In the parliamentary debates that followed the Brussels meeting between Papandreou and Ozal, Mitsotakis accused Papandreou of abandoning the cause of Cyprus, of surrender and lack of preparation, and of having embarked in negotiations with Turkey without a mutual declaration of respect of their common borders, and of the relevant international agreements, without making substantive talks contingent on a Turkish troop withdrawal from Cyprus, and without Turkey's acceptance of a recourse to the ICJ for the delimitation of the continental shelf.

Papandreou's decisions appear to have been made at the highest political level, with minimum, if any, input from the experts at the Ministry of Foreign Affairs. This may have reflected a contemporary trend in the making of foreign policy. It may have also been a sign of lack of trust in the Greek career diplomatic service. Consequently, these decisions caused the resignations of three senior career diplomats, ambassadors Serbos, Stoforopoulos and Dountas.[19] In numerous newspaper articles Dountas provided a most articulate critique of the manner by which Papandreou proceeded in his negotiations with Turkey, without any evidence of change in its policy or in the policy of the United States on Greek–Turkish differences and Cyprus. Moreover, he expressed concern on the negative impact of these initiatives on Cyprus. Dountas cautioned that such rash policies would create long-term problems for Cyprus and Greece, and raised the problem of the Muslim minority of western Thrace as one of those long-term problem areas that Turkey would exploit.

In the year that has passed since the dramatic initiatives that brought about the three summit meetings between Papandreou and

Ozal, no further progress has taken place in Greek–Turkish relations. Papandreou, due to health, personal and domestic political problems, was unable to return Ozal's visit as originally planned. The domestic political problems that confronted both prime ministers undermined further their power base and their ability to undertake major foreign policy initiatives. Thus, the 'spirit of Davos' appears to have expired during the course of 1989. The situation may have been further complicated by the lack of progress on the Cyprus problem. Despite months of face-to-face negotiations between the president of Cyprus, George Vassiliou, and the Turkish–Cypriot leader, Raouf Denktash, and reassessment meetings in the presence of the UN Secretary-General, the Turkish Cypriots appear even more intransigent than in the past. The proposals they presented early in February 1989 for a resolution of the Cyprus problem amount to the partition of Cyprus under the guise of a loose confederal system. Moreover, Ozal appears unwilling or unable to deal with Denktash, who enjoys the support of the hard-liners in the Turkish ministries of defence and foreign affairs. This became apparent when Ozal fully endorsed Denktash's decision late in the summer of 1989 to suspend the high-level talks with President Vassiliou; to reject de Cuellar's framework for a solution of the Cyprus problem; and to set new conditions for the resumption of the negotiations.

Other serious problems arose during 1989. These include: (1) the growing number of Turkish violations of Greek airspace; (2) provocations regarding the Muslim minority in western Thrace, especially during the Greek electoral campaign for the June 1989 elections; and (3) Turkey's failure to take steps to restore the property rights of the Greek minority of Istanbul. Moreover, there is no evidence that the discussions at the committee level have produced new ideas for the resolution of the problems identified earlier in this chapter, such as the delimitation of the continental shelf. Instead, the fears of enclaving the Greek Aegean islands have been further enhanced by the unilateral Turkish proclamation of search-and-rescue areas in the Aegean, whose boundaries are similar to those claimed by Turkey for the delimitation of the continental shelf and for airspace control purposes. Nor has any progress been made in the implementation of the Rogers' Agreement under which Greece returned to the military command of NATO. Finally, the European Community has not undertaken any serious initiatives to influence Turkey's behaviour, whether on the Cyprus problem or the other Greek–Turkish differences. Any such action would require some reciprocity on the Turkish application for membership of the Community, something that the twelve are not ready to do at this time.

Since 1974, the cycle of confrontation–negotiation–confrontation between Greece and Turkey has been a familiar one. This cycle is likely to be repeated in view of the issues dividing the two countries. However, despite domestic pressures and ideological bravado, resort to force has been avoided even though in 1974, 1976 and 1987 Greece and Turkey came dangerously close to war. Under both conservative and socialist governments, pragmatism has prevailed. Pragmatic necessity brought about the Davos meeting, without presumably any compromise on the fundamental Greek positions regarding these Greek–Turkish differences. In view of the consensus underlying Greek foreign policy, it is doubtful that any future freely elected Greek government would moderate the position that Greek sovereign rights will not be subverted. Greek pragmatism has not been the result of weakness, nor is it a bluff. However, pragmatism will not survive long in the face of new provocations, especially over the Muslim minority of western Thrace, and/or a new *fait accompli* by Turkey in Cyprus. A solution to the Cyprus problem may help improve the political climate between Greece and Turkey, but it is not a panacea. Greek–Turkish problems have their own momentum and affect other vital interests. The steps taken at and since Davos, along with the reaffirmation of the 'no war' option, are vital to the peaceful coexistence of the two states. The fact that these bilateral talks did take place is a welcome sign of maturation. It also shows the understanding that solutions can be found through negotiations, but only where legitimate issues exist and without the threat of force and/or provocation. The success of any future talks will depend on confidence-building measures before any of the substantive issues can be resolved. Finally, conflict resolution and peaceful coexistence ought to be pursued because of the benefits that *détente* can bring to both sides, and not because of the desires and pressures of powers outside the region. *Détente* and peaceful coexistence are possible if each state accepts the other's equality, sovereignty and legally established rights. The challenge is monumental, but not impossible.

NOTES

1. Van Coufoudakis, 'Greek–Turkish Relations, 1973–1983: The View from Athens', *International Security*, vol. 9 (Spring 1985) no. 4, pp. 185–217.
2. Perhaps the best summary can be found in Andrew Wilson, *The Aegean Dispute*, Adelphi Paper no. 155 (London: International Institute for Strategic Studies, Winter 1979–80).
3. Van Coufoudakis, 'Greek Foreign Policy since 1974: Quest for Independence', *Journal of Modern Greek Studies*, vol. 6 (May 1988) no. 1, pp. 55–79.
4. Greek–Turkish relations; Cyprus; defence co-operation with the United States; NATO; the European Community.
5. Van Coufoudakis, 'Greek–Turkish Relations, 1973–1983', pp. 202–3.
6. Van Coufoudakis, 'Greco-Turkish Relations and the Greek Socialists: Ideology, Nationalism and Pragmatism', *Journal of Modern Greek Studies*, vol. 1 (Fall 1983) no. 2, pp. 373–92.
7. The dispatch of oceanographic research vessels escorted by Turkish navy warships in disputed as well as in Greek areas of the continental shelf, overflights in Greek airspace, and so on.
8. For the appropriate texts, see Christos Sazanides, *Hoi Hellino-Tourkikes Scheseis Sten Pentaetia 1973–1978* (Thessaloniki: published by the author) pp. 81, 204–10.
9. Including ambassadorial meetings in Athens and Ankara; meetings between the secretaries-general of the respective ministries of foreign affairs; meetings of experts on technical problems; meetings of foreign ministers in the context of NATO meetings; and three summit meetings. Karamanlis met Demirel in Brussels, 31 May 1975; Ecevit in Montreux on 11 March 1978, and at Blair House in Washington, 30 May 1978.
10. The Greek appeal to the Security Council and the Council's decision 395/76 can be found in Sazanides, *Hoi Hellino-Tourkikes Schesis*, pp. 288, 316–17. For the decision of the ICJ, see *International Legal Materials*, vol. 15 (September 1976) no. 5, pp. 985–1009.
11. P. Tsakaloyannis, 'The European Community and the Greek–Turkish Dispute', *Journal of Common Market Studies*, vol. 19 (Spring 1980) no. 1, pp. 35–54. For the Commission's opinion on the Greek membership application, see European Community Information Service, Background Note 6/1976 (30 January 1976).
12. For the sources and causes of pragmatism, see Van Coufoudakis, 'Greek Foreign Policy since 1974', pp. 63–5.
13. Van Coufoudakis, 'Greek–Turkish Relations, 1973–1983', pp. 212–13.
14. Such as the cancellation of the exercises 'Deterrent Force 1/82' and 'Distant Drum' in May 1982, and exercises excluding the use of the island of Lemnos in the autumn of 1982 and 1983. This policy remains in effect to this day.
15. *The Week in Review*, Greek Embassy Press and Information Service, Washington, DC (9 March 1987) no. 10/87, p. 2.
16. Some Papandreou critics have disputed the seriousness of the incident, or even that this incident ever occurred.

17. For the communiqué issued at Davos see *The Week in Review*, Greek Embassy Press and Information Service, Washington, DC (1 February 1988) no. 4/88. For the Brussels communiqué see *The Week in Review*, Greek Embassy Press and Information Service, Washington, DC (7 March 1988) no. 9/88. For the Athens communiqué see *Greece – Information*, Greek Embassy Press and Information Service, Washington, DC (20 June 1988) no. 23/88.
18. Greek defence spending as a percentage of GDP in 1987 was 6.2 per cent, the second highest in NATO after the United States. In contrast, Turkey ranked fourth at 4.4 per cent. United States, Department of Defense, *Report on Allied Contribution to the Common Defense* (Washington, DC: USGPO, 1989) p. 96.
19. Serbos headed the Turkish affairs section of the Ministry of Foreign Affairs. Stoforopoulos was Greece's ambassador to Cyprus. He was recalled from his post because of his public criticism of Papandreou's decisions. Dountas, the old Cyprus hand, was Greece's ambassador to Moscow at the time.

5 Turkey's Relations with Greece: Motives and Interests

HEINZ KRAMER

To talk about motives and interests of a country's foreign policy is, to a large extent, an exercise in speculation. This is due to the highly imprecise meaning of the two concepts, which are characterised by a lack of a clear, commonly accepted and operational definition. Nevertheless, 'interest' or 'national interest' is a prominent concept in the analysis of international relations or foreign policy.[1] I will refrain, here, from another exercise in adding a further definition or categorisation to the already existing ones. Instead, I will content myself with a rough 'working definition' for the purpose of this presentation. If, in the following, I speak of 'motives' this is in the meaning of basic factors which guide the foreign policy behaviour, whereas 'interests' are more or less synonymous with 'goals'. And, as both imply also non-material, psychologic factors or issues, it is also evident that sometimes (or even more than sometimes) the distinction between 'motives' and 'interests' is far from clear and in many cases arguable. But despite these obvious conceptual weaknesses, this may be one possible way to get a better understanding of the background of Turkey's foreign policy towards Greece.

In the following I will mainly develop three arguments. The first concerns the background of the relationship that is created by the common history of both countries and the imprints that this history has left on the collective psychological map of both publics. Secondly, I want to argue that the general motives of Turkey's foreign policy are also applicable to her relationship with Greece, that is the Turkish behaviour towards the Aegean neighbour country is no deviating case, although since the mid-1950s this relationship ranks very prominently in the foreign policy hierarchy of Turkey and takes the first place during the 1970s. And, thirdly, I try to show that the actual policy of the Ozal government towards Greece is based on the assumption that the possible advantages by far outweigh the possible risks that may be linked to a process of controlled Greek–Turkish reconciliation.

THE GENERAL BACKGROUND OF THE RELATIONSHIP

Before starting to analyse Turkish foreign policy behaviour towards Greece it seems to be helpful to have a short look at the general background of the relationship between the two Aegean states. This relationship cannot be understood correctly unless seen in the light of the common historical heritage which, up to the present, plays an important role in explaining their perception of each other and of their respective behaviour. In Greece as well as in Turkey the relationship between the two countries is seen as being loaded with traumatic historical experiences.[2] These touch directly and very fundamentally upon the problem of national identity. Modern Greece establishes her national identity to a large extent on the successful struggle against the Ottoman yoke, which in the Turkish view is identical with the acceleration of the decline of the Ottoman Empire. On the other hand, the Republic of Turkey owes her existence, *inter alia*, to a successful 'war of independence' in which Greek occupational troops in western and central Anatolia were the main enemy. What is for the Turks the birth of their state is for the Greeks the definite end of some type of neo-imperialistic ideology. Thus, both states link their very existence and an important part of their national identity to events that have been highly detrimental to the other side.

Up to the present, this perception of history, of the respective national identity, and of certain dangers to it, which could be the result of the behaviour of the other side, have been crucial elements for the conduct of both states in their mutual relationship. This has led to a state of affairs characterised more by mutual feelings of distrust and by a deterrent political behaviour than by mutual trust and efforts for co-operation. Until the very recent past this perception and conduct of affairs have been reinforced on both sides by national 'agencies of socialisation' such as schools, media and the academic community.[3]

A certain contrast to this picture is created by the fact that on a personal level one can very often find a much more open and relaxed attitude on both sides. It is by no means an exception to find a Turk who says that he has nothing against the Greek people and that he does not believe that the Greeks want to harm the Turkish people. And vice versa. That is to say that the image of the other side as the 'arch-enemy' is more a collective image than one that concerns the individual. It should be added here that in general even this collective image is not very widespread in the Turkish public. The general attitude of the Turkish people towards the Greeks can better be characterised as indifference rather than as emotional interest.

It is this politico-psychological background, this mixture of historical events and collective images, which have been created by the biased perception of these events, that has to be taken into account if one wants to analyse Turkey's motives and interests. These are not solely determined by objective factors of geographic, economic or military considerations, which also play an important role but do not tell the whole story.

TURKISH MOTIVES AND INTERESTS

One of the leading motives of Turkey's foreign policy can be derived from the general political aim of the country since the founding of the republic. That is that the foreign policy shall not negatively interfere with the economic and societal development process which shall bring the country to the level of contemporary civilisation. Domestic development clearly has a priority over foreign relations as long as national integrity and sovereignty remain intact. This leads directly to the guiding principle of Turkish foreign policy: peace at home, peace in the world. The political practice derived from this principle is largely characterised by an anti-revisionist, status quo orientation.

This goes together with a political practice that stubbornly looks after the preservation of the Turkish nation-state as it was created and internationally recognised by the Treaty of Lausanne in 1923. The notions of 'nation', 'nationalism', 'nation-state', 'national interest' and 'national integrity' are not only recurrent leitmotifs of Turkish constitutions since 1924 but also of the country's relations with the outside world.

Both these elements – priority of national development and preservation of national integrity – form the background of the general mix of Turkey's foreign policy.[4] This mix is characterised on the one hand by attempting not to become involved in disputes between regional forces that may have negative repercussions on Turkey. Or, to put it positively, Turkey tries to establish smooth working relationships with all countries in her extended neighbourhood. Examples of this foreign policy practice can be found since the times of Atatürk. Among these the early Turkish–Soviet friendship, the reconciliation with Greece after the war of independence, the Balkan Pact and the Saadabad Pact rank prominently. Actual examples of this line of foreign policy are the carefully balanced relationship with Iran and Iraq, as well as Turkey's readiness to join the recent efforts for increased co-operation between the Balkan countries.

On the other hand, Turkey has never hesitated forcefully to defend her national interests as she perceives them. But in doing so, she has always tried to abstain from the use of military means and relied more on diplomacy and legal arguments. Thus, the young republic has been successful in regaining the unshared sovereignty over the Turkish straits as well as achieving the incorporation of the Hatay area.

The same can be said about the general Turkish approach in relations with Greece. The process of reconciliation started by Atatürk and Venizelos after the war of independence was crowned by the Treaty of Friendship and Co-operation of 1933. And since the mid-1950s when the relationship between both countries was again marked more by conflict and tensions than by friendship and reconciliation, every Turkish government has tried to reach a solution by direct bilateral negotiations and has normally abstained from the use of force. And if Turkey sometimes had recourse to force, this normally did not go beyond the form of demonstrative acts and/or threats and was accompanied by a policy of careful crisis management which avoided a large-scale military confrontation.[5]

This is not to say that Turkey did not make use of military means at all in order to defend her interests. But these means have been mostly put into action against what official Turkish language calls domestic 'separatist forces' that endanger the territorial integrity of the country. But in her desire to destroy the bases of Kurdish forces which lie across the border with Iraq, Turkey has again generally fallen back upon diplomatic efforts in order to gain the support of her neighbours against the Kurds.

But it is in connection with issues that touch upon elements of national sovereignty and national integrity that Turkish foreign policy shows a more rigid attitude. Among these issues the preservation of territorial integrity, the preservation of the international legal bases of the republic, and the fate of Turkish minorities in neighbouring countries rank most prominently.

With respect to *territorial integrity*, it was the Soviet attempt at the end of World War Two to incorporate parts of north-eastern Turkey into the Soviet Union that facilitated the abandoning of Atatürk's foreign policy principle of 'non-alignment' by his follower Ismet Inonu.[6] This led finally to the firm inclusion of Turkey into the Western state system. For the Turkish political élite, preservation of territorial integrity means not yielding an inch of what was established and internationally recognised as the Republic of Turkey at Lausanne in 1923.

This principle normally does not create problems for Turkey's neighbours unless issues occur that were not dealt with at Lausanne or with respect to which new international developments occur. This is mainly the case with questions concerning international waters. Thus the problems of the delimitation of the continental shelf and the territorial waters in the Aegean have become a contentious issue between Greece and Turkey. It is in these cases that Turkey reacts like any state, that is she tries to get as much as possible. And by declaring these issues to be cases of national interest in the sense outlined above, they have become parts of the collective political psychological map of Turkey on which a compromise is very difficult to reach because this is closely related to the notion of 'defeat'. Therefore it is very important that any solution to the problem not only is satisfactory in material terms but is also free from any inclination that it has been brought about by sacrifices with respect to the integrity of the Turkish nation and its territory.

From what I have said about the historical background of Greek–Turkish relations and its politico-psychological connotations in both countries it becomes immediately clear why a question, which on first sight seems to be of a technical nature, is so difficult to solve in the case of Greece and Turkey. This is mainly because the sensitivity with respect to national integrity and sovereignty is highly developed on both sides.

Another motive of Turkish foreign policy connected with the issue of national sensitivity is the uncompromising *preservation* of what is seen to be the *international legal base* of the republic. This legalistic approach is sometimes very hard for outsiders to understand, especially when the issues involved do not seem to pose concrete difficulties for Turkey or restrict her room for international political activity. Thus, Turkey's position concerning the remilitarisation of the Greek islands in the eastern Aegean seems to be more determined by this legalistic approach than by real concern with respect to the country's security. And indeed, it is hard to conceive a threat to Turkish security by the stationing of a Greek brigade, which is earmarked for NATO, on the island of Lemnos or by the militarisation of the Dodecanese Islands, given the overall military balance between the two Aegean states and the clear strategic superiority of Turkey.

Perhaps this legalistic approach can be explained by what a Turkish scholar has called the 'state tradition' of Turkish politics.[7] Although Metin Heper has restricted his concept to domestic political developments, it seems to have a foreign policy aspect as well.[8] Another explanation for this legalistic attitude could be the fear that compromising on the international legal base of the Turkish Republic in one respect, that is the Treaty of Lausanne, might tempt other states to try a revision of other parts of this base, that is the Soviet Union might try again to revise the Convention of Montreux as she had done after World War Two. But, if one takes into consideration that the question of the militarisation of the eastern Aegean islands is one that concerns two NATO allies and, to a certain extent, the context of the alliance as such, whereas a Soviet desire for a revision of the regime of the Turkish straits is at least an issue of East–West relations, the Turkish legalism remains difficult to understand.

And one should not overlook the amount of opportunism that accompanies this Turkish legalism. The Turkish government, as any other, only takes recourse to legal texts if it is sure that they are in favour of its own position. In the case of the Greek–Turkish disputes this can be demonstrated by the different approach that Ankara takes to different issues at stake. With respect to the militarisation of the Aegean islands, Turkey invokes the rulings of the treaties of Lausanne (1923) and Paris (1947), that is she takes a strictly legal approach, as she also seems to do with respect to some matters of air traffic control, whereas with respect to questions related to maritime issues she has carefully avoided becoming involved with the international legal developments that have taken place in the context of the various UN conferences on the law of the sea and, generally, favour positions that are not in the Turkish interest.

Concerning the fate of *Turkish minorities* in neighbouring states, Ankara seems to apply the same skilful mix of diplomatic efforts, which aim at the creation of a favourable climate in the bilateral relations with the respective state, and a controlled recourse to more substantial means. In any case, this policy is backed up by the creation of a domestic public opinion that delivers the justification for any concrete step taken by the government. This is not difficult to attain due to the role that 'national issues' play in the collective mind of the Turkish public. Although the political leaders of the republic since the days of Atatürk carefully avoided any inclination towards pan-Turkist ideologies,[9] the process of creating a Turkish nation-state on the remnants of the Ottoman Empire has unavoidably been accompanied by a process of nation-building which cannot abstain from stressing the ethnic components.[10] This has led to a high public sensitivity with respect to the fate of Turks all over the world and especially with respect to the fate of larger groups of Turks living in foreign countries.

The means applied by Ankara to protect the interests and the well-being of Turkish minorities show a great variety which seems to depend on the room for political manoeuvre under the given circumstances. The situation of Turkish 'guestworkers' in western Europe, especially in the Federal Republic of Germany, is mainly influenced by means of bilateral governmental agreements and through the Turkish press at home and in western Europe. Concerning the fate of the Turkish minority in Bulgaria, the government in Ankara seeks solutions through bilateral talks which are backed by an anti-Bulgarian campaign in international organisations such as the Council of Europe and in the CSCE framework. But Turkey strictly refrains from any activity that could be interpreted as a threat by the Bulgarian government. In doing so Ankara takes into account that her relations with Bulgaria are affected by the larger framework of East–West relations and the important role that Bulgaria plays as a transit country for a large amount of traffic between Turkey and the other European countries.

Concerning the Turkish minority in Greece, one has to take into account the existence of a Greek minority in Turkey. Although it is much smaller in number, its significance is enhanced by the fact that the seat of one of the leading personalities of the Greek Orthodox Church is located in Istanbul. Notwithstanding the fact that the stipulations of the Treaty of Lausanne provide a clear legal base for the independence and freedom of action of the Ecumenical Patriarchate, the Turkish government is in a position to influence heavily the factual day-to-day development of this situation. As the history of Greek–Turkish relations since the mid-1950s reveals, both sides are well aware of their respective minority in the other country functioning as a sort of hostage.[11] This has led to the very low profile of Turkey's policy regarding the situation in western Thrace.[12] It has mainly been restricted to some lobbying in Western fora in order to condemn what in Ankara is seen as a discriminatory Greek policy. This has, of course, been accompanied by extensive media coverage in Turkey, which, however, normally does not arouse public interest abroad.

The only exception to this generally modest approach of Turkey's policy with respect to the minorities abroad is the case of Cyprus. Here, the Turks took recourse to the use of military force in order to protect the physical integrity of the Turkish–Cypriot community. But Cyprus can be seen as an exception with respect to almost any issues of the Greek–Turkish dispute. This is mainly due to some differences in the historical development of the Cyprus issue in comparison with the general Greek–Turkish relationship. Cyprus is the only place where some influential role has been assigned to Turkey by an international treaty after she had lost the territory. The role of a guaranteeing power attributed to Turkey by the treaties of Zurich and London formally establishes, in Turkish eyes, the possibility of military action without the implication of expansionist aims or aggressive behaviour. Thus, for the Turks the military intervention of 1974 does not constitute a deviation from the general philosophy of Turkish foreign policy, according to which the territorial boundaries of the republic have been established once and for all by the Treaty of Lausanne and that therefore there is no need for military action aimed at occupying foreign territory.[13]

One last motive of Turkey's foreign policy in general, which also has implications for her behaviour towards Greece, derives from the *Western orientation* of the country. Since Atatürk's days the essence of Turkish politics can be seen in the efforts that have been made to bring the country to the level of contemporary Western civilisation. More than sixty years of Turkish domestic and foreign policy have served the realisation of this goal. Today a large part of the Turkish élite is of the opinion that it has been reached, especially so after the country became a member of the Western political and economic system after World War Two. The foreign policy since 1947 had no other aim than firmly anchoring Turkey to the West in order to finalise the process begun by Atatürk.[14]

Turkey conducted this foreign policy under one very important precondition: the country was to be treated as an equal among the other Western states.[15] As the high sensitivity of this issue has often not been fully recognised by Turkey's allies, their behaviour towards the country gave rise to suspicion among the political leadership and other opinion leaders that the West recognises Turkey only as a strategic-military asset on the periphery of the Western system and not as an integral part of this system. This has led to the growth of mixed feelings among the Turkish political class about the usefulness of an unrestricted Western orientation of the country. These doubts were accompanied by a discussion about the basic foreign policy interests of Turkey which was especially lively during the 1970s but calmed down again after 1980. Today the necessity of a firm Turkish commitment to the West seems again to be the overwhelming public consensus.[16] But after the experiences with US policy towards Turkey in 1964 and after 1974 and those with the EC countries after 1980, this public consensus is an 'enlightened' one and the insistence of Turkish foreign policy on full equality is stressed even more, as can be seen from Ankara's argumentation with respect to EC membership.

Given the special psychological background of Turkey's relations with Greece, the Turkish sensitivity with respect to equal treatment and uncompromised recognition as a Western country had certain repercussions on the situation between the two Aegean states. Turkey is well aware of the fact that Greece, unlike herself, is regarded as a 'natural' part of the West and of Europe. Therefore, for Turkey it was always an issue of utmost importance not to be discriminated against in favour of Greece. This can clearly be seen with respect to NATO membership, relations with the EC and relations with the United States, which form the main institutional frameworks of Turkey's affiliation to the West. This link between Turkey's membership in the core institutions of the Western state system and the Greek–Turkish relationship often transforms the latter in a very subtle way into a triangular one with the third corner being either the United States or NATO or the European Community or one of its members.[17] Up to now, this configuration has not been very helpful for the solution of Greek–Turkish disputes but it offered for both sides some leverage in order to gain additional material support from their allies.

It is this part of the general Turkish problem of establishing a Western national identity that makes the Turkish élite and part of the Turkish public believe that some of the Greek positions concerning disputed issues in the Aegean are motivated by the desire to isolate Turkey from Europe, that is from the West. And it may be this psychological syndrome that is, apart from all material considerations, behind the Turkish efforts to get a certain share of the Aegean, and to prevent the Aegean from becoming a 'Greek sea'. As the Aegean is a European sea, any country that can claim to be an

Aegean country is a European country as well. In any case, one should not underestimate these collective psychological undercurrents in dealing with certain Turkish positions and actions with respect to Greek–Turkish disputes.

THE ACTUAL SITUATION[18]

The motives and interests outlined above can be found in the foreign policy of almost any Turkish government after 1950 and they form also the base of Turgut Ozal's approach and his policy towards Greece after he came to power in December 1983. From the very beginning, that is in his first governmental programme, he outlined what became known in Turkey as the 'policy of the olive branch'. The starting-point of this policy is Ozal's firm conviction that there is no reason for the Aegean states to continue with a confrontational policy. In his opinion the common interests in good neighbourliness and economic co-operation by far outweigh the issues separating the two countries. A solution of the conflict can only be to the profit of both states. As a consequence of this basic conviction, Ozal repeatedly offered to open talks with the Greek government about all issues – especially co-operation in the spheres of economics and tourism – without any preconditions. As a signal of her goodwill, Turkey in 1984 abolished the visa requirement for Greek citizens who wanted to visit the country.

This approach is in concordance with the 'classic' motive of Turkish foreign policy that the economic and social modernisation of the country can best be achieved if Turkey has orderly and peaceful relations with her neighbouring countries. In view of his ambitious economic and political plans to prepare the country for EC membership and transform it into the leading economic force in the eastern Mediterranean, Ozal has much interest in reducing foreign policy pressure on Turkey. This not only holds true with respect to the relations with Greece. The pronounced Turkish neutrality towards the conflicting parties of the Iran–Iraq war, the recent intensification of relations with Syria, and Turkish attempts to come to terms with Bulgaria – both countries with which Turkey has some serious disputes – all point in the same direction. And as Ozal can claim that by following this line of foreign policy he is in full conformity with the Kemalist tradition of Turkey's foreign policy, he does not encounter principal opposition at home. The criticism of the political opposition and in parts of the Turkish press is directed at procedural or tactical questions or consists of warnings against too early or too far-reaching Turkish concessions which may not be met by equivalent Greek moves.

Ozal's readiness to respond favourably to Papandreou's conciliatory signals after the last severe crisis of March 1987 was further supported by the rather undogmatic and unideological personal political style of the Turkish prime minister. His generally pragmatic approach towards politics made it easy for him to react to Papandreou's moves by setting aside normal principles and concerns about possible Greek *arrière-pensées*. This personal flexibility of the Turkish prime minister should not, however, be confused with a readiness for a hasty abandonment of political positions. On the contrary, Ozal generally has a very precise idea of his policy goals and the pros and cons of his activities. This could be seen very clearly during the 'Davos process' when Ozal refused any moves that went beyond the phase of confidence building and could give rise to the impression that he might be ready to deal with the substantial issues of the Greek–Turkish conflict.

The advantages for Turkey of a *détente* in her relations with Greece are obvious. First, Ankara could concentrate its security policy efforts completely on the situation in the south-east, which is seen as critical, and on the traditional Turkish security concern towards the north. The Turkish reactions to the new Greek security policy doctrine could be undone. In view of the burden on the Turkish and national economy in general that is created by the security policy measures, even a minor relief is welcome.

Secondly, extensive Greek–Turkish co-operation in the tourism sector could enhance the profitability of the potential presently existing on the Turkish Aegean coast. The development of, for example, 'integrated package tours' that include the Greek islands and the Turkish coast could be a measure that would also be advantageous for the tourist facilities on the islands. And, in general, a higher degree of permeability of the borders in the eastern Aegean could be economically advantageous for both sides. Besides this, the generally low level of economic interpenetration between both countries indicates that there is room for mutually advantageous economic co-operation.

Thirdly, a *détente* in the Aegean would have positive repercussions on Turkey's relations with the US Congress, which since 1974 has not been free from recurrent tensions. Here, Turkey may, above all, hope for the abolition of the 7:10 ratio in American military aid to the Aegean states which is strictly adhered to by Congress. But there may also be some hopes in Ankara that American politicians would ease their criticism about Turkish policy with respect to Cyprus and the Armenian issue if the 'Davos process' leads to some positive developments in Greek–Turkish relations.

Fourthly, the Turkish government knows very well that a solution to the bilateral problems in its relationship with Greece as well as a solution to the Cyprus problem is of paramount significance with respect to the chances of the Turkish application for EC membership. It is hardly conceivable that the political circles in Ankara really are convinced that a final solution to these problems could be postponed until Turkish entry has taken place and that one could use EC fora to these ends, although one can sometimes find such opinions among Turkish officials and politicians. Therefore, one can expect strong Turkish efforts in order to clear the situation in the Aegean if the Community would declare in principle its readiness to accept Turkey. But it should not, however, be expected in Brussels or the leading political circles of the member countries that Turkey will soften her position before the Community has cleared the way to membership.[19]

Fifthly, the Turkish government knows very well that it can only realise its interests in the Aegean if the Greek side is ready to enter into talks and negotiations. Therefore, one can see a constant interest of all Turkish governments since 1974 to enter into a dialogue with Athens. This interest is due to the Turks' realisation that contrary to what happened on Cyprus where the Greek junta delivered the welcome occasion for a unilateral intervention, there is no possibility for a unilateral Turkish action in order to realise its goals in the Aegean. Unilaterally Turkey is only able to maintain the status quo, which is felt to be unsatisfactory in Ankara as well as in Athens.

These advantages or hopes, which are linked by the Turkish government to the opening of a dialogue with Athens, are not endangered by serious risks or disadvantages. Due to the national consensus about the basic motives of Turkish foreign policy as outlined above, no government in Ankara that tries to enter into a dialogue with Athens runs the risk of being confronted with a fundamental political opposition. The domestic political risk, therefore, is rather limited as long as the Turkish interlocutors carefully respect national sensitivities and display the necessary amount of caution with respect to the content and course of the dialogue. Any

Turkish government can only deviate from what seems to be an established national consensus about Greek–Turkish affairs if it is able to present to the public a considerable Greek return offer. The behaviour of the Ozal government in the course of the 'Davos process' so far shows that the Turkish prime minister is very well aware of these domestic terms of his Aegean policy.

In her relations with her main Western partners, too, Turkey will not encounter any difficulties by opening talks with Greece. Quite the contrary. Relations with the government of the Turkish separatist state in northern Cyprus could only become strained if the Turkish Cypriots gained the impression that they could become victims of a Greek–Turkish *détente*. But given the high rank of the Cyprus issue in the hierarchy of Turkish national interests, such a development seems to be very improbable. After a certain initial irritation, Denktash has realised this as well, although he also had to recognise that he could not decouple the development in Cyprus from the dynamics of the Greek–Turkish *rapprochement*. In this his position does not differ very much from that of his Greek-Cypriot counterpart. But so far the Turkish position with respect to Cyprus has remained unchanged, that is a solution of the problems has to be reached in direct negotiations between the representatives of the two communities and Ankara will only accept a solution that assigns Turkey a role as guarantor for the security of the Turkish community on the island.

This short overview of Turkish motives and interests in the actual situation of relationships between the Aegean states shows clearly that there are no special obstacles that could prevent Ankara from entering into a dialogue about the ways and means of a solution to the bilateral problems. For the Turkish side this has always been the best way to realise its interests. Besides this, for the Turks, too, the principle holds true that to talk together in any case is preferable to shooting each other. This is what Andreas Papandreou expressed by summing up his Davos meeting with Turgut Ozal in the sentence: 'The agreement is: no war.'

NOTES

1. See, for instance, the article 'National Interest' by J. N. Rosenau, *International Encyclopedia of the Social Sciences*, vol. 11, pp. 34–40 or J. Rochester, 'The Paradigm Debate in International Relations and its

Implications for Foreign Policy Making: Toward a Redefinition of the "National Interest"', *Western Political Quarterly*, vol. 31, no. 1 (1978), pp. 48–58. See also F. A. Sondermann, 'The Concept of the National Interest', *Orbis* vol. 21 (1977) pp. 121–38.
2. See G. Hering, 'Ein historischer Überblick über den griechisch-türkischen Konflikt', a paper given at the conference, 'Der griechisch-türkische Konflikt', Mühlheim/Ruhr, (1984) and N. Wenturis, 'Die politische Kultur Griechenlands unter dem Aspekt des Konflikts mit der *Türkei*', paper given at the same conference. See also the respective parts in K. Grothusen (ed.), *Griechenland* (Göttingen: Vandenhoeck & Ruprecht, 1980) and in K. Grothusen (ed.), *Türkei* (Göttingen: Vandenhoeck & Ruprecht, 1985).
3. This is indirectly confirmed by the fact that an effort to purge the respective national textbooks of distorted views of common historical events and of biased characteristics of the other country ranks prominently in the list of tasks set up in the 'Davos Agreement' between Papandreou and Ozal. For an account of the biased views in the media, see M. Dabağ and Ch. Viallourides, *Der griechisch-türkisch-zypriotische Konflikt als internationaler Modellkonflikt* (Bochum: Ruhr Universität Bochum, 1985). Another evidence for the (past) role of the media can be seen in the publication of two leaflets about the 'Aegean question' by the respective association of journalists of Athens and Istanbul in which only the respective official positions are expressed. This gives to an outsider the image of the press as acting like a government spokesman instead of being an independent public institution. What is said about the academic community can very easily be confirmed by a glance at the respective publications of scholars from both countries in which a 'dissenting opinion' is a very rare exception.
4. See for this M. Gonlubol, 'Atatürk's Foreign Policy: Goals and Principles', in T. Feyzioglu (ed.), *Atatürk's Way* (Istanbul: Otomarsan, 1982) pp. 255–302.
5. The incidents with the Turkish research vessels *Candarli* and *Sismik 1* in 1974, 1976 and 1987 are indicators for this policy of calculated brinkmanship, which, of course, carries a certain risk of turning from cold into hot war. On the other hand, the Turkish desire to prevent critical situations from developing into a military confrontation can be substantiated by the de-escalative behaviour with respect to some border incidents during which soldiers on both sides were shot.
6. See for this period of modern Turkish history, F. Erkin, *Les relations turcosoviétiques et la question des détroites* (Ankara: Basnur Natbaasi, 1968) and B. Kuniholm, *The Origins of the Cold War in the Near East: Great Power Conflict and Diplomacy in Iran, Turkey and Greece* (Princeton, NJ: Princeton University Press, 1980).
7. M. Heper, *The State Tradition in Turkey* (Beverley: Eothen Press, 1985).
8. This argument is based on the fact that the Foreign Ministry mainly recruits the higher echelons of its personnel from the same educational institutions as do some other 'backbones' of Turkey's civil bureaucracy. As far as the concept of 'state tradition' is applicable to them it seems to be applicable to the Foreign Ministry as well. The reliance on legalism as

well as a certain 'imperial attitude' seem to be part of the 'state tradition' in Turkish foreign policy.
9. The only exception to this is the political movement led by the ex-colonel Türkes which in the form of the Nationalist Action Party as one of the minor partners of Süleyman Demirel's 'National Front' coalition governments exerted some influence on the Turkish politics during the 1970s. But this position always remained a minority one and could not really lead to a change of the bases of Turkey's foreign policy. For the role of pan-Turkist ideas in Turkish policy, see J. Landau, *Pan-Turkism in Turkey: A Study in Irredentism* (London: C. Hurst, 1981) and M. Agaogullari, 'The Ultranationalist Right', in I. Schick and E. Tonak (eds), *Turkey in Transition* (New York and Oxford: Oxford University Press, 1987) pp. 177–217.
10. See F. Georgeon, 'A la recherche d'une identité: le nationalisme Turc', in A. Gokalp (ed.), *La Turquie en transition: Disparités, identités, pouvoirs* (Paris: Maisonneuve et Larose, 1986) pp. 125–53.
11. This has been very clearly demonstrated by the Turkish behaviour towards the Greek minority in Istanbul during the 1955 riots, the extradition of Greek citizens living in Turkey in 1964, which was accompanied by the famous Kararname Decree, and with respect to the fate of the Greek inhabitants of the islands of Imroz and Tenedos. In all cases the Turkish government did nothing against the ill-treatment of Turkish citizens of Greek origin but instead contributed to the development of situations that led to the exodus of the majority of the Greek population. For the 1955 events, see H. Bagci, *Die türkische Au en politik während der Regierungszeit Menderes von 1950 bis 1960* (Bonn: doctoral dissertation, 1988) pp. 190–4; see also B. Spuler, 'Religiöse Minderheiten', in Grothusen, *Türkei*, pp. 613–20.
12. For this issue of Turkish politics, see Y. Inan 'Aren't There Any Turks in Western Thrace?', *Dis Politika–Foreign Policy*, vol. 14, no. 1/2 (1988) pp. 77–88, and, as the most reasonable Turkish study so far, B. Oran *Turk–Yunan Iliskilerinde Bati Trakaya Sorunu* [The Question of Western Thrace in Turkish–Greek Relations] (Ankara, 1986).
13. There have been remarks by some leading Turkish politicians in the 1970s which can be interpreted as a wish to deviate from this orientation of Turkish foreign policy with respect to Greek territory in the Aegean. In assessing these remarks one should, however, take into account that they never had a chance to become the official political line of that time and one should also consider the domestic political situation of those days, which was generally characterised by a hot climate and radical verbalism. In this respect there is a certain resemblance to the behaviour of the PASOK leadership when the party was in opposition.
14. This is the official Turkish line of reasoning but it should be noted that one could also argue that Turkish membership in one of the great power blocs which evolved after World War Two means a deviation from the Atatürkist approach which can be interpreted as a forerunner of non-alignment. For the first (official) view, see Gonlubol, 'Atatürk's Foreign Policy', and *Modern Turkey: Continuity and Change* (Opladen: Leske & Budrich Verlag, 1984) pp. 115–30. The second position can be found in

more revisionist interpretations of the Turkish political development after 1945: H. Keskin, *Die Türkei: Vom Osmanischen Reich zum Nationalstaat* (Berlin: Olle & Wolter, 1981) or R. Poschl, *Vom Neutralismus zur Blockpolitik: Hintergründe der Wende der türkischen Außenpolitik nach Kemal Atatürk* (Munich: Minerva, 1985).

15. For this element of Turkish foreign policy and its meaning for Turkey's relation with the Western countries, see K. Grothusen, 'Außenpolitik', in Grothusen, *Türkei*, pp. 92–7.
16. For the domestic debate about the appropriateness of Turkey's foreign policy conduct, see F. Ahmad Feroz, *The Turkish Experiment in Democracy, 1950–1975* (London: C. Hurst, 1977) pp. 407–24; M. Boll, 'Turkey's New National Security Concept: What it Means for NATO', *Orbis*, vol. 23 (1979) no. 3, pp. 609–31; see also D. Sezer, *Turkey's Security Policies*, Adelphi Papers no. 164 (London: IISS, 1981).
17. This has been analysed for the Greece–Turkey–United States triangle by Th. Couloumbis, *The United States, Greece and Turkey: The Troubled Triangle* (New York: Praeger, 1983).
18. For a concise overview of the most recent developments in Greek–Turkish relations, which have become known under the label of the 'Davos process', see H. Laipson, *Greek–Turkish Relations: Beginning of a New Era*? (Washington, DC: CRS Report, 1988) and A. H. Axt and H. Kramer (eds), *Griechisch–türkische Beziehungen: Von der Konfrontation zur Annäherung? Die jüngste Entwicklung vor dem Hintergrund des Ägäiskonflikts* (Ebenhausen: SWP, 1989). This section borrows heavily from pp. 98–102 of this study.
19. The role of the 'Greek factor' in the context of Turkey's application for EC membership is elaborated in more detail in H. Kramer, 'The Greek–Turkish Dispute and its Implication for an Eventual Turkish Accession to the EC', in *Future Relations Between Turkey and the European Community*, special supplement to '*Türkische Wirtschaftswelt*' (Munich) vol. 4 (April 1988) no. 4, pp. 11–17 and H. Kramer, *Die Europäische Gemeinschaft und die Türkei: Entwicklung, Probleme und Perspektiven einer schwierigen Partnerschaft* (Baden-Baden: Nomos Verlag, 1988) pp. 265–281.

6 Linkage Politics Theory and the Greek–Turkish *Rapprochement*

GEOFFREY PRIDHAM

INTRODUCTION

There is a revived and increasing interest in the explanatory power of the 'linkage politics' approach, an approach that focuses on the relationship and particularly the interaction between domestic political processes and foreign or defence policy-making. It also reflects what Hanrieder has called 'a new convergence of international and domestic political processes' in industrialised countries, 'with consequences that are most likely irreversible'.[1]

While the pursuit of 'linkage politics' has been inhibited in the past by disciplinary divides, this revival of 'linkage politics' is evident not only in international affairs, for comparativists are showing greater appreciation of the international dimension of political systems and their operation.[2]

Broadly, linkage politics has been concerned with (domestic) institutional processes and constraints on political choice; with 'boundary-crossing' events and mechanisms; and, at a deeper level, with the notion of 'penetrated systems'. Clearly, any realistic assessment of the political dynamics of decision-making has at least to take into account the impact or likelihood of domestic constraints as well as international influences: we have, therefore, to look not merely at the formal context but also at the complex environment in which policy is formulated and played out. At the same time, it is necessary to avoid being overdeterministic in this approach.[3]

Obviously, as comparativists will point out, there is significant scope for cross-national variation in developing and pursuing the approaches of linkage politics. In Greece and Turkey, we have two countries where 'boundary-crossing' events and patterns have been visible and not uncommon and may be said to represent one theme of their modern historical experience. Indeed, the former with its history of foreign interventions is virtually a classic example of a 'penetrated system'. The exercise adopted in this chapter is, however, not to confront the full range of Greek–Turkish relations over time, but instead to focus on a recent and relevant case study, one that has at least raised the hope of some new departure in these relations. Any viable assessment of this development cannot forego theoretical perspectives from linkage politics in order to confront its complexity, not least because its dynamics depend significantly on domestic factors. Attention will therefore turn on the possibilities for new initiatives and the difficulties that face their implementation. But, first of all, it is perhaps necessary to look rather more closely at concerns in linkage politics, especially at those that may assist this particular case study.

THEORETICAL PERSPECTIVES FROM LINKAGE POLITICS

Generally, linkage politics has been concerned with a two-directional process: with inner-directed linkages, or the impact of the international environment on the domestic arena; and with outer-directed linkages, with the way in which domestic developments and actors impinge on external relations. It is understandable, though also unfortunate, that comparativists have tended to dwell on the former direction and international affairs students on the latter. For it is usually the combination of the two directions, specifically their interaction, that provides the best potential for analysing the dynamics of foreign policy-making. However, the virtue of theoretical work on linkage politics has been to emphasise the need for differentiation in both directions – the nation-state should not be treated automatically as a unitary actor, nor should the international environment be regarded vaguely as some uniform entity.

One starting-point is to broach the general notion of 'penetrated systems', which featured in earlier literature and has reappeared in some more recent studies and is pertinent to the two countries in question. Originally, this formed part of dependency theory in explaining the structural position of developing states in the international system, although it has also come to be applied to some cases of more advanced countries. Rosenau was at pains to argue that 'penetration' implied more than 'interdependence', for 'a penetrated system is one in which non-members of a national society participate directly and authoritatively, through actions taken jointly with the society's members, in either the allocation of its values or the mobilisation of support on behalf of its goals'.[4] This involves a certain 'fusion of national and international systems in certain kinds of issue-areas',[5] although Rosenau recognised that some differentiation between those states where penetration is thorough and those where it is limited was necessary.[6] For him, penetrating agents could be either other states or international organisations, where clearly an example of the former would be the role of the United States in postwar Europe. Rosenau also talked about 'fused linkages' in this respect, with particular reference to the integrative potential of supranational organisations.[7] According to him, a 'linkage' is any recurrent sequence of behaviour that originates in one system and is reacted to in another in an input/output fashion: 'since boundaries can be crossed by processes of perception and emulation as well as by direct interaction, allowance must be made for both continuous and intermittent sequences'.[8] Hence, interest lies in patterns rather than one-off boundary-crossing events with short-lived repercussions. In developing this approach, Rosenau drew attention to different linkage phenomena and noted these could include non-governmental actors as well as official institutions.

But Rosenau, in line with the trend of international-affairs thinking, was primarily concerned with outer-directed linkages. Nevertheless, the concept of 'penetrated systems' drew attention to the other direction and implied some connection between them both. It is also conceivable that the degree of 'penetratedness' might be different where there is also an outer-directional element. This recalls Deutsch's suggestion that 'foreign events may have an effect on the memories of people'.[9] For instance, US intervention and influence in postwar Greece and the association between this and the colonels' regime has accounted largely for the theme of anti-Americanism in Greek foreign and defence policy in the recent period, especially under the PASOK government with its populist line in external affairs. Undoubtedly, this has coloured the style and also perhaps to some extent the content of policy. Similarly, as Veremis has pointed out, 'the Cyprus crisis was the catalyst for all changes in Greek foreign and defence policy after July 1974; a threat from the Warsaw Pact was no longer perceived as the primary security consideration, and disillusionment with the United States and NATO contributed to a reconsideration of Greece's defence orientation'.[10] Certainly, any basic explanation of a country's line in external relations has to take into account an historical as well as a geopolitical dimension, but the question still remains how one specifically identifies its function. Historical memory about the relationship with Turkey is clearly embedded in the Greek popular mind – rather more than with Turkey – but is it merely a story of its reactivation in given circumstances? Or, how much is this theme utilised instrumentally and by what agents?

A rather more elaborate framework for linkage politics is Brecher's approach to studying foreign policy systems.[11] Deriving this from the idea of inputs and outputs and generally from systems analysis, Brecher argued that the concept of system was no less valid for foreign-policy analysis and that it required identifying crucial variables and establishing relationships among them.[12] His research design involves dividing inputs into operational environment (external and internal), communication (especially the media) and the psychological environment (attitudinal prism, élite images), the process into formulation and implementation, and then outputs are simply defined as the substance of decisions.[13] The internal operational environment includes political structure: type of political regime, character of party system, civil–military relations of control and the extent of continuity and stability of the authority structures in the system.[14] Brecher, as have others such as Geller, opened up new areas of theoretical discussion such as regime coherence and levels of domestic strain; therefore, about how far élites and leadership are able to exercise authority and take decisions or are constrained by a variety of determinants, for example strength and impact of political opposition; and the potential for public opinion concern with foreign issues.

The question of constraints on policy-makers has surfaced in more recent literature on linkage politics. Thus, Hagan's agenda for comparative research on political influences looks in particular at the problem of regime fragmentation and vulnerability.[15] His definition of 'regime change' is primarily about leadership changes and changes in the cohesion or balance of power in ruling groups. Constraints may appear when 'pronounced political divisions within a regime and the occurrence of strong political pressures threatening to remove the regime from power are likely to have a broad impact on foreign policy'.[16] Other chapters in the same volume discuss constraints and opportunities in policy-making, including 'influence and instrumentality' deriving from international organisations. It is noted that intergovernmental organisations are 'the institutional components of many regimes', for they 'can be treated as variables within a complex interdependence system that impinges on national governments; they provide opportunities for national decision-making at the same time they add to the constraints under which states must operate'.[17]

Such approaches focusing on cause and effect help in measuring the relationship between outer- and inner-directed linkages and therefore, more specifically, in assessing the interplay between external and domestic actors and other phenomena in a dynamic framework. Above all, they identify the scope for different actors in the operational environment and warn against overrating the importance of individual ones when treated in isolation. Thus, Brecher usefully pays attention to political socialisation as providing insight into the world-view of decision-makers, an aspect also considered by Geller in reference to the personal characteristics of leaders. 'Men who make foreign policy decisions, like all men engaged in public affairs, are predisposed to view their environment through a distinctive lens or prism; this derives in part from their political culture'.[18] At the same time, one has to bear in mind how far these predispositions are allowed to come into play, and this relates to authority and concentration in decision-making. Domestic constraints might act as a counter-influence here, for certainly leaders might choose to play down their personal preferences when their authority is seriously challenged. Again, inclusion of the communication network is important given that the media can either act as the channel for the impact of public opinion, forcing leaders, at least in the short term, to adopt a different line, or they may in other systems (such as where there is government control over the media) act as a quasi-official arm to reinforce the political choices of leaders.

To summarise, linkage politics identifies a whole range of possible actors or influences in foreign and defence policy-making and attempts to categorise and group them. In terms of inner-directed linkages, we are talking about such variables as geopolitical location, the international economy, the role of international organisations, bilateral links with other states and standing commitments such as through treaties, not to mention the overall dynamics (positive, negative or changing) in a given geopolitical region. With outer-directed linkages, variables range from political structures to different élite groups (both political and non-political, for example economic and military) and other actors such as political parties and interest groups as well as the media. One may also take into account socio-economic variables and such matters of clearly direct relevance as the state of military capability. Some theoretical work in international affairs has utilised these categories in a broader or a narrower context. Couloumbis, for instance, has grouped these variables into four categories: individual level, national level, regional level and international system level. Indeed, he applied this framework to the very case study of Greek–Turkish relations to which we now turn.[19]

THE GREEK–TURKISH *RAPPROCHEMENT* 1987–9: A CASE STUDY

The aim here is not to describe in historical detail the 'Davos process', which was launched with the first summit between the Greek and Turkish prime ministers early in 1988 following some improvement in their relations in previous months: rather, it is to use this particular case study to reveal themes and problems that relate to linkage politics, and to apply lessons from the latter to understanding the former. This analysis is based primarily on a variety of quality press sources with some reference to literature where applicable.[20]

Two initial points may be made. Firstly, there has been a strong personal element in this process given the momentum from their commitment to it on the part of the Greek and Turkish leaders. This had predictably been highlighted in press coverage; as one commentator put it: 'Davos, in a way, remains very much a private enterprise of the two Prime Ministers, who seem to have staked their prestige on it.'[21] This is one line of explanation arising from the way in which the Davos meeting was prepared, when a series of personal messages were exchanged; indeed also from the defusion of the March 198˙ crisis over the Aegean, when the two countries came close to war Ozal's intervention is said to have been crucial in preventing escalation of the conflict. This personal element also merits some emphasis in view of the strong part played by both prime ministers in their countries' foreign policies. Papandreou, in particular, very much dominated his government's policies and foreign and defence polic˙ especially (he was for some years also defence minister), and i˙ known for occasional volte-faces, suggesting he has enjoyed signifi˙ cant room for manoeuvre. At the same time, this personal elemen˙ made the process in turn vulnerable to political difficulties facin˙ either leader.[22] Secondly, the complex of problems facing Greek Turkish relations are of such magnitude as in any case to cas˙ immediate doubt on how far two leaders, however powerful, may b˙ able or free to overcome or at least neutralise this in more than an˙

short-term sense. As Chipman has remarked, 'individually, the issues that divide Greece and Turkey (except for the special case of the resolution of the Cyprus problem) are not major, but taken together they form a package of problems that can easily be exacerbated and serve to reinforce mutual suspicions'.[23] Karasmanoglu elaborates:

> Disagreements over Cyprus and the Aegean are at the basis of present hostility. Although both parties usually formulate their claims in precise legal terms, the disputes are essentially political and the issues are often dominated by nationalistic perceptions and historically defined attitudes. . . . Greek–Turkish differences in the Aegean stem partly from the geographical peculiarities of the region, and partly from the respective historical perceptions of the disputants.[24]

In short, the personal initiative of the two leaders and their 'meeting of minds' (Ozal and Papandreou apparently established a personal rapport at Davos) are probably not sufficient to carry through a new policy direction, in addition to launching it. Once started, such a process and its prospects cannot be assessed without considering a range of international and domestic variables that come into play.

Of course, any effective breakthrough in establishing better relations between the two countries must be seen as historical. But the previous attempt at such an initiative, a decade before, only occasions scepticism. Karamanlis and Ecevit met for a summit at Montreux in January 1978 to establish a dialogue and broach the familiar problems dividing the countries.[25] Karamanlis was at this time concerned with paving the way for Greek membership of the European Community where some solution of these problems might encourage European opinion – a linkage theme with a familiar ring in 1987–9, with Turkey now seeking entry to the Community. It was also felt then that Karamanlis had the political authority at home to carry through any settlement, but the Montreux summit failed to create any momentum for change. The US move to lift the Turkish arms embargo aroused suspicions in both countries, deadlock between the two Cypriot communities was confirmed, then Evecit suffered electoral defeat in 1979.[26] Of course, there have been periods when Greek–Turkish relations have been distinctly better, such as in the 1930s and again after World War Two (when both countries faced the common Soviet threat), but significantly that was before the onset of the Cyprus issue.

While, seen broadly, the history of this region serves to caution against the possibility of any rapid alteration in Greek–Turkish relations, it is nevertheless instructive to focus more closely on the *rapprochement* in the late 1980s to evaluate how far, despite setbacks, this has presented a chance of leading eventually to any substantial improvement. The following discussion will therefore address itself to these questions: what were the motives on both sides for *rapprochement*, and how far could they be seen as a variation on the theme of linkage politics? What was the follow-up to Davos, and how competently were subsequent steps handled? And how important was the overall impact of domestic pressures and constraints on policy-making?

As to motives, it is not difficult to identify a variety of these from the evidence; but it is less easy to assess how far stated motives are perhaps genuine, and more importantly, what has been their relative importance. Common to both sides, it is generally recognised, was the feeling of profound shock that they should have come close to war in March 1987. Both leaders attested to this in public: Ozal remarked after the Davos summit that the March crisis had been a 'turning-point', and the Davos communiqué said that 'such a crisis should never be repeated'. There were also particular concrete reasons allied to or reinforcing the 'anti-war' motive. On the Greek side, for instance, the high command issued a report stating that in the March crisis, if it had escalated, the military could have checked the Turkish army for only three days, and hence Greece would have lost the war.[27] Given the timing of the move towards Davos, in the wake of this crisis, there is no reason to doubt this motive, but it still leaves significant room for others to be present. Among these, very evidently on the part of Ankara, was the Turkish determination certainly Ozal's strong commitment here, to gain entry to the European Community – an application had recently been sent to Brussels – and the belief that the road to securing this lay via Athens. Greece as an established member-state, had the right to veto the Turkish application. While the Turkish government hoped that dialogue would help to undermine the Greek intention to use a veto, Papandreou certainly saw this issue as a clear chance for leverage over Ankara and therefore as a possible means for extracting concessions over Cyprus.

It has also been suggested that both leaders had in common a desire to reduce the conflict in order to perform more freely an international role in the wider region of the Balkans, the Middle East and the eastern Mediterranean. For instance, this would allow Turkey freedom to concentrate on military threats from the East, including of course from the Soviet Union.[28] In so far as this would also make them stronger *vis-à-vis* the United States too, there was a logic to this motive; for example on the Greek side, it would enlarge Papandreou's room for manoeuvre over the forthcoming issue of the agreement on US bases. On the Turkish side, there was also concern over the Near East, for an end to the Iran–Iraq war was not yet in sight. That both leaders wanted to achieve something to secure a visible place in the history books is possible, but not sufficient as a motive (although with Papandreou, his age and declining health gave some credence to this explanation). Perhaps, too, the general world tendency to solve a number of long-standing problems of conflict was influential, but that could hardly explain the dynamics of Davos. Common to both sides, predictably, business interests urged reconciliation to take advantage of expanding bilateral trade. As the president of the Greek Federation of Industry said, once the politicians gave the green light, businessmen on both sides were all set to ride 'this wave of euphoria' after Davos. This was evidently one example of where political initiative at the top could set in train a process of *rapprochement* at different levels.

Finally, there were motives exclusively concerned with domestic politics. These included the desire to cut back on military expenditure to relieve other areas of policy concern. On the Greek side, in particular, the link was made between increased military expenditure and the failure of various government policies, given also the decline in popularity of PASOK from late 1986. There is also the familiar hypothesis that foreign crises or achievements may act as a diversion from domestic problems, a syndrome that has marked Papandreou's conduct of government at various points of time.

Thus, it is the usual story of invariably mixed motives – some clearly international in character and others more domestic in origin. It is, of course, difficult with some motives to distinguish an essential difference, or – in other words – there is an actual or likely interaction between policy determinants. For instance, the 'anti-war' motive for Papandreou illustrates this problem: an outbreak of hostilities with Turkey and Greece's probable defeat would have represented a disaster for his government, all the more as his policy stance had consisted of a pronounced line of rhetorical aggression towards Ankara. Such an outcome would have had immediate domestic repercussions leading to the almost certain fall of Papandreou. Also, election pressures are a standard item in domestic constraints on foreign policy. Papandreou apparently waited until Ozal's re-election in the autumn of 1987 before pursuing the idea of a first summit, for he then knew that the Turkish leader's domestic position was assured. Of course, the opposite perhaps applies in the Greek case because the proximity of the 1989 national elections was bound to come increasingly into play, perhaps inducing Papandreou to move too fast. It also suggested that Papandreou's sudden transformation into a 'peacemaker', in contrast to his previous line towards Turkey, contained a good degree of political opportunism. But this requires us to consider the process after the Davos summit, which was the first of three meetings between the two leaders during 1988.

The Davos summit itself ended with a number of agreements, such as the establishment of a direct telephone link between the two prime ministers, the idea of yearly meetings and the formation of two committees (one on specific items such as economic co-operation and tourism; the other political, to search for solutions of divisive issues). As such, it represented some form of initial breakthrough, just as the meeting had an historic importance – not to mention that it showed a change of attitude by Papandreou, who had opposed any such meeting until Turkey withdrew some troops from Cyprus. Furthermore, the decision to separate micro-issues from major problems of conflict was a wise diplomatic move. Some self-restraint was also demonstrated as there occurred at this very moment demonstrations by Turkish minorities living in western Thrace. One may see this element of self-restraint repeated later in the spring, when the meeting of the EC/Turkey Association broke down over the Cyprus issue. Although the Turkish government was very keen for this Association ('frozen' after the 1980 military coup) to be reactivated, Ozal chose not to let this setback spoil the Davos process. Furthermore, there followed a series of bilateral meetings at different levels involving economic and cultural contacts, a visit by the mayor of Istanbul and then a meeting of the political committee in Athens. Papandreou and Ozal met again in Brussels in early March, when they confirmed the 'Davos spirit' agreeing to establish further committees of diplomats and military experts to examine contentious issues of military exercises and the control of airspace in the Aegean.

In terms of formal procedures, therefore, there was much to be said for the way in which both sides carried through *rapprochement* in the months after Davos. Evidently, the commitment of the two prime ministers seems to have acted as a spur to these developments in their effort to consolidate the movement achieved at Davos. The process went further than the attempted follow-up to the Montreux summit a decade before, but once again the issue of Cyprus proved simply unavoidable and presented a serious stumbling-block to further progress. Moreover, the steps described above outlined the process at the official level. Élites, however, do not act in a vacuum, and this is where policy-making becomes more complicated. By the time of the third summit at Athens in June, other determinants had come more into play, showing how much domestic constraints can be influential. In fact, a forewarning of this problem had come a month-and-a-half beforehand at the aforementioned meeting of the EC/Turkey Association Committee, for the Greek government had raised the Cyprus issue 'under strong domestic pressure'.[29]

One of the significant problems facing this *rapprochement* was that of expectations. These were undoubtedly high as a result of the euphoria attached to the Davos summit, for the 'spirit' that emerged stimulated hopes that were really unrealistic. There were also some mixed or more cautious reactions, but on the Greek side in particular it was expected that Papandreou might return from Davos with something of an 'Aegean victory'.[30] At least, the fact that the Greek prime minister had changed his position by meeting Ozal was seen as an argument for some form of concession from Ankara. However, the political opposition, New Democracy, was compelled to support Papandreou, since it had advocated *rapprochement* before his change of line. Pressure on New Democracy meanwhile increased because of fears of the government stealing its policy. In a parliamentary debate in mid-March, New Democracy launched an attack on Papandreou's policy, accusing him of party-political motives and playing 'secret diplomacy'.[31] Meanwhile, the Greek press, which had initially been sceptical about the 'Davos spirit' now created doubts and pressed for substantial rewards. The Greek-Cypriot community had furthermore started to express concern that its interests might not be fully taken into account. When the mayor of Istanbul visited Athens in early May there were demonstrations against him by Cypriots and Kurds. Another point of resentment that surfaced in Greece was the alleged imprisonment of Greek Cypriots in the TRNC. Ozal's visit to Athens in June was met by further demonstrations, this time by Armenians as well as Kurds and Greek Cypriots.[32] By then, the Cyprus issue had come to the forefront of the Davos process, and Greek indignation was so strong that the Athens summit had done nothing to help solve it. Ozal's preference for dealing first of all with the micro-issues before – eventually – coming round to tackling the difficult problems was, while a standard diplomatic technique, now proving impracticable, for example his offer to support Greece's application for hosting the Olympic Games in 1996 did little to check the turn of events. The Greek press was very critical of Papandreou's cautious position and began to write off Davos as a 'mistake'.[33]

In other words, Papandreou came under increasing domestic pressure from different quarters. To some extent the same was also true of the Turkish side, although this was not marked by the same intensity of domestic debate as in Greece. This was largely because the Davos process did not involve essentially a change of policy line on the part of Ankara, which under Ozal had pressed for dialogue and co-operation.[34] However, there were vigilant elements (notably military and diplomatic circles), that acted as a constraint on Ozal even at the time of the original Davos summit. This counter-pressure came into play all the more when the Cyprus issue became prominent. Hostile statements about Cyprus and also the Aegean question started to reappear. Rumours that the Turkish government might, after all, make some concessions over Cyprus (these were voiced in the Greek press) only served to increase hard-line pressure in Ankara. As one source commented, 'in Turkey, hard-liners remain sceptical that anything other than an iron fist policy can impress Greece'.[35] There remained too the underlying problem that civil–military relations in the evolving Turkish system had not been fully clarified. It was noted that, 'the one thing that seems to shake his [Ozal's] unflappable exterior is suggestions that he is in no real position to make proper concessions on Cyprus because he has not put the army properly back in its cage'. In any case, President Evren made it clear before the Athens summit that not a single Turkish soldier would leave Cyprus before an agreement on the island's future was reached that would guarantee the safety of Turkish Cypriots.[36]

It was a case, therefore, of growing domestic pressures on the two leaders threatening to undermine the confidence-building approach of their policies. Leaders may, of course, try to reformulate their approach – Papandreou engaged in his familiar tactical balancing act of trying to win over Greek support – or they may delay developments, although in a case like this that might impair the dynamics of the process. It was, however, the trend of public opinion against both leaders in their respective countries that did much to take the steam out of the *rapprochement*, combined eventually with other political difficulties at home. Despite the series of bilateral meetings that occurred during these months, the popularity of Papandreou and Ozal declined during the year. This mattered more on the Greek side because the former faced re-election sooner, and in any case his government was already in a weak and vulnerable position. In late May, a poll indicated that only one-third of the Greek public supported *rapprochement*; a few weeks later another survey showed that 30 per cent saw Ozal's forthcoming visit to Athens as a 'provocation'. At the same time, 45 per cent of the Turkish public rejected absolutely any partial removal of Turkish troops from Cyprus.[37] There was some suggestion that the two leaders 'clearly underestimated the strength of their atavistic mistrust', in reference to the two publics, for 'both men found that the Davos "no war" deal was unpopular not just with the public, but even with top-ranking officials and aides'.[38] Because of this, both leaders ran some risk of becoming politically isolated in their respective domestic contexts. It may appear ironic, but in the end Papandreou became constrained by the very public feelings that he had previously aroused against Turkey. In effect, he was unable to carry opinion with him over this particular change of policy direction. One should point out here that the exclusive style of both leaders in this process, in relation to their own governments, only exacerbated domestic disquiet and therefore rebounded on their *rapprochement*.

In the short period since the Athens summit, there have been no further initiatives to revive the 'Davos spirit'. A return visit to Ankara by Papandreou for a further summit was discussed, but did not take place. The Greek presidency of the European Community in the second half of 1988 monopolised his government's external activity; and meanwhile Papandreou's government was crippled by his illness and slipped into a mire of financial scandals. Similarly, on the Turkish side, Ozal became enmeshed in various other political concerns, including internal party opposition and the business of a constitutional referendum.[39] One remains doubtful about the future of the process inaugurated in early 1988, given this loss of momentum. At least, there has been some improvement in the atmosphere of Greek–Turkish relations and various secondary measures; on the other hand, there has been a failure to consider permanent policy changes.[40]

CONCLUSION

Clearly, this case study illustrates the impact of some linkage mechanisms and not others. That is, third parties or other states stood aside during this *rapprochement*, although the widespread view was one of encouragement and relief that, at least in Western eyes, it might reduce internal tensions within NATO in the important southern flank. It was not as such an example of penetrative activity in the direct sense, although memories of past penetration – of Greece by Turkey – have remained as an emotional historical legacy, with a considerable potential to influence policy. During the period examined, the press in both countries tended to denounce compromises as a 'betrayal'. Certainly, to use Brecher's term, the psychological environment came forcefully into play: as indeed did the communication network (the media) in the operational environment. Above all, the Greek–Turkish *rapprochement* of 1987–9 is a convincing example of domestic constraints in policy initiative. While there was no real party-political polarisation over the matter – in Greece, New Democracy could not attack the initiative as it was consistent with its own policy, although it did criticise the manner of pursuing it – it was the mobilisation of hostile groups and of opinion in general that increasingly weighed in the balance. Some élites, notably economic ones, were, however, in favour of the process.

What this case study represents is that it is essential to look at the interaction between both inner- and outer-directed linkages in order to assess the dynamics of the process. One source commented at the time that the difficulties encountered 'are a classic example of what can happen when heads of government ignore the cautious processes of international relations in favour of making a splash'.[41] It became gradually clear that the two leaders were not being successful in building a consensus to secure the chances of their personal initiative. Whether those chances were in any case strong at this point of time is perhaps doubtful, given that the negative dynamics in relations between Greece and Turkey were difficult to check, let alone reduce. Increased demands by one side (whether official or not) only stiffened opinion on the other side, which in turn increased constraints on the government in question. Altogether, this case study shows that leaderships very often have only limited room for manoeuvre, whatever the element of personal commitment to a policy and whatever formal power they may enjoy. 'Dynamics from above' often do not suffice alone to secure an historical breakthrough in policy approach.

NOTES

1. W. F. Hanrieder, 'Dissolving International Politics', *American Political Science Review* (December 1978) p. 1280.
2. For example, C. Hermann, C. Kegley and J. Rosenau (eds), *New Directions in the Study of Foreign Policy* (London: Allen & Unwin, 1987); G. Boyd and G. Hopple, *Political Change and Foreign Policies* (London: Frances Pinter, 1987).
3. See P. Gourevitch, 'The Second Image Reversed: the International Sources of Domestic Politics', *International Organisation* (Autumn 1978) p. 900.
4. J. Rosenau, 'Pre-theories and Theories of Foreign Policy', in R. B. Farrell (ed.), *Approaches to Comparative and International Politics* (Evanston, Ill.: Northwestern University Press, 1966) p. 65.
5. Ibid., p. 53.
6. Ibid., pp. 70–1.
7. J. Rosenau, *Linkage Politics* (New York: Free Press, 1969) p. 59.
8. Ibid., p. 45.
9. K. Deutsch, 'External Influences on the Internal Behaviour of States', in Farrell, *Approaches to Comparative and International Politics*, p. 25.
10. T. Veremis, 'Greece and NATO', in J. Chipman (ed.), *NATO's Southern Allies* (London: Routledge, 1988) p. 274.
11. M. Brecher, *The Foreign Policy System of Israel* (London: Oxford University Press, 1972).
12. Ibid., p. 1.
13. Ibid., p. 3.
14. Ibid., pp. 8–9. See also D. Geller, *Domestic Factors in Foreign Policy* (Cambridge, Mass.: Schenkman, 1985).
15. J. Hagan, 'Regimes, Political Oppositions and the Comparative Analysis of Foreign Policy', in Hermann *et al.* (eds), *New Directions*, pp. 339–65.
16. Ibid., p. 348.
17. M. Karns and K. Mingst, 'International Organisations and Foreign Policy', in ibid., p. 457.
18. Brecher, *The Foreign Policy System of Israel*, p. 249.
19. Th. Couloumbis, 'Assessing the Potential of US Influence in Greece and Turkey: a Theoretical Perspective', *Hellenic Review of International Relations* (1983–4) pp. 27–50.
20. The following discussion is based mainly on the British and West German quality press coverage of these developments.
21. *The Times*, 13 June 1988. See also H.-J. Axt and H. Kramer, *Griechisch–Turkische Beziehungen: von der Konfrontation zur Annaherung?* (Ebenhausen: Stiftung Wissenschaft und Politik, 1989) pp. 114–16.
22. Axt and Kramer, *Griechisch–Turkische Beziehungen*, p. 115.
23. Chipman, *NATO's Southern Allies*, p. 77.
24. A. Karaosmanoglu, 'Turkey and the Southern Flank', in ibid., p. 339.
25. J. Alford, *Greece and Turkey: Adversity in Alliance* (Aldershot: Gower, 1984) p. 109.
26. Ibid., pp. 109, 115.
27. *Observer*, 12 June 1988.

28. Axt and Kramer, *Grieschisch–Turkische Beziehungen*, p. 100.
29. *Observer*, 1 May 1988.
30. *Observer*, 17 January 1988.
31. *Frankfurter Allgemeine*, 14 March 1988.
32. *The Times*, 14 June 1988.
33. *Frankfurter Allgemeine*, 24 May 1988 and 15 June 1988.
34. Axt and Kramer, *Grieschisch–Turkische Beziehungen*, pp. 92, 98.
35. *The Sunday Times*, 12 June 1988.
36. Ibid.
37. *Frankfurter Allgemeine*, 10 June 1988.
38. *The Times*, 14 February 1989.
39. Axt and Kramer, *Grieschisch–Turkische Beziehungen*, pp. 115, 131.
40. Ibid., pp. 113–14.
41. *Observer*, 1 May 1988.

Part II

Domestic Perceptions of Challenges to National Security

7 Greece's Strategic Doctrine: In Search of Autonomy and Deterrence*

ATHANASIOS PLATIAS

INTRODUCTION

Strategic doctrine is viewed, in this chapter, as a state's 'theory' about how it can best 'produce' security for itself.[1] Strategic doctrine may be conceptualised as a means–end relationship, in which military means are connected to political objectives.[2] Ideally it should include an explanation of why the theory is expected to work in practice. Actual events test the validity of the state's national security 'theory' and serve to show whether the 'theory' helps the state achieve its political goals.

A strategic doctrine must identify threats and devise remedies for those threats. A more crucial function of the doctrine is to set priorities. Priorities must be established between both threats and remedies because the number of possible threats is usually great and the resources are scarce.[3] Other things being equal, this is particularly true for small states because limited resources force them to make hard choices.

Greece in the last sixteen years (since 1974) has been trying to develop its own doctrine that will perform the tasks outlined above. It is the objective of this chapter to construct a rough map of Greece's strategic thinking by identifying a central core of generally shared ideas concerning Greece's security.

In its 'grand' sense, strategic doctrine incorporates economic, moral, demographic and other factors upon which the security of a

---

* The author wishes to thank D. Constas, F. Kikiras and G. Poukamissas for their helpful comments on an earlier draft of this chapter. All errors and opinions are of course the responsibility of the author. For support during the preparation of this chapter he thanks the SSRC–MacArthur Fellowship Program in International Peace and Security.

state is built in various ways.[4] This chapter will not deal with 'grand strategy', nor will it address the operational elements of the doctrine, but will focus, more specifically, on the political–military elements of Greece's doctrine.

Since strategic doctrines often develop in an incremental way, and are not fully fleshed out right from the beginning, they need to be inferred from a variety of sources.[5] The conceptualisation of the Greek strategic doctrine developed in this paper has been drawn from a number of sources, namely: studies on Greek security policy; speeches, articles and books written by both civilian and military decision-makers; close study of diplomatic and military practice; and finally, from the examination of the evolution of the force posture of the Greek armed forces.

This chapter is divided into two parts: the first part deals with the threat perceived by Greek decision-makers and the factors that condition the perception of the threat; the second part discusses the remedies that Greece has devised to deal with the perceived threats. In particular, the second part discusses the two main political–military elements of Greece's doctrine: autonomy and deterrence.

CONDITIONING FACTORS

The Threat

Historically, the two persistent concerns of Greek security have been the Turks and the Balkan Slavs. The intensity and the direction of threat have changed several times during the last two centuries. Immediately after World War Two, world communism was the overriding concern, and this meant that the 'enemy' came from the north. This situation changed dramatically in the 1960s. The threat from the north diminished to the point of disappearing, while the threat from the east increased to the point of becoming imminent. As a result, the probability of a war between Greece and Turkey became more likely than the chances of a military exchange with the Warsaw Pact countries.

Currently, Greek doctrine includes an intensive and extensive view of the Turkish threat. The view held in Athens is that Greece's NATO ally, Turkey, has adopted a revisionist policy aimed at changing the status quo which was established by the treaties of Lausanne (1923), Montreux (1936) and Paris (1947).[6] Greek strategic analysts, political élites and the public all believe that the ultimate Turkish objective is westward expansion. This perception cuts across party lines; there are no significant party differences on the evaluation of the Turkish threat.

Threatening signals interpreted by Greek strategic analysts as indicators of impending danger include: (1) statements by leading Turkish politicians; (2) diplomatic initiatives; and (3) military preparations.

Threatening statements
Threatening statements have been persistently made by Turkish officials, ever since Turkey's invasion of Cyprus in 1974, regardless of whether the government in power was civilian or military. Below is a brief example of such statements which Greek officials consider indicative of Turkey's ultimate intentions:

> I will not cede the Aegean to anyone. Half of the Aegean belongs to us and all the world must know it. (Prime Minister Sadi Irmak, *Hurriyet*, 18 January 1975)

> It is natural that the rights and responsibilities of a nation which is the sovereign of Anatolia should extend at least into the middle of the Aegean. No Turkish government can ignore this fact which is a matter of national security. (Defence Minister Hasan East Isik, *Turkish Daily News*, 17 March 1987)[7]

> In the Aegean, one must necessarily pursue a dynamic policy. The conditions today are different from the conditions in 1923. Turkish power has grown. . . . Cyprus is the first step toward the Aegean. (Foreign Minister Esenbel)[8]

Diplomatic initiatives[9]
Since 1973, Turkey has undertaken several diplomatic initiatives designed to undermine Greek sovereignty in the Aegean and western Thrace:

1. At the *continental shelf level* it granted oil exploration licenses for portions of the continental shelf in the Aegean claimed by Greece; sent research vessels, accompanied by warships, to carry out research on the continental shelf claimed by Greece; and proposed joint exploration of the 'disputed' area (i.e. the Greek area).

2. At the *territorial sea level* it raised questions in NATO fora relating to naval arrangements in the Aegean; threatened war if Greece were to extend its territorial waters to the internationally accepted twelve-mile limit; conducted research on maritime pollution in the entire Aegean under the cover of implementing an international programme sponsored by the United Nations, without requesting Greece's permission; and tried to secure from the relevant international authorities the control of the rescue operations in the Aegean.
3. At the *airspace level* it issued a notice to airmen (NOTAM 714) to the ICAO, demanding that all aircraft crossing the median line of the Aegean report to Turkey; challenged the ten-mile limit of Greek sovereignty in the air, often in large formations; challenged Greek operational air control of the Aegean; and refused to report the flight schedules of its military planes in the Greek FIR.
4. At the *territorial level* it accused Greece of illegally militarising the eastern Aegean and Dodecanese Islands; tried to undermine the strategic value of the Aegean islands in various allied fora; and tried to raise the issue of the Turkish minority in western Thrace in order to lay claim to western Thrace itself.[10]

Military preparations
The Greeks consider the actual deployment of Turkish armed forces a further threat indicator. The First Turkish Army is deployed across from western Thrace, the Second is across from the island of Cyprus, and the Fourth (ominously called by Turkey the Aegean Army) across from the Aegean islands. According to Greek officials, the First Army has an 80–100 per cent degree of readiness, much higher than that of the Third Army, deployed along the Soviet borders, whose degree of readiness does not exceed 50 per cent.[11]

As far as the Aegean Army is concerned, Greek officials claim that it has a total force of 150 000 men and includes two infantry divisions, a division of marines, an airborne division with 204 helicopters and Turkey's entire parachutist force.

The Aegean Army, which is not under NATO command but remains under exclusive Turkish control, is also supported by a fleet of 100 transport planes, 150 landing craft and some 400 rubber boats.[12] Each boat is capable of carrying 8–10 fully armed soldiers, and they are suitable for short-distance landing operations on coastlines where access is difficult. As the then Deputy Minister of Defence Antonis Drossoyannis said in an interview: 'Even for those not versed in military affairs, it is obvious that the presence of the aforementioned forces constitutes a threat to our islands.'[13]

Based on these threatening signals, and recent historical experience – the 1974 Turkish invasion of Cyprus – Greek strategic analysts expect that Turkey is likely to adopt a *fait accompli* diplomacy against Greece when the following two preconditions are fulfilled: (1) the opening of the 'window of vulnerability' for Greece, that is when Greece is not capable or willing to resist, and (2) the opening of the 'window of opportunity' for Turkey, that is when it is expected that the superpowers will not oppose the Turkish invasion.

In short, current Greek strategic thinking includes an intensive and extensive view of the Turkish threat. On the other hand, the threat from the Warsaw Pact is viewed as secondary and indirect. It is based on the premise that Greece can only be attacked from the north as part of a wider conflict. But in the 1990s, this conflict appears extremely remote.

Constraints

Threat, of course, is not perceived in a vacuum. Greek strategic thinking has been influenced by four important factors: Greece's small population compared to that of Turkey, its geography, its comparatively meagre economic resources and superpower interests in the region.

Population

There are only 10 million Greeks in Greece which is a country of limited military and economic resources. In contrast, the Turkish population is over 55 million. It is projected that by the turn of the century 11 million Greeks will have to face 73 million Turks.[14] Greece is therefore vastly outnumbered in terms of sheer manpower. Turkey has been able to maintain a huge standing army of more than 650 000 (excluding paramilitary forces[15]), an army potentially capable of making a swift transition to attack from its peacetime position.

The manpower limitations make Greece vulnerable to surprise attack on the one hand and vulnerable to extended strategies of attrition[16] on the other.

Geography

The country's geography is largely implacable to defensive arrangements. The absence of strategic depth in the east (and the north) and the tremendous length of the border have plagued Greek strategists for a long time.

Geography creates problems for Greece in all possible theatres of war with Turkey. Cyprus is 600 miles away from Greece but only 60 miles from Turkey. Furthermore, major Greek islands are very close to the Turkish mainland. Important population centres and military installations are within Turkish artillery range.

To complicate matters, the air defence of the islands is extremely difficult because of the short warning time available for interception of penetrating enemy aircraft. Lastly, Greece's land border with Turkey in Thrace is far away from Greece's main strategic centres and access to it is limited by the existing transportation network. In short, the geography of the Greek–Turkish land and sea borders does not give Greece the advantage of interior lines, that is does not provide it with the capacity rapidly to concentrate forces in one front and then to shift them to another.

Economic resources

Because of the sheer size of Turkey, Greece has always faced a disparity of economic resources. Until recently the Greeks believed that they might compensate for this disparity by generating a more advanced economy. This hope has been eroded over the last decade by Turkey's rapid economic growth and Greece's problems.

Great power interests

External actors have a substantial impact on Greek–Turkish relations in various direct and indirect ways. The most important external actor is the United States, which has a strong interest in both sides. It seems, however, that Turkey is considered more important than Greece in the US scale of priorities.[17] This explains why the United States tilts in favour of Turkey in almost every crisis. Hence, American interests in the area have conditioned Greek security concerns and have defined the international constraints of the country.

REMEDIES

The Past: Pre-1974 Period

The security of Greece after World War Two was determined to a large extent by its bilateral and multilateral commitments. By its alignment with the United States and NATO, Greece placed its security considerations in the broader framework of NATO's security policy in the area. Greek armed forces became unduly dependent on decisions taken by the Atlantic Command. The extent and the intensity of NATO involvement in Greek defence planning, with the foremost example being the period of the 1950s, froze any and all Greek initiatives.

The prescribed role of the Greek armed forces was based on the US premise that the main security problem was one of an internal rather than an external nature. Greece was to have 'a military establishment capable of maintaining internal security in order to avoid communist domination'.[18] The legacy of the civil war was apparent in this role prescription.

Once the role of domestic control was accomplished, the alliance obligations of the Greek armed forces were to a very large extent considered fulfilled, since defence against an external threat was considered a secondary task of the Greek armed forces. In case of Warsaw Pact aggression, the Greek army was supposed only to cause some delay to the enemy.[19] The premise was that the United States and NATO would provide reinforcements to Greece in the event of such an attack. Hence, under NATO plans in the post-World War Two period, Greece's role was limited to that of a trip-wire whose destruction would set into motion the Alliance's powerful components.[20]

The military implication of these role assignments (namely internal security and delay action) and the resulting force posture – lack of strong air and naval components – was that Greece was not able to defend itself autonomously against attack. This was demonstrated clearly in the summer of 1974. The Turkish invasion of Cyprus of that year caused Greece to reconsider its post-World War Two defence posture.

Returning to our introductory remarks that the state's 'theory' of how to 'produce' security for itself is tested against events, it is evident that the country's strategic doctrine was tested against events and failed. The Atlantic Alliance proved incapable of protecting Greece from the threat from the east. This incapacity raised some broader questions. Like other small states, Greece is obliged to trade-off independence for security. In order to improve security and obtain protection, Greece traded away some of its independence by joining the Alliance. But in 1974, the Greek strategists discovered that the country paid the cost of alignment with NATO and the United States (namely loss of independence) without enjoying the benefits that the alignment was supposed to provide, namely protection. Greek policy makers discovered in 1974 that the country did not move from insecurity to security. It was both insecure and dependent.

In short, the humiliation of the 1974 Cyprus crisis demonstrated to Greek policy-makers that the defence posture designed by Greece's allies at best was not compatible with and at worst was contrary to national interest. The perceived Turkish threat completely undermined the post-World War Two premise of relying on allied reinforcements, and contributed to the Greek search for a more autonomous defence policy.

The Present: Post-1974

In search of autonomy
The underlying principle of post-1974 Greek defence policy is that the country has to develop an autonomous security policy, drawing upon its own resources, in order to deal with the Turkish threat. In international relations theory this is called a strategy of internal balancing.[21] Hence, the country substituted external balancing (the expectation of allied reinforcements) for internal balancing (mobilisation of the country's own resources).

The autonomous defence policy within an allied context can be labelled a 'NATO plus' strategy. Two types of arrangements are incorporated into it. First, the Greek armed forces assigned to NATO will regain their full independence from the alliance at any moment if Greece's vital interests are imperilled by Turkish actions. The other arrangement is the establishment of forces under exclusive national command. To implement the 'plus' element of the 'NATO plus' strategy, the post-1974 governments took the following measures:

1. They strengthened the élite groups (that is the *special forces*), which were placed under exclusive national command. In fact, the current ratio of special to regular forces is the highest among the NATO countries.

2. They dramatically strengthened the *naval* and *air components* neglected during the pre-1974 period. This is clearly reflected in the budgetary allocations among the services where the army's share of the budget declined while the navy's and air force's share increased.
3. They strengthened the Military High Command for Interior and Islands (ASDEN), which is not assigned to NATO.
4. They minimised the high degree of vulnerability resulting from dependence on foreign arms suppliers by adopting the counter-dependency strategies of *domestic production* and *diversification*. Diversification proved to be a viable and quite effective strategy for reducing vulnerability dependence in a relatively short time. Within the last fifteen years, the degree of dependence upon a single supplier has diminished from more than 80 per cent in 1974 to approximately 40 per cent.[22] Indigenous production, on the other hand, is a long-term strategy. Currently, 20 per cent of the defence needs are satisfied by domestic production.[23] The long-term objective is a 50:50 share between imports and indigenous production.

This trend toward a more autonomous strategy within the alliance was further accelerated with the announcement of Greece's new policy of national defence (8 January 1985).[24] The new defence policy intensified the trend toward internal balancing by initiating the process for the establishment of a *militia army* in the Aegean islands and western Thrace to supplement the existing standing army based on the conscript system. In addition, the new defence policy has introduced some rudimentary elements of *total defence* by initiating that all defence resources of the Greek nation must be utilised.[25] As a first step toward a total defence organisation of the entire country, defence considerations will affect almost all aspects of life in the Aegean islands and western Thrace, including the economic infrastructure, road network, municipal organisation, the medical care system and the electric power system.

In search of deterrence
As a status quo country, Greece wants only to deter its opponents. Thus, the broad purpose of the Greek strategic doctrine is the *deterrence* of Turkish aggression.

Deterrence is a policy that seeks to persuade Turkey that the costs of using military force against Greece will outweigh the benefits. Deterrence in Greece's strategic thinking takes four different forms:

national deterrence, international deterrence, extended deterrence, and active deterrence.

National deterrence. The Greek policy of deterrence seeks to present Turkey with a *credible threat* of exacting a very high price in the event of aggression. This price can take many forms, including *denial* of battlefield objectives, damage to military forces and other values (namely *retaliation*).

The credibility of the deterrent threat depends upon Greece being perceived as possessing (1) the *military capability* to inflict a burdensome cost on Turkey and (2) the *will* or the *intention* to use those capabilities as necessary.[26]

Deterrence is stronger when a state invests in its military capability. Following this principle, the post-1974 Greek governments almost doubled the military expenditure. In particular, Greece spends the highest percentage of its gross domestic product – approximately 7 per cent – for defence purposes of any NATO country. In absolute terms, Greece spends as much as Turkey for defence. Another factor that must be taken into account is the share of manpower devoted to defence. Greece devotes more manpower to its defence – approximately 6.1 per cent of the labour force – than any other NATO country.[27]

The quest for quantitative symmetry with Turkey, however, has inherent limitations. As the then premier Andreas Papandreou mentioned in parliament (January 1987), 'our competition with Turkey along the quantitative dimension leads nowhere. Hence, emphasis should be given primarily to the qualitative improvement of our defense system in its entirety.'[28] In fact, Greece seeks to achieve *qualitative superiority*. Toward this end, the Greek government during the 1980s has taken measures which, *inter alia*, include: intensification of training; emphasis on combined arms operations; use of capital-intensive systems of warfare; maintenance of a relatively modern arsenal; increased readiness and sustainability; use of force multipliers such as Command, Control, Communication and Intelligence (C^3I) systems; reduction of turnaround time and so on.

In short, to counter its quantitative asymmetry, Greece's doctrine has placed emphasis on qualitative superiority. Coupled with the intensive exploitation of the country's economic and manpower resources, this is expected to strengthen Greece's *military capacity*, the first requirement of deterrence.

The second requirement for a credible deterrence is the *commit-*

ment to respond to an attack and, of course, the *communication* of that commitment, Indeed, Greek governments have repeatedly stated that 'Greece claims nothing from any other country, but equally is not prepared to make any concession at the expense of its national territory.'[29] To increase the clarity of its commitment, the Greek government has drawn some 'red lines' in advance, called *casus belli*. A *casus belli* is something like an automatic trigger of war or, to put it differently, it is an event that may be a cause of a general war or a large-scale military action. The advance declaration of *casus belli* serves three general purposes: it lessens the possibility of miscalculation; it provides a clear signal that deterrence has failed; and it establishes a foundation of international legitimation in the event of Greek military action.

At least two *casi belli* have been explicitly stated: a Turkish attack on Cyprus, and any Turkish attempt to exploit the continental shelf of the Aegean.

International deterrence. Greece is a member of the Atlantic alliance and hosts several US and NATO bases on its territory. This brings some 'unintended benefits'. Western presence in the country has increased the costs and risks associated with an attack against Greece. Any attack on Greece from Turkey and the resulting Greek–Turkish war would inevitably result in the destruction of military installations and weapons (on both sides) that are partially or even exclusively financed by NATO and the United States for the purposes of the common defence. Such a regional war would place the security of the US and NATO bases in Greece and Turkey at risk. Even a short (but intensive) war would completely wipe out NATO's infrastructure in the region. Hence, NATO and the United States have every reason to try to deter any conflict between Greece and Turkey and, if deterrence fails, to intervene to stop it. This in turn, strengthens Greece's deterrence for as long as the country has adequate capacity to 'rock the boat'.

The Soviet Union would also have an incentive, after a certain point, to intervene and stop the conflict – before it turns into a war of attrition – in order to maintain its vital access to the Mediterranean Sea.

Extended deterrence. Greece's national interests extend beyond its borders to include the security of another state, namely Cyprus. As a result, when Cyprus is threatened with military force by Turkey, decision-makers in Athens must prepare to come to its defence by threatening *retaliation* against Turkey. This is the essence of the Greek strategy of extended deterrence.

To project the shadow of one's military forces into another country is a difficult task. As Thomas Schelling explains, 'the difference between the national homeland and everything "abroad" is the difference between threats that are inherently credible, even if unspoken, and threats that have to be made credible'.[30]

The credibility of such an extended deterrence threat depends upon Greece's capacity to *deny* the Turkish objectives in Cyprus, that is to employ adequate forces in a timely fashion in Cyprus. However, this is extremely difficult to achieve in a theatre of war that is far away from Greece and much closer to Turkey. Hence, the credibility of Greece's extended deterrence in Cyprus is not based on the threat of *denial* but on a threat of *retaliation*, namely on the threat of all-out war. This is the meaning of the concept of 'horizontal escalation' in current Greek strategic thinking. According to this concept, response to Turkish aggression need not be symmetrical (that is reacting to the threat at the same location and level of original provocation). 'Horizontal escalation' implies an *asymmetrical response* which involves shifting the location or nature of one's reaction into terrain better suited to the application of one's strength against the adversary's weakness.

The credibility of the extended deterrence threat also depends on the *will to fight*, if necessary. In this regard, Greece's credibility suffers from past behaviour. Indeed, extended deterrence threats work better when the side making them has defended its interests in a similar situation in the past. Clearly Greece's performance was not up to par in 1974 and hence the country damaged its reputation for defence.

To re-establish the credibility of Greece's deterrence in Cyprus, the Greek governments, and particularly the Papandreou governments (1981–9), adopted the following strategies.

Casus belli. The Greek governments have drawn the 'red line' very clearly. As Papandreou declared in parliament,

> in order to avoid misunderstanding, it should be known to friends and foes alike that in case of an attack or invasion against the Greek-Cypriot positions, Greece will not stay out. I have warned that this is a casus belli. We hope that our partners in the EEC and our allies in NATO will understand the sincerity of our decision to

defend Cyprus because if Cyprus is lost, Greece eventually will be lost.[31]

Reputation for firmness and recklessness. Greece proved in the post-1974 crisis that she can stand firm and, if necessary take high risks (for example the March 1987 crisis). Indeed, extended deterrence threats work better when the side making them has built a reputation for being risk-seeking.
Trip-wires. Greek forces have been stationed in Cyprus. Hence, any Turkish attack on the island would automatically involve the Greek forces positioned there and would drastically raise the likelihood of an all-out Greek–Turkish war.

Active deterrence. Active deterrence is the strategy of threatening or inflicting punishment on the opponent in order to dissuade him from continuing some undesired action. It threatens use of force to stop an adversary from doing something he has *already* undertaken. In essence this strategy involves initiating an action that can cease, or become harmless, *only if* the opponent responds. This strategy is illustrated by the actions taken by the Greek government in March 1987 in order to stop Turkey from exploring the Greek continental shelf in the Aegean.

In March 1987, Turkey's National Security Council ordered the oil exploration vessel *Sismik 1* to sail through the Dardanelles under naval escort to start prospecting in the Aegean. At the same time, the Turkish government published a map of the area the research vessel was supposed to explore. It became immediately apparent that *Sismik* had been ordered to investigate the continental shelf in the Aegean claimed by Greece.

Predictably, the crisis took its course. Greece considered such an infraction of its territorial rights as a cause of war. Thus, in a response to the Turkish move, Greek armed forces rushed to the eastern border in a state of full alert.

To increase the credibility of its threat, the Greek government placed itself in a position from which it was difficult to retreat: it committed itself to a response by putting on the line the nation's honour and diplomatic reputation.[32] As the prime minister declared in an emergency television broadcast, 'the maps published by Turkey show clearly that the planned route of the Sismik lies 95% within the area under which the Greek continental shelf extends. . . . It is our decision not to allow the Sismik to go on with its seismic research in the Aegean. It is our duty to defend both our borders and our sovereign rights.' It was very fortunate, the premier said, that this ship 'has not showed up as yet in Aegean waters'. But if it did, and a war situation arose, he warned, 'a catalytic change might also occur in the entire Balkan area, even in the very defense system of the West, that is NATO itself'.[33]

Clearly, the Greek government decided to run the risk that unilateral escalation (namely general mobilisation and orders to the navy to sink the vessel) could precipitate an equally forceful response by Turkey. As a result, the pace of military events could outstrip the time needed for diplomacy to come into the picture. But it was precisely the manipulation of the risk of war that made deterrence work. The initiation of the process that carried the risk of disaster for both sides contributed to Turkey's decision to take a step backward.

The March 1987 crisis showed that to find the balance between deterrence *stability* and *credibility* is a demanding task. A *stable deterrence* posture must maintain a delicate balance between the demonstration of firmness and the readiness to use force on the one hand, and on the other, it must not provoke the opponent.[34] Establishing the *credibility* of deterrence is also a difficult task. For credibility enhancement it is usually crucial to demonstrate firmness. This implies issuing threats and adopting an uncompromising bargaining position. Again, these are serious risks associated with this course of action (for example provocation, escalation). In practice, achieving an effective balance between credibility and stability has been a precarious task for policy-makers.[35]

Greek strategists try to design a deterrent posture that is both stable *and* credible. Three basic options are available to Greece: *intransigent strategy*, that is adoption of firm and unyielding position vis-à-vis Turkey; *firm-but-flexible strategy*, that is adoption of a mixed strategy of standing firm in response to the Turkish demands while offering compromise based on reciprocal accommodation; and *appeasement strategy*, that is adoption of a strategy of unilateral concessions vis-à-vis Turkey.

The problem with the intransigent strategy is that Greece's deterrence credibility is maximised at the expense of deterrence stability. This means that the chances of escalation are high. In addition, an intransigent stance by Greece can discredit the moderate policy-makers in Turkey who advocate compromise and enhance the position of hard-liners (for example the military establishment).

On the other hand, appeasement strategy avoids the problems

associated with an intransigent stance and in this manner strengthens deterrence stability. However, unilateral concession may encourage further Turkish demands.

Appeasement is an effective strategy only if the adversary is motivated solely by defensive goals. Turkey is clearly not motivated by defensive goals. It aspires to change the prevailing status quo in the region. Thus, Greek policy-makers have concluded that the policy of sacrificing a great deal to avoid war (that is appeasement) is dangerous.[36] The credibility of Greece's commitment would be weakened and thus Turkey might be tempted to attempt further coercion.

For Greece the most effective stance is a mixed strategy in which opposition to the demands of Turkey is coupled with conditional compromise.[37] This firm-but-flexible strategy was adopted in the March 1987 crisis. At that time, Greece demonstrated its determination to escalate (that is mobilisation and preparation of pre-emptive strike) and subsequently accepted a compromise to break the deadlock (it gave assurances to Turkey that it too will refrain from drilling in disputed areas). The Greek conditional offer of compromise signalled to the Turkish leadership the possibility of taking the necessary step backward without damaging its bargaining reputation and its domestic position. If Greece had not taken this position, and had not offered a face-saving way out, the Turkish leadership may have found it difficult to retreat under pressure.

CONCLUSION

Small states trying to develop their own strategic doctrines have fewer options and less freedom than the great powers. Indeed, very few small states (namely Sweden, Switzerland, Finland, Israel) have actually managed to develop their own original doctrines. Small states usually develop an original doctrine after realising that the doctrines of the bigger powers have only limited applicability to their problems.

Turkey's invasion of Cyprus in 1974 showed Greece that its national security 'theory' was not valid: it was tested and it failed. Full reliance on NATO for its own strategic needs did not prove to be a guarantee of protection. Greece in 1974 realised that it was both *insecure* and *dependent*. The events demanded a new theory, one consistent with the new realities. Greece then devised new approaches to the mounting threat from the east. The new strategic doctrine attempts to 'produce' security by maximising *autonomy* while simultaneously strengthening *deterrence*. The future will tell whether the new doctrine will fulfil its objectives, or whether it too, like its predecessor, will not live up to expectations.

NOTES

1. See Barry Posen, *The Sources of Military Doctrine: France, Britain and Germany Between the World Wars* (Ithaca, NY: Cornell University Press, 1984) p. 13.
2. See Carl von Clausewitz, *On War*, ed. Michael Howard and Peter Paret (Princeton, NJ: Princeton University Press, 1976); Edward M. Earle (ed.), *Makers of Modern Strategy* (Princeton, NJ: Princeton University Press, 1971) p. viii; Bernard Brodie, *War and Politics* (New York: Macmillan, 1973) pp. 1–29; and Basil Liddell Hart, *Strategy* (New York: Frederik Praeger, 1967) p. 335. For a completely different conceptualisation, see Timothy Lupfer, 'The Dynamics of Doctrine', *Leavenworth Papers No. 4*, Fort Leavenworth, Kan. (July 1981) p. vii.
3. See Arnold Horelick, 'Perspectives on the Study of Comparative Military Doctrine', in Frank B. Horton (ed.), *Comparative Defense Policy* (Baltimore, Md.: Johns Hopkins University Press, 1974) p. 155, and Posen, *The Sources of Military Doctrine*, pp. 13–14.
4. See Edward N. Luttwack, *Strategy: The Logic of War and Peace* (Cambridge, Mass.: Harvard University Press, 1987).
5. It should be noted that for the sake of presentation we may have imposed greater coherence on Greek doctrine than is actually the case.
6. See Van Coufoudakis, 'Greek–Turkish Relations, 1973–1983: the View from Athens', *International Security* (Spring 1985) pp. 201–4.
7. The statements by Irmak and Isik are quoted from *Greece: A Profile* (Athens: International Studies Association, 1988) Appendix I, p. 33.
8. The statement by Esenbal is quoted from *Turkish Officials Speak on Turkey's Aims* (Athens: Institute for Political Studies, 1985).
9. This part of the chapter draws heavily on Athanasios G. Platias, 'High Politics in Small Countries: an Inquiry into the Security Policies of Greece, Israel and Sweden', Ph.D. Dissertation, Cornell University (1986) pp. 161–5.
10. Turkey even complained that Greece has no right to place on its own soil in Thrace emigrants returning from the Soviet Union. See *Ta Nea* (4 January 1990) p. 7 (in Greek).
11. These data have been presented to parliament by the Greek prime minister. See *Journal of Parliamentary Debates* [Praktika Voulis] (24 May 1987) p. 6240 (in Greek). See also Robert McDonald, 'Alliance Problems in the Eastern Mediterranean – Greece, Turkey and Cyprus: Par

II', in *Prospects of Security in the Mediterranean, Adelphi Paper No. 229* (London: International Institute for Strategic Studies, 1988) p. 74.
12. Ibid.
13. Interview with A. Drossoyannis, *Military Technology* (October 1984) p. 5.
14. For a projection of the Turkish population see *Turkey: A Country Study* (Washington, DC: Library of Congress, 1988) p. 378.
15. See *The Military Balance, 1989–1990* (London: International Institute for Strategic Studies, 1989) p. 76.
16. Because of the great superiority in human resources, Turkey could benefit from any military encounter that reduced Greek military strength even if its own losses were much higher, so long as the ratio of Turkish to Greek losses does not exceed the overall ratio of strength in their favour.
17. See, for example, Jed Snyder, *Defending the Fringe: NATO, the Mediterranean and the Persian Gulf* (Boulder, Col.: Westview Press, 1987).
18. See US Department of State, *Foreign Relations of the United States, 1951* (Washington, DC, 1974) p. 452, and Yannis Roubatis, 'The United States and the Operational Responsibilities of the Greek Armed Forces, 1947–1987', *Journal of Greek Diaspora*, vol. 6 (Spring 1973) pp. 41–9.
19. See Petros Garoufalias, *Greece and Cyprus: Tragic Mistakes and Lost Opportunities* (Athens: Bergadis, 1982) p. 47 (in Greek). See also Yannis Roubatis, 'The US involvement in the Army and Politics of Greece, 1946–1967', Ph.D. Dissertation, Johns Hopkins University (1980).
20. See John Iatrides, 'Greek Security Policy under Andreas Papandreou', paper delivered at the Peace Studies Program, Cornell University (30 April 1986) p. 4 (mimeograph copy).
21. See Kenneth Waltz, *Theory of International Politics* (Reading, Mass.: Addison-Wesley, 1979) p. 168.
22. See the yearly reports of the US Arms Control and Disarmament Agency, *World Military Expenditures and Arms Transfers*.
23. Data presented to the parliament by the Greek prime minister. See *Journal of Parliamentary Debates* (23 January 1987) p. 2915 (in Greek).
24. See *Ta Nea* (9 January 1989) p. 18 (text in Greek). The new policy aimed *inter alia* at the rationalisation of the country's force structure and deployment. This caused some eastward and southward shift of the Greek land forces. The inherent flexibility of the air and naval forces minimised the need for a reorientation of the peacetime deployment.
25. See *Journal of Parliamentary Debates* (23 January 1987) p. 2915.
26. For the classic formulation of the requirements of deterrence, see William Kaufmann, *The Requirements of Deterrence* (Princeton, NJ: Center for International Studies, 1954) pp. 6–8.
27. See NATO Press Service, *Press Release*, M-DPC-2 (86) 39 (4 December 1986).
28. See *Journal of Parliamentary Debates* (23 January 1987) p. 2914 (in Greek).
29. See the announcement of the new defence policy, *Ta Nea* (9 January 1985) p. 18 (in Greek).
30. Thomas Schelling, *Arms and Influence* (New Haven, Conn.: Yale

University Press, 1986) p. 36.
31. See *Journal of Parliamentary Debates* (23 January 1987) p. 2915.
32. For a theoretical analysis of this tactic see Edward Rhodes, *Power and Madness* (New York: Columbia University Press, 1989) pp. 107–34.
33. *Ta Nea* (28 March 1987) pp. 14–15.
34. For an analysis of this problem, see Richard Smoke, *War: Controlling Escalation* (Cambridge, Mass.: Harvard University Press, 1977) pp. 239–97, and Robert Jervis, *Perception and Misperception in International Politics* (Princeton: Princeton University Press, 1976) pp. 58–113.
35. For an analysis of this problem, see Paul Huth, *Extended Deterrence and the Prevention of War* (New Haven, Conn.: Yale University Press, 1988) pp. 11–14 and 33–55.
35. For an analysis of this problem, see Paul Huth, *Extended Deterrence and the Prevention of War* (New Haven, Conn.: Yale University Press, 1988)
36. In fact in the Greek strategic *débâcle* the term 'appeasement' is used with the pejorative connotations that derive from the Munich debate. See *Journal of Parliamentary Debates* (24 May 1987) p. 6240 (in Greek).
37. For a theoretical analysis of the advantages of this strategy, see Glenn Snyder and Paul Diesing, *Conflict Among Nations: Bargaining, Decision Making and System Structure in International Crises* (Princeton, NJ: Princeton University Press, 1977) pp. 254–80; Huth, *Extended Deterrence*, pp. 51–5; and A. George, D. Hall and W. Simons, *The Limits of Coersive Diplomacy* (Boston, Mass.: Little, Brown, 1971).

8 The Strategic Matrix of the SEM: A Turkish Perspective

DUYGU SEZER

INTRODUCTION

The strategic milieu currently evolving in the SEM is a combined function of the politico-military developments and trends that have been taking place at three levels: the East–West, the regional, and the local.[1]

This chapter will survey the relevant developments at each level and point to their impact, operating singly and collectively, on the strategic matrix of the SEM.

TRENDS IN EAST–WEST RELATIONS

Momentous developments in East–West relations and within the Soviet Union and eastern Europe at the close of the 1980s have created the basis to recast entirely the strategic balances, calculations and dynamics that have prevailed in Europe since the dawn of the Cold War. It is only logical that changes of such profound politico-military nature draw within their orbit of influence the strategic interaction in the SEM, particularly in view of the fact that Greece and Turkey, the two major players of this region, have been intimately associated with the institutional expressions of the East–West conflict.

The Gorbachev Factor

President Mikhail S. Gorbachev should be credited for having been the primary force behind the evolution in East–West relations since 1985 towards political co-operation and military accommodation. Granted, as Michael Howard argues,[2] that most of what he has proposed and eventually agreed to had been proposed initially by the

West, Gorbachev is nevertheless responsible for actually having made the return to a dialogue possible with his willingness and readiness to meet the West on several of the latter's terms. He allowed the process of military accommodation to pick up momentum not simply by yielding to Western positions on many important points but, perhaps more significantly, by attacking with his 'new thinking' several crucial long-standing politico-military concepts, policies and practices associated with the Soviet Union.

Gorbachev's conceptual and policy initiatives have received a favourable reception in Turkey in general, as elsewhere in the world. On the other hand, an element of caution, the desire to wait until words are translated into deeds, in particular in the realm of Soviet military doctrine, seems to be the pervasive attitude.[3]

Arms Control: INF Treaty and CFE Negotiations

Among Gorbachev's contributions, in fact one of the most fundamental, is the INF Treaty – a source of positive input into the strategic picture in the SEM.

How does Turkey view this historic step towards nuclear disarmament in Europe, removing a class of nuclear weapons that had formed an integral part of NATO and Warsaw Pact defence strategies and arsenals?

In general, the response has been highly enthusiastic. At the more specific level, however, the INF treaty brought to the fore, for Turkey the urgency of two interrelated issues: the imbalance in conventional forces between NATO and the Warsaw Pact; and the possibility of the modernisation of NATO's short-range nuclear weapons.

The conventional force balance
Turkey felt that her portion of NATO's southern flank was greatly outnumbered by Soviet/Warsaw Pact forces.[4] Therefore, she was strongly in favour of the initiation of East–West negotiations on conventional force reductions 'from the Atlantic to the Urals'.

At the Conventional Stability Mandate Talks of the twenty-three members of NATO and the Warsaw Pact two issues presented difficulties for Turkey: the globalist versus the regionalist approach in assessing the security needs of individual countries; and the delimitation of areas of exclusion.

Turkey advocated a globalist approach. The preoccupation by the West with the stability of the centre, and, conversely, the tendency to relegate the flanks to marginality for European defence and arms reductions, apparently shaped Turkish apprehensions over the centre's creeping regionalism. Greece also seemed to be disappointed with the centre-oriented regionalism.

Determining the areas of exclusion from the pending negotiations was the other thorny issue. Turkey proposed to exclude a portion of her territory in the south-east on the grounds that countries bordering that area, namely Iran, Iraq and Syria, were not subject to the CSCE regime. The Soviet Union eventually yielded to Turkey on this point. Greece objected to the exclusion of the port of Mersin. The dispute was resolved at the end of the mandate talks in an ambiguous compromise.

Since they resumed in March 1989, progress at the negotiations on CFE have helped relax noticeably Turkish anxieties over the conventional imbalance with the great northern neighbour. At the end of 1989, Turkey seems to entertain greater confidence that the Soviet Union might indeed be serious about her declared position in favour of a defensive military doctrine and strategy.

Nuclear weapons modernisation

Turkey was not enthusiastic about the proposals for the modernisation of short-range nuclear weapons. Her nuclear arsenal consists of nuclear bombs, Honest John rockets and 8-inch and 155-inch artillery.[5] To the relief of Turkey, the matter was closed in May 1989 when President Bush yielded to West German demands not to proceed with modernisation plans.

The Greek stance towards nuclear weapons was more ambivalent. Turkey has assigned a deterrent value to the tactical nuclear weapons, however obsolete, on her soil. In contrast, Papandreou's government consistently declared them undesirable, and vowed to remove 'the American nuclear weapons' unilaterally.[6] Some but not all of their nuclear inventory, also obsolete, were indeed removed in later years. Greece was also in the forefront of the proposals for a nuclear-weapon-free-zone in the Balkans, which Turkey never considered with favour. Anyhow, the notion has been overtaken by the larger disarmament and arms control process in Europe.

DEVELOPMENTS IN ADJOINING REGIONS

South-West Asia

The cease-fire in the Iran–Iraq war and the withdrawal of Soviet troops from Afghanistan have brought to south-west Asia an important degree of stability since the latter part of 1988.

The war between her two neighbours, Iran and Iraq, had forced Turkey to be on guard against the threat of being drawn into armed hostilities inadvertently as a result of several mutual concerns, namely the heightened ethnic unrest among the Kurdish populations in all three countries, border crossings into Turkey in hot pursuit, and the vulnerability of the Kerkuk–Iskenderun oil pipeline to possible bombings by Iran in an attempt to undermine Iraq's oil exports.

The developments in Afghanistan are likely to engender indirect rather than direct politico-military repercussions on the SEM, largely because of the geographical distances involved and the absence of direct stakes in the conflict. Yet, because Turkey has been traditionally apprehensive about the role of socialist internationalism in Soviet foreign relations, Gorbachev's policy of retrenchment from Afghanistan has come a long way in rectifying the image of the Soviet Union in Turkish eyes.

In 1989 the forty-year-old Arab–Israeli conflict failed, once again to reach the negotiating table despite some hopeful signs such as Yasser Arafat's diplomatic success with the United States that same year. Lebanon continues to be the target of manipulation and influence by all the major players in the region and their proxies.

The United States and NATO have specific interests in south-west Asia, such as the free flow of oil, resulting in the identification of regional conflicts there as out-of-area issues. The proximity of SEM to a region recognised by the Atlantic alliance as an important source of out-of-area challenges to its vital interests explains why Greece, Turkey and Cyprus continue to enjoy special strategic importance for the West.

The fact that the region is, at the same time, the major supplier of international terrorism adds to the difficulties and risks of being geographically adjacent to this trouble-spot of world politics. The experiences of Greece with international terrorism and the ensuing strain in US–Greek relations are a case in point.

Theoretically speaking, militarily significant and peace-oriented developments since 1988 in south-west Asia could have led to reduced superpower military presence in the region. Other than the Soviet troop withdrawals from Afghanistan, however, there is no indication of major cutbacks in primary elements of their respective military strength in the region, that is from naval units in the Indian Ocean, the Gulf, and the eastern Mediterranean.

Eastern Europe and the Balkans

Developments in eastern Europe, and especially in the Balkans, have historically possessed an almost irresistible potential to influence the strategic picture in the SEM. The successive liberal revolutions in eastern Europe in late 1989, more or less replicating the Polish example of the spring of the same year, have ushered in a thoroughly new chapter in the structure of threat perceptions in Europe. They have registered the final stroke to whatever reciprocal perception of threat might have lingered on in eastern and western Europe in the expanding atmosphere of East–West accommodation. The military alliances, if not the national military establishments, have truly began to look like anachronisms.

Similar observations apply in the SEM. Greece had already officially declared in 1984 that she perceived no Soviet/Warsaw Pact threat. The recent developments in eastern Europe and the Soviet Union have only increased the legitimacy of her claims in this respect. Greece had previously mended her relations with her Balkan neighbours, in particular with Bulgaria, entering into what seemed like an anti-Turkish coalition with Bulgaria in 1988 with the Greek–Bulgarian non-aggression declaration.

Turkey has only recently and gradually begun to redefine her perception of the threat from 'the north', and in this task she has been assisted by the wave of liberalisation in eastern Europe.

The fall of Tudor Jivkov's regime in Bulgaria has been of special relevance to Turkish–Bulgarian relations. These had deteriorated in summer 1989 when the six-year-old assimilation policy against the ethnic Turkish minority culminated in the mass exodus of 300 000 Turks to Turkey. The crisis destroyed the optimism generated earlier in 1988 when the Balkan Conference met in Belgrade with the participation of all the six Balkan states. The new government under Petar Mladenov has offered to restore the rights of the Turkish minority, mobilising in turn a pro-Jivkov backlash to the proposed concessions. On the other hand, the prevalent sense of uncertainty about the new regime's ability to consolidate its power rules out predictions about how the problem might evolve.

Quo Vadis NATO's Southern Flank?

The SEM forms a major portion of the southern flank of NATO. It also falls within the south-western theatre or military district (TVD) of the Soviet Union. What, then, is the nature of the rivalry in this region between the two military alliances against the context of dramatic change in the international environment?

The analysis in the preceding pages leads to one logical response only: that the NATO–Warsaw Pact military confrontation is rapidly eroding in this region as elsewhere in Europe. It is eroding under the impact of several related developments, some of which are carefully orchestrated by governments, for example the CFE negotiations, the CSCE process and Soviet/Warsaw Pact declarations of non-offensive military doctrines and unilateral force cuts, while others have erupted spontaneously in response to popular demands, for example the liberalisation in Europe.

Deep substantive changes notwithstanding, both military alliances still maintain their institutional structures. Officially NATO's military strategy of flexible response is still in force intact. In contrast, the Soviet/Warsaw Pact declarations have announced the adoption of a defensive military doctrine and strategy.

This mixed picture of both change and continuity in the military contours of the alliances finds its reflection in the SEM, too. Change has occurred in two major areas. The first concerns the threat perception. The second concerns the nature of the relationship of the local allies, that is Greece and Turkey, with the United States, the alliance leader.

As mentioned previously, Greece had already redefined 'the threat' back in 1984. In the 'new defence dogma' Turkey was defined as the real threat, not 'the north'. It is only logical that the present era should further reinforce this perception, especially in view of the lack of progress on any substantive issue between Greece and Turkey. Change in the Turkish threat perception has been a slow process but it is already a fact of life for many in the security community. While the traditional assessments of the Soviet Union as the most important source of threat are being moderated, the potential in the south (Syria, Iraq and Iran) and from Greece is being upgraded.

Allied Relations: The United States, Greece and Turkey

Recent trends in and attitudes towards military assistance and basing rights can be viewed as the expression of the creeping distancing between the United States and her smaller allies on the southern flank. Broadly speaking, the US desire to reduce her security com mitments to her transatlantic partners has been well known for several years now. On the subject of bases, the United States may not have yet reached that point where she could feel confident that she no longer needs to rely on these bases and facilities for her own and the West's security.

The level of American assistance, quite generous in the early 1980s in view of the crisis and instability in south-west Asia caused by the Iran–Iraq war and the Soviet invasion of Afghanistan, began a steady decline after 1985. Congressional sympathies for Greece cushioned the impact of the decline by increasing the value of excess equipment transferred to Greece under the so-called Southern Region Amendment (1987) to the US Foreign Assistance Act, shifting the 7:10 ratio in Greek: Turkish military aid to nearly 8:10.[7] US military assistance to Greece declined from a high of $588.6 million in 1984 to an estimated $357.1 in 1988. For Turkey, respective figures were $1005.7 and $545.2 million.[8]

Statistics sometimes conceal important dynamic forces at work behind the numbers. The aid levels to Greece in the first half of 1980s hide, for example, the fact that the deterioration in US–Greek relations while Papandreou was in power, his anti-US and anti-NATO posturing did not deprive him of US assistance. In the case of Turkey, the increasing levels of assistance in the early 1980s skilfully hide the powerful Congressional opposition to Turkey on several counts but most notably because of the Cyprus question.

The subject of basing rights was a singularly relevant topic for the United States, for whom access to military bases and facilities in Greece and Turkey has provided one of the main instruments of the broader post-war strategy of containment in this part of the world.

Greece and Turkey approached the question of US bases and facilities in the 1980s with differing philosophies. Greece under Papandreou's government seemed to have been categorically opposed to the continuation of what it defined as the 'American', as distinct from NATO, bases. Despite this opposition in principle, however, a new base agreement was renegotiated in 1983, to last until 20 December 1988. While in office, Papandreou was reported to have stated that should a new agreement with the United States be reached, it would have to be approved by the Greek people through a national referendum.[9] The agreement has not been renegotiated yet, as domestic political developments in the wake of the national elections in June 1989 apparently pushed it into the lower echelons of the politicians' priority scale.

Turkey, in contrast, did not object in principle to the continued operations of allied bases and facilities in Turkey. She viewed their role exclusively within the framework of NATO responsibilities. The current US–Turkish DECA, negotiated in 1980, runs until 18 December 1990. Turkey has threatened to abrogate base-rights if and when the anti-Turkish, pro-Armenian draft resolution is voted upon by the US Congress.

Greece and Turkey both have argued for higher levels of American military assistance in return for continued American access to the bases and facilities. Turkey seemed to be more careful not to appear to be linking base-rights with assistance, preferring instead to blend the two concepts into one within the larger term of 'defence cooperation'. Both countries have also been careful not to become associated with US actions that they perceived as having served unilateral US policies and interests. The question of allied responsibility in 'out-of-area' conflicts, that is the Iran–Iraq war, Lebanon and terrorism often lurked as a hidden source of tension through the 1980s in US–allied relations on the southern flank.

Congressional attitudes towards countries where the US has base-rights is being hardened, too, as a result of several factors. The changing international politico-military climate has probably been the most powerful influence in bringing about a change in perceptions concerning the need for forward deployment of US forces around the periphery of the Soviet Union. The peaceful picture of the world and the constraints of a huge federal deficit have led powerful forces in the Congress to argue for cuts in foreign aid and to resist linkage between American assistance and base-rights. These trends found new expression when Section 562 of the Foreign Assistance Appropriations Act of 1 October 1988 (PL 100–461, HR 4637) gave the US president the authority to reprogramme funds[10] earmarked for assistance to a base-right or base-access country.

In short, Greek objections and Turkish reserve concerning access to the bases and facilities by the United States were not received with enthusiasm in Washington.

The basic question concerning the levels of US military assistance levels and US base-rights could be framed in a larger perspective: how long is the United States likely to need to rely on Greek and Turkish bases for her security? For the West's security? The answer seems to be 'at least a while longer'. Verification of the arms control treaties and the continuing turmoil and turbulence in the larger Middle East requires the United States to have continued access to these bases.

Allies as Adversaries: Greece and Turkey

If two states cannot sustain, at the very minimum, normal bilateral relations, membership in a multilateral alliance may come to be valued more for its potential role in constraining the adversary than for its contributions to collective security against a third party.

Greek–Turkish relations evolved in the 1970s and 1980s along the lines proposed above. Not only did bilateral allied co-ordination cease since the Cyprus crisis of summer 1974, but those multilateral activities on the southern flank that required Greek and Turkish participation and co-ordination, that is military exercises and arrangements for air defence, have fallen hostage to the Greek–Turkish conflict. This state of affairs has led a recent study on the southern region to conclude: 'Until progress is made, NATO's military position in the region will be at a gross disadvantage, however much the balance of forces is improved in NATO's favor'.[11]

Outstanding issues that remain stalemated include the command and control question and the question of the rearmament of certain Greek islands, in particular the island of Lemnos. The Rogers' Agreement of 1980, worked out to address the issue of command and control arrangements in the Aegean, turned into an instrument of one-sided advantage upon the rejection of its full implementation by the incoming Greek government of Papandreou in 1981. On the question of Lemnos, national interests are again pitted against alliance interests because Turkey insists that the island remain demilitarised, hence closed to NATO, while Greece presents an armed Lemnos as an asset to the defence of NATO's southern flank. The dispute over the rearmament of Lemnos threatened for a while agreement within the NATO High-Level Task Force on a new force comparisons document.[12]

NATO–Warsaw Pact Balance in the SEM

NATO released its conventional force balance data in November 1988; the Warsaw Pact released their's in January 1989. In other words, the public has only recently been informed of the official figures on the military balance. This should serve as a reminder that any discussion on the subject should proceed with caution. With this reservation in mind, only general trends will be outlined here.

Naval superiority is a marked feature of NATO forces in general. This aspect of the balance applies on the southern flank, too. The Sixth Fleet furnishes the backbone of the Atlantic alliance's naval power in the region. Its strength currently consists of one or two carriers, nine or ten other surface combatants, four submarines, an amphibious ready group of between three and five ships, and a variety of support ships.

The Soviet Mediterranean Squadron maintains an average strength of forty ships. Five or six of them are major surface combatants drawn from the Black Sea Fleet and five or six are submarines from the Northern Fleet. Soviet Naval Aviation Backfire bombers greatly enhance the firepower of the Soviet Navy in the region.

The Black Sea Fleet clearly constitutes a much more potent source of Soviet naval power in the region, with an overseas base under construction at Tartus (Syria). The primary role of the fleet is assumed to be to support operations in Thrace in conjunction with the Mediterranean squadron. Its secondary role is sea control off the Turkish coast.

The dominance of Soviet naval power in the Black Sea region creates a Soviet–Turkish balance that is quite the reverse of that which holds in the southern region as a whole. NATO plans presumably rely on the firepower of the Sixth Fleet for the defence of the Turkish straits and Thrace, as well as on the reinforcements it would make available through its control of the sea lanes of communication.

Naval forces have been excluded from the conventional arms control negotiations in Europe. Hence, the question of the naval balance in the Mediterranean and the Black Sea is not likely to be addressed, at least during the current phase of the negotiations. Nor does there seem to be much receptivity in the West to long-standing Soviet proposals for a Mediterranean freed from nuclear weapons, foreign troops and bases. The United States, in particular, would not wish to lose its dominance over the Mediterranean, which allows it to control not only NATO's southern region but the Middle East and northern Africa as well. In practically every hypothetical arms control scenario in the Mediterranean, the Soviet Union, in contrast to the United States, would continue to enjoy a natural advantage simply by being a Black Sea power.

The NATO–Warsaw Pact balance on the ground and in the air in the SEM shows a vastly different picture. Most of the literature of Western origin on the subject refers to a marked disparity between the NATO and Warsaw Pact forces not merely in quantitative terms but perhaps more importantly in qualitative terms. On the other hand, Gorbachev seemed to reject this general contention initially during his visit to Washington in December 1987, maintaining that rough parity existed. Similarly, data released by the Warsaw Pact on the conventional force balance continued to assess the picture as one of rough parity. CFE negotiations have focused on finding a common ceiling at lower levels.

The strong belief in Turkey in the existence of a huge imbalance with Soviet/Warsaw Pact forces provided an apparently unceasing pressure for force modernisation. Currently, that modernisation drive seems to parallel the CFE negotiations.

The Turkish and Greek drives for weapons modernisation are probably viewed in Washington and Brussels with some degree of scepticism rather than with full support since many outside the two countries believe that it is the Greek–Turkish conflict that is primarily responsible for fuelling the race for arms modernisation.

THE LOCAL STRATEGIC PICTURE AMONG GREECE, TURKEY AND CYPRUS

It is a well-known fact that Greek–Turkish strategic interaction has two contradictory facets: the countries are both state-to-state adversaries and NATO allies. Because the latter aspect of the Greek–Turkish relationship was discussed in the previous section, attention here will be paid only to the former aspect.

Neighbours as Adversaries: Greece and Turkey

The adversarial relationship between Greece and Turkey has for long overpowered the allied one. The tension that flows from the Aegean disputes and the Cyprus conflict has brought the two countries to the brink of war at least twice in the 1980s, the last occasion being in March 1987.

In January 1988 the historic Davos initiative was launched by prime ministers Papandreau and Ozal. The mutually declared purpose was to resume the bilateral dialogue and to prevent the outbreak of war. In retrospect, it looks more like an attempt at personal diplomacy and dialogue between two leaders, motivated largely by political instincts, rather than between two governments. The process was shelved quietly as Papandreou was drawn into political and personal problems in the latter part of 1988 and throughout 1989.

On the other hand, Davos offered a ray of hope, if not in resolving the substantive issues, at least in piercing through the thick cloud of suspicion that separates the two countries. For a while there appeared to be a definite reduction in tensions. Both sides seemed to exercise greater restraint, thus making an important contribution to lessening the threat of war. In Greece, official talk of the 'new defence dogma' subsidied. In Turkey, officials ceased to talk about *casus belli* and the Aegean Army.

The 'no peace, no war' state of affairs between the two countries since the launching of the Davos initiative may testify once more to the high degree of rigidity in the respective positions of the two countries concerning the issues dividing them. Feelings are also being aroused on both sides concerning respective ethnic minority questions. Turkish public opinion had hoped that the completion in late 1989 of the restoration of the buildings of the Greek Patriarchate in Istanbul after decades of official obstruction would provide the occasion for some improvement in the climate, but it has not.

The Greek–Turkish Military Balance

The arms race between the two countries has been a permanent feature of their interaction since the Cyprus crisis of 1974.

Greece has steadily committed a higher percentage of its GDP to defence spending (Table 1). In this sense, Greece has in fact been the biggest spender in NATO almost regularly since 1974; moreover, she has been investing more heavily in equipment – at nearly twice the rate of Turkey between 1980 and 1984 (Table 2).

As to the size of their armed forces, according to the *Military Balance* (IISS) 1988–9 figures, the Greek armed forces on active duty number a total of 214 000 in a population of 10 055 000. The Turkish armed forces on active duty number a total of 635 300 in a population of 51 385 000. The same source provides the figures on key equipment deployment of the national forces shown in Table 3.

The Cyprus Conflict

Great disparities continue to exist in the respective visions of the Greek-Cypriot and Turkish-Cypriot communities on the essentials for a settlement: the nature of the Cypriot state that would institutionalise and codify the political and geographical aspects of intercommunal coexistence, and the future of the Turkish military force in Cyprus. The failure of UN-sponsored Denktash–Vasiliou exchanges in the first half of 1989 bears witness that the deadlock persists.

TABLE 1 *Defence expenditures as percentage of gross domestic product (based on constant prices)**

	Av. 1970–4	Av. 1975–9	Av. 1980–4	1980	1984	1985	1986	1987	1988
Greece	4.7	6.7	6.6	5.7	7.1	7.0	6.1	6.2	6.6
Turkey	2.8	4.5	4.3	4.6	3.9	4.0	4.2	3.8	3.8

* Adapted from *NATO Review*, no. 6 (December 1988) p. 31.

TABLE 2 *Equipment expenditures as percentage of total defence expenditure (based on constant prices)**

	Av. 1970–4	Av. 1975–9	Av. 1980–4	1980	1984	1985	1986	1987	1988
Greece	8.2	19.3	17.4	18.8	15.3	14.5	15.8	17.2	24.4
Turkey	3.9	19.2	9.1	4.7	13.1	13.6	17.9	21.1	22.5

* Adapted from *NATO Review*, no. 6 (December 1988) p. 31.

TABLE 3 *Deployment of key military equipment by Greece and Turkey*

	Main battle tanks	Artillery Multiple rocket launchers	Combat aircraft	Armed helicopters
Greece	1893	1336	297	10
Turkey	3600	2033	522	0

Historical and political facts inform one that it may never be possible thoroughly to disentangle the Cyprus conflict from the Greek–Turkish conflict and vice versa. In fact, the Cyprus conflict has never had an independent life of its own. For a brief period in 1960–3, the opportunity presented itself. The young Republic of Cyprus possessed then the freedom to distance itself from the legacy and burden of the Greek–Turkish connection and to press ahead to consolidate a Cypriot state on the foundation of a distinct Cypriot national identity. That opportunity was not seized.

It is highly likely that the stalemate in the bicommunal dialogue will continue to resist movement until and unless there is a radical conceptual and philosophical breakthrough in each community's thinking and feeling about the other. The prospects of such change occurring are very much interlinked with the prospects for a similar process in Greek–Turkish relations. Merely calling for the withdrawal of the Turkish military forces does not look like a persuasive negotiating position if it is not accompanied by credible assurances that those circumstances that brought the Turkish military force to Cyprus nearly fifteen years ago could never be repeated again. And those assurances would have to be inherent to the structure of the future Cypriot state. Turkey, on her part, could try to assuage the fears of the Greek-Cypriot side by stating in an unequivocal fashion that she maintains an armed presence in Cyprus only as an interim measure until internal settlement is reached between the two communities.

On the other hand, the international climate is likely to pose itself as a powerful source of pressure on Turkey and the Turkish Cypriots. The European Community named the continuing Greek–Turkish and Cyprus conflicts among the reasons for its refusal in December 1989 to consider the Turkish application for membership. The tearing-down of the Berlin Wall has set a powerful example to all the interested parties to look for a new strategy and counter-strategy. There is a general expectation for a similar lifting of the green line in Nicosia. But as long as emotional and attitudinal walls continue to divide the minds and hearts of the two communities, how durable could a physical wall-less and line-less life be?

CONCLUSION

The second part of the 1980s has witnessed momentous developments in the nature of contemporary international relations whose origins were founded in the early post-war years. Even though it is too early yet to conclude that the outstanding features of the post-war international system have definitely become *passé*, it is possible to argue that important forces and developments have already challenged many of the underlying concepts, assumptions and structures of that system. For a while the one area where change was simultaneously occurring and holding out the promise of major revisions to the post-war world order seemed to be confined to the military security domain. The liberal revolutions in eastern Europe have expanded the boundaries of change enormously to include the political, economic and cultural domains.

The SEM falls within the explicit boundaries of the East–West system of interaction by virtue of the fact that two major state-actors in this sub-region, Greece and Turkey, have formed part of the West's military structure there since 1952. It is in many ways inevitable, therefore, that a major change in East–West relationships, the central force in international relations, should be reflected in East–West relations on the periphery, that is the SEM. It is no surprise, therefore, that threat perception has been changing concomitantly with the change in East–West relations. This is true especially for Turkey, for Greece had already officially ceased to designate the north, meaning the Soviet Union and the Warsaw Pact, as a source of threat to her security.

In the more immediate sense, it is the nature and pattern of interactions between Greece, Turkey and Cyprus that make a direct imprint on the strategic scene in the SEM. The implicit and explicit threat of the use of military force was a permanent feature of Greek–Turkish relations since at least summer 1974. The Davos initiative dimmed that threat during its brief life span.

Several circles in both Greece and Turkey argue that the Davos process was a failure simply because it did not solve any of the substantive issues. Yet the Davos summit has set in motion a vitally important dialogue. How can a dialogue be expected to resolve a set of serious inter-state conflicts unless it is first given a chance to address the issues, to hear out the parties and to test intentions, over a period of time?

Furthermore, the Davos initiative brought forth a mutual pledge not to go to war. This is a fundamental step towards war prevention. The expression of a mutual determination to prevent a Greek–Turkish war and to pursue a dialogue should be seen as a credible manifestation of a rational search for conflict resolution. The international atmosphere could also be helpful in sustaining this mutual determination. Many of the confidence-building measures adopted first at the Helsinki Conference (1986) and at the Vienna Conference (1989) could easily be utilised with resourcefulness and goodwill to pierce through the thick shield of hostility and suspicion separating the two countries.

The Greek–Turkish interaction may be entering a qualitatively new stage in the closing years of the 1980s, specifically under the influence of the momentous changes taking place in Europe. Of these only one has direct relevance to Greek–Turkish relations, namely the decision rendered by the European Community in December 1989, postponing until at least the mid-1990s the consideration of Turkey's application for membership.

Others have indirect, though immense, potential influence. The growing Western consensus on the phasing out of the Soviet/Warsaw Pact threat, the concomitant weakening of NATO, the integrationist momentum within western Europe and the liberalisation of eastern Europe have, together, culminated in a general expectation of a peacefully reunited and prosperous Europe in the near future. Greece, already securely positioned in western Europe, will take her place almost automatically in the new Europe of whatever institutional structure. For Turkey, the prospects are full of ambiguities and uncertainties. The basis of her association with Europe is not only less secure but her position may be further undermined by the inevitable weakening of NATO in the face of the new era of European peace. In these circumstances, Turkish diplomacy might soon have to cope with the challenge of defining, and delivering, a proper place and role for Turkey in the reunited Europe of the near future. Given the recent rebuff by the European Community, the task would seem to be all the more formidable unless the European framework that might eventually emerge is a loose one, something along the lines of Gorbachev's 'Common European House'. The evolving CSCE process might also eventually transform itself into a more permanent European framework, promising to secure Turkey's links with and place in Europe.

On the Cyprus question, the chances of resolution still seem to rest ultimately in the hands of the two ethnic communities who will have to agree on the nature and structure of their own independent state. This, however, should not imply an oversight of the fact that organic relations tie Cyprus to both Greece and Turkey.

Finally, the fluidity and uncertainty in the new stage of international relations, implying the eventual break-up of the alliances and their transformation into something radically different, may bode ill for regional conflicts rather than having the beneficial effects so far encountered in Europe, where political and cultural dynamics are rather unique. From this perspective, the fundamental challenge facing the local actors in the SEM in the next few years hinges on their ability to restrain pressures to take advantage of the new-found freedom offered by the erosion of alliance discipline and loyalty. Equally dangerous is the general picture of instability and turbulence in the Middle East. The countries of the SEM, in particular Turkey, will live with a sense of vulnerability to the plethora of conflicts – big and small – in the Middle East.

NOTES

1. This definition is adapted from Louis J. Halle, *The Elements of International Strategy: A Primer for the Nuclear Age* (1984) p. 4, quoted in Barry Buzan, *Strategic Studies: Military Technology and International Relations* (London: Macmillan, 1987) p. 4.
2. Michael Howard, 'The Gorbachev Challenge and the Defense of the West', *Survival*, vol. XXX (November/December 1988) no. 6, p. 489.
3. These views have been obtained from I. Biren (Admiral, Turkish Navy, now retired), 'Nato's Security in the Mediterranean', *Turkish Review* (Istanbul) vol. 2 (Winter 1987) no. 10, pp. 11–17; *Diplomatic Pulse* (Abstract of Turkish Daily Press, *Antalya*) (14 March 1989); V. Halefoglu (then Minister of Foreign Affairs), 'Allies and Partners', *NATO Review*, vol. 34 (February 1986) no. 1, pp. 1–6; Ministry of Foreign Affairs, *Budget Report, Fiscal Year 1988*, Turkish Grand National Assembly, Office of Minutes, Ankara (3 November 1988) (in Turkish); Ministry of Foreign Affairs, *Press Release*, Ankara, 9 December 1988; T. Ozal (then Prime Minister), 'Turkey in the Southern flank', *Defense Yearbook 1989* (London: Brassey's, 1989) pp. 3–9; E. Vuralhan (then Minister of Defence), *Statement Before the Commission on the Plan and the Budget of the Grand National Assembly of Turkey*, Ankara (18 November 1988) mimeographed records (in Turkish); E. Vuralhan, *Opening Statement*, Eurogroup Round Table Meeting, Washington, DC (28 November 1988); M. Yilmaz (Minister of Foreign Affairs), 'Burden-Sharing From Turkey's Perspective', *NATO Review* (October–November 1988) pp. 1–3.
4. NATO released its data on the conventional force balance in Europe in November 1988; the Warsaw Pact released its data in January 1989. The NATO document points to disparities in favour of the East; the Warsaw Pact sources refer to 'virtual parity'. Evidently the Turkish view reflects the NATO assessment.
5. William M. Arkin and Richard W. Fieldhouse, *Nuclear Battlefields: Global Links in the Arms Race* (Cambridge, Mass.: Ballinger, 1985) p. 102.
6. William M. Arkin, 'Greece's Balancing Act', *Bulletin of the Atomic Scientists*, vol. 43 (March 1987) no. 2, pp. 11–12.
7. Center for Strategic and International Studies (CSIS), *NATO's Southern Region: Strategy and Resources for Coalition Defense* (mimeographed report, Washington, DC, 1988) p. 19.
8. Richard F. Grimmett, *Current Issues with the Base-Rights Countries and their Implications* (Washington, DC: Congressional Research Service, 5 December 1988) p. 33.
9. Ibid., p. 9.
10. Ibid., p. 18.
11. CSIS, *NATO's Southern Region*, p. 29.
12. International Institute for Strategic Studies (IISS), *Strategic Survey, 1987–88* (London, 1988) p. 51.

Part III

Systemic Influences on an Intra-alliance Conflict

9 Systemic Influences on a Weak, Aligned State in the Post-1974 Era
DIMITRI CONSTAS

The aim of this chapter is to trace those factors in the post-1974 international system that may have affected external balancing efforts by a 'weak', 'aligned' state which is also experiencing a major threat against its security interests emanating from within rather than from outside its alliance. Although the specifications 'weak', 'aligned' and, especially, 'threatened by an ally' appear too restrictive, it is the hope of the author that certain conclusions from this chapter could transcend the narrow parameters of the Greek–Turkish conflict (and Greece's place in it as perceived by a Greek scholar) and serve theory-building efforts in the area of 'intra-bloc conflicts'.

The characteristics of an international system can be categorised by a variety of criteria. Kal Holsti, in his influential work on the subject, has defined five important aspects of an historic international system.[1] This chapter will focus on three items in Holsti's list: 'structure', 'interaction' (especially level of 'tension') and, to a much lesser extent, 'rules'.

Conventional wisdom and scholarly opinion generally concur that external sources of strength are more crucial to the weak states than to the great powers. There is nevertheless little agreement regarding the criteria that would place a state in one of these two categories.[2] A plausible way out of the labyrinthine problem of defining the concept of a 'weak state' is to measure its capabilities not against all other states but in relation to its neighbours especially its regional rivals, while taking into account the degree to which its strength matches its national goals.[3] A comparison of Greece's capabilities with the state with which it interacts on a conflictual level – Turkey – would be sufficient to classify her in the 'weak states' category. A criterion suggested by Athanasios Platias adds weight to this designation:

size/strength (of Greece) compared to the country (the United States) whose actions have profound influence on her national interests.[4]

The effects on Greece of developments on the systemic level are further qualified by her status as an aligned state attached to one of two military coalitions that continue to dominate the international scene in the 1972–87 period. Indeed, the bipolar structure of the post-1972 international system[5] manifests itself in the extraordinary concentration of military power in the hands of two states (the United States and the Soviet Union) and their respective alliance configurations, primarily NATO and the Warsaw Pact. Earlier predictions of rapid transformation of this structure into tripolar (China) or multipolar configurations (western Europe, Japan and the Third World) have not as yet materialised.[6] Actors competing with the two superpowers have not managed to put together that optimum combination of economic wealth and military might that would allow the pursuit of foreign policy objectives on a global scale. At the same time, the bipolar configuration of military power is loose rather than tight in a double sense. First, the vast majority of states, including some with significant bases of power, stayed apart from the two contending blocs or occasionally shifted allegiances from one to the other. Secondly, members of the two alliances retained, throughout the post-1974 period, a measure of autonomy effectively resisting pressure to return to the monolithic behaviour patterns of the Cold War era.[7]

Within this loose bipolar system, modes of interaction underwent substantial change during three time intervals: *détente* (1974–9), tension (1980–5), back to *détente* (1985 to the present). What distinguishes the years 1980–5 from the other two periods is a trend evident in both antagonists' attitudes to render co-operative patterns of interaction subordinate to conflictual ones. In those years the arms race gained momentum as demonstrated in the deployment of new, formidable weapons systems (Cruise, Pershing II and SS20 missiles) and the beginning of research and development of new technologies that could undermine the current 'balance of terror' (SDI), the abrogation of arms-limitation agreements (ABM, SALT II) and interruption of related negotiations, various kinds of boycotts ranging from trade to athletic events (Olympic Games: Moscow, 1980; Los Angeles, 1984), wars by proxy in the Third World (Afghanistan, Angola and the Nicaraguan conflict), aggressive action against civilian targets (the Korean airliner incident), suppression of reformist movements (Poland) and inflammatory rhetoric.

In principle, a weak state would expect to benefit from tense superpower relations. Superpowers, depending on the weak state's strategic value, might be tempted to compete for its favours: alignment or, at least, neutrality.[8] Peaceful coexistence can offer no such rewards. Nevertheless, a weak state's discretion to trade loyalty for additional security and other advantages is subject to a variety of restraints when it happens to be already aligned to one of the two rival blocs, especially if it seeks to bridge, as in the case of Greece, a national security gap caused by an ally rather than the 'common', 'external' enemy.

In order to pursue alternative, external, balancing options, the weak aligned state must overcome several obstacles. For one, its own domestic political and socio-economic structure might effectively resist policies departing from established modes of external interaction. Also, military aid, technological procurement and similar dependencies[9] make today's alliances 'relatively binding' and preclude adjustments of power allocation through realignment.[10]

Furthermore, the internal rivalry within one coalition might discourage the other from opening its doors to the weak state concerned, especially if its rival is regarded as a 'bigger catch'[11] or might cause regional complications. Even without going as far as defection and realignment, for a superpower to overtly take sides in a fraternal feud within the other camp is perhaps the less expedient of the available strategies to weaken the opponent. Finally, the post-war record (Hungary, Czechoslovakia, Poland) shows that superpowers are too apprehensive of nuclear escalation to engage openly in policies that the other side might regard as provoking defection of one of its allies.

These are significant obstacles blocking the way to defection and the use of this threat, but certainly they do not rule out cautious, low-key arrangements between the weak state and the other side. Nevertheless, with its options restricted, the weak, threatened, aligned state must focus on its own camp and compete with its rival partner for allied resources with its sole consolation the fact that similar limitations apply to its opponent as well. The crucial factor becomes each partner's real or perceived contribution to the collective goals of the alliance and the degree to which their roles are complementary. Each will endeavour to demonstrate how crucial is its role and how current world and regional conditions enhance its strategic value. Commitment to the allied cause is an asset, proudly advertised, while the other side's infidelity and irresponsible moves are eagerly exposed. While the 'weaker' of the rivals tries to sensitise the other partners to the security vacuum it is experiencing and calls frequently upon them to take that reality into account in determining aid levels and regional defence planning, the 'stronger' dismisses those fears as fabricated and suggests adherence to the 'traditional' allied duties: deterrence of potential external rather than internal aggressors.

Co-operative or conflictual trends in systemic interactions have a marginal effect on the process toward an agreed settlement of an intra-bloc rivalry. In times of *détente*, pursuit of national objectives might take priority over the collective interest of the alliance on the assumption that the other side will be less disposed to exploit the conflict.[12] By the same token, relaxation of tensions might reduce the incentives of the dominant power in the bloc to make the sacrifice needed to restore allied unity or for the rival partner, who expects to lose from such hegemonic interference, to pay the cost involved.

When the state of affairs between the two coalitions is in turmoil there might be more powerful incentives for effective mediation in the fraternal dispute. The 'external threat' might also predispose the rival partners toward moderation. But in its quest for intra-bloc coherence the dominant partner should take into account the rivals' comparative value for allied strategies. The risk of alienating the 'stronger' of the two opponents under conditions which underline its importance must be weighted against the expected gains from the restoration of unity with consequent easing of the pressures applied.

In short, prevailing levels of tension in the loose bipolar system will do little to enhance the posture of a weak, aligned state facing a threat from inside its own coalition. There is little chance that a military alliance will offer to make up for an internal power assymetry which the 'weaker' aligned state is unlikely to balance from outside its camp.

This gloomy overview of the post-1974 world structure and interactions along with the bleak external balancing prospects for a weak, threatened ally looses part of its gloom when other aspects of the situation are introduced into the analysis. While bipolarity is the prominent feature in the military field, other issue areas such as the balance of payments, international currency fluctuations, raw material prices and so on – vital items in contemporary international politics – are liable to multicentric power configurations.[13] The two superpowers, restrained from taking advantage of their military supremacy by the traumas of Vietnam and Afghanistan and fears of nuclear escalation, found themselves entangled in hard bargaining with allies and foes alike over a broad range of interlinked issues.[14]

Bipolycentrism,[15] the articulation of different power configurations coexisting with *military* bipolarity, became during the 1970s a prominent feature of international politics. The new era was formally inaugurated in August 1971 when President Nixon announced a series of measures that put an end to American hegemony in world trade and financial affairs. Developments suggesting spectacular improvement of East–West relations – US withdrawal from Vietnam; Nixon's visits to China and Moscow; the ABM and SALT I treaties between the United States and the Soviet Union – also contributed to bipolycentrism. Friends and comrades within or outside the two blocs would no longer be restrained by an external threat in their fierce competition against a superpower's economic interests around the globe. Western Europe, China and Japan consolidated their status as prominent, semi-autonomous economic and political centres and their patterns of interaction with aligned and non-aligned countries often transcended barriers posed by East–West military rivalries. EC-Europe in particular, enlarged with the accession of the United Kingdom, Denmark and Ireland, saw in the post-1973 oil crisis period both the necessity and the opportunity for more vigorous and independent involvement in Middle Eastern, Mediterranean and world affairs. As tension gradually built up in US–Soviet relations, EC-Europeans, deeply concerned over scenarios of limited nuclear war and policies insensitive to their apprehensions, expanded trade ties[16] and other economic transactions[17] with eastern Europe. It was at the peak of the confrontation over INF that the concept of a 'European defence community to protect détente' took roots in European public opinion and the minds of policy-makers.[18]

For a weak, aligned state disenchanted with its status in a power hierarchy formed on the basis of military capabilities and global strategic considerations, these developments have had two positive implications. First, they created external balancing opportunities through a regional (western European) integration scheme that attached more value to economic and political development than to military might and involved none of the previously discussed realignment costs. Secondly, active involvement in a regional co-operation arrangement bringing together members of the two blocs (for example inter-Balkan co-operation) emerged as a 'legitimate' method to enhance a weak, aligned state's security posture and political manoeuvrability.

In the post-1972 era, multipolarity in the economic and technological sphere became a constructive influence easing the intensity of East–West conflict and precluding a return to the monolithic bloc relations of the past. But for the vast majority of states outside the First and Second Worlds, inclusion in the networks of interdependence failed to boost their collective status in economic power stratification. Widespread optimism in the aftermath of the oil embargo that commodity cartels would force industrialised countries to concessions leading to a more equitable economic order, evaporated as it was realised that the conditions that had allowed the use of oil as an economic weapon in 1973–4 could not be reproduced. Oil-price hikes brought to the surface cleavages segregating oil-exporters from oil-importing, non-industrial states and the newly industrialising states that attained success under the existing international economic rules.[19]

The years that followed the embargo provided to neither of these groupings the opportunity to enjoy economic prosperity. The gap between the Fourth World and the rest of the less-developed world widened. The indebtness of most of the newly industrialising states grew at alarming rates. Finally, oil-exporters failed to convert their accumulated wealth into a solid, effective infrastructure that could perpetuate economic expansion. They also fell short in their goal to preserve the coherence and efficiency of their cartel and keep oil prices in line with inflation-adjusted prices of industrial goods. The 1979–80 world recession, precipitated by the last 'successful' operation of the oil cartel, hurt severely all three groupings; a disheartening prelude for the rise to power of the Greek socialists had made economic co-operation with Third World countries, especially the Arab nations of the Mediterranean, an essential feature of their foreign policy electoral platform.

Clearly, the anticipated emergence of the Third World as a pole of nascent economic power fell short of expectations. Also, lack of policy coherence[20] and economic might precluded that group of countries from converting their domination of UN General Assembly into a substantial locus of political power. The growth of UN membership (from 139 in 1974 to 159 in 1984) whose net beneficiary was the African–Asian–Latin American group (which grew from 104 in 1974 to 125 in 1984)[21] along with the spectacular increase in UN General Assembly resolutions (from 187 in 1974 to 343 in 1984)[22] did little to strengthen the social restraint[23] emanating from the world's most representative forum. The growing self-realisation of a distinct cultural identity by the Islamic countries added to the strain created by economic disparity, and older, radical–moderate differences further complicated consensus formation among the Third World coalition.

For a weak state regarding international organisation/international law functions as important parts of its external balancing strategy these were frustrating developments. Greek and Cypriot efforts to mobilise UN General Assembly support for the imposition of tangible sanctions against Turkey that went beyond the mere verbal condemnation of the 1974 invasion and the continued occupation of Cypriot territory were unsuccessful.[24]

The process of setting and implementing international rules that could serve weak state, external balancing efforts was further hindered by the policies of the Reagan administrations. US 'unilateralism'[25] in foreign-policy formulation, a distinct feature of the 1980s, was manifested at the level of the international system in different but complementary forms. First, US support for the United Nations, its organs and specialised agencies, withered for reasons ranging from a desire to punish the UN majority for behaviour perceived as hostile to US interests and values to resentment of financial practices of these bodies perceived as wasteful. Consequently, the overall trend of US contributions to the United Nations during the 1980s flattened out and eventually began to fall.[26] Although Congress, rather than the administration, is primarily responsible for imposing cuts to UN financing – the 1985 Kassebaum Amendment representing the high-water mark in that respect – the administration's rhetoric and practices were instrumental in shaping such negative Congressional attitudes.[27]

Naturally, such policies undermined the effectiveness of UN conflict-resolution efforts including those of the Secretary-General, the official entrusted by all parties concerned, including the United States with the handling of the Cyprus problem. This contradiction between words and deeds is made plain in the support provided by the United States to the UNFICYP. The United States, a most vocal supporter of UNFICYP's role on the island, reduced its contribution from $9 million in 1985 to $7.3 million in recent years.[28]

Withholding of financial contributions ran parallel to moves showing disenchantment with the whole UN process, for instance US withdrawal from UNESCO or their refusal to sign the 1982 UNCLOS, a treaty framework, accepted by Greece, stipulating rules and procedures directly applicable to maritime boundary delimitation in the Aegean region. Again, rejection by the United States of the jurisdiction of the ICJ in a case brought by Nicaragua as a legal remedy for alleged American involvement in the mining of Nicaraguan ports certainly made no contribution to international adjudication.

This brief exploration of trends in post-1974 international politics related to the capabilities of a weak, aligned, threatened state is not sufficient to develop reliable estimates of future behaviour patterns. At the same time the analysis has suggested a number of probable regularities that deserve further examination.

A synopsis of such likely regularities allows the formulation of three propositions. First, under a (loose) bipolar structure in the area of political/military issues, fluctuations of intra-bloc conflict will only marginally influence the external balancing potential of a 'weak', 'aligned' state, 'threatened by an ally'. Secondly, 'bipolycentrism' might increased external balancing opportunities that carry no realignment costs, provided that the weak state's inferiority *vis-à-vis* its intra-bloc rival is limited to the military/security domain. Thirdly, in a loose bipolar system the social restraint, inherent in international norms, is adversely affected by a superpower's efforts to reassert its dominant position in world politics and/or by deepening divisions within the non-aligned group of countries.

It is hoped that future research will falsify, modify or affirm these propositions, thus gradually breaking the ground for theory-building endeavours in a neglected field of enquiry.

NOTES

1. K. J. Holsti, *International Politics: A Framework for Analysis*, 5th edn (Englewood Cliffs, NJ: Prentice-Hall, 1988) p. 24: boundaries, characteristics of political units, structure, interaction and rules. Others, for example J. Wilkenfeld *et al.*, *Foreign Policy Behavior* (London: Sage, 1981) pp. 76–7, suggest much more elaborate taxonomies for the different features of an international system and for systemic variables in general.
2. See on this issue O. De Raeymaeker *et al.*, *Small Powers in Alignment*, Catholic University of Leuven, Studies in International Relations, no. 2 (Leuven: Leuven University Press, 1974) pp. 17–20; also D. Vital, *The Inequality of States: A Study of the Small States in the International System* (Oxford: Clarendon Press, 1967) and *The Survival of Small States: Studies in Small Power/Great Power Conflict* (London: Oxford University Press, 1971); R. W. Tucker *The Inequality of States* (New York: Basic Books, 1977).
3. M. Handel, *Weak States in the International System* (London: Frank Cass, 1981) p. 53.
4. Athanasios G. Platias, 'High Politics in Small Countries: An Inquiry into the Security Policies of Greece, Israel and Sweden', unpublished Ph.D Dissertation, Cornell University (August 1986) p. 491.
5. For a comprehensive review of the variety of meanings that has been attached by scholars to the concept 'international system', see M. Brecher and P. James, *Crisis and Change in World Politics* (Boulder, Col.: Westview, 1986).
6. See the discussion in W. S. Jones, *The Logic of International Relations* (Glenview, Ill.: Scott, Foreman, 1988) pp. 284–301.
7. B. Russett and H. Starr, *World Politics: The Menu for Choice* (New York: W. H. Freeman, 1981) p. 104.
8. Handel, *Weak States*, p. 181.
9. Th. Couloumbis, 'The Structure of Greek Foreign Policy', in R. Clogg (ed.), *Greece in the 1980s* (London: Macmillan, 1983) pp. 95–122, after reviewing a number of important indicators of Greece's international profile such as arms purchases, direction of trade, major treaty partners and so on, concluded that with the exception of energy dependency 'most of the other roads lead to the direction of Western Europe and the United States'.
10. Ch. Kegley and E. Wittkopf, *World Politics: Trend and Transformation* (New York: St Martin's Press, 1981) p. 389.
11. For example Soviet reluctance to induce Greek realignment should be attributed to a series of factors such as the Dardanelles Straits, long common borders creating mutual dependencies with Greece's arch-rival as well as to a long history of cordial Soviet–Turkish relations that date back to the early 1960s. Two developments, both originating from White House initiatives, set the ground for this upward trend in the relations between two countries burdened with a long past of competitions and hostilities. These were, first, Kennedy's decision in 1963 to withdraw – in the aftermath of the Cuban missile crisis – US Jupiter missiles from

Turkish territory; and, secondly and much more important, Johnson's warning, one year later that there will be no NATO guarantee against Soviet aggression in the event of Turkey invading Cyprus. Liberalisation of the Turkish political scene during the same period, evident in the introduction of a 'left-of-centre' philosophy by the RPP and the entrance into the Assembly of a Marxist political party, contributed to a reassessment of the 'Soviet threat' and set the stage for a more independent policy, friendlier to the Soviet Union. Between 1964 and 1974 bilateral political and economic relations thrived; this is illustrated in the orientation of Soviet policies towards Cyprus (see Duyugu Sezer, 'Turkey's Security Policies', in J. Alford (ed.), *Greece and Turkey: Adversity in Alliance* (Aldershot: Gower House, 1984) pp. 43–89). The Soviet Union 'anxious not to jeopardize the progress that it had made in its relations with Turkey' avoided condemning the 1974 invasion of Cyprus. The US arms embargo to Turkey strengthened the pro-Western bias of the Greek government and led to a dramatic upsurge in Turkish–Soviet relations that is likely to be difficult to overcome in the future. By 1978 Turkey had become the largest recipient of Soviet aid outside the Comecon, 'aid which exceeded that given by any Western state to Ankara' (Michael M. Boll, 'Turkey's New National Security Concept What it Means for NATO', *Orbis*, vol. 23 (Fall 1979) no. 3, pp. 609–31 see esp. p. 622).

12. It is pertinent at this point to quote from Sezer's analysis, 'Turkey' Security Policies', p. 71: 'in the 1960s the Cyprus conflict was seen as a potential East–West issue and it seemed better to freeze the situation in Cyprus rather than to resolve it. It therefore persisted into the 1970s. But whereas Turkey could obediently yield in the 1960s, before détente, she did not yield in the 1970s when she felt less threatened by the Soviet Union. That neither the US Sixth Fleet not the Soviet Eskarda would move against her are likely to have figured in the Turkish calculation when the decision was taken to intervene in Cyprus.'
13. Stanley Hoffmann, 'The Diplomatic–Strategic Chessboard', in W. Olson et al., *The Theory and Practice of International Relations* (Englewood Cliffs, NJ: Prentice-Hall, 1983) p. 30; see also J. Rosenau's criticism of Morton Kaplan's international system models: 'addressed to the issue area bounded by questions of military and national security which, while important, are far from a predominant majority of the external problems with which societies must contend' (J. N. Rosenau, *The Scientific Study of Foreign Policy*, rev. and enlarged edn (London: Frances Pinter, 1980) p. 329).
14. D. Allen, 'Foreign Policy and the Contemporary International Environment', in M. Clarke and B. White (eds), *An Introduction to Foreign Policy Analysis: The Foreign Policy System* (Ormskirk, Lancashire: G. W. K. A. Hesketh, 1981) pp. 95–111.
15. The term is defined by Kegley and Wittkopf, *World Politics*, pp. 394–5
16. In 1978–80, that is at the peak of East–West confrontation, the total volume of EC–Comecon imports and exports increased by almost 25 per cent, see *EEC External Trade – Monthly Bulletin* (Special Issue, July 1981).

17. In 1981 the Soviet Union agreed to a construction of a 3000 mile pipeline to supply five EC members: Belgium, France, Holland, Italy, West Germany *plus* Austria with 40 billion cubic metres of natural gas. Also, in 1980–1 the European Community continued efforts to establish formal ties with Comecon that led to the conclusion of a treaty in 1988.
18. G. Craig and A. L. George, *Force and Statecraft: Diplomatic Problems of Our Time* (New York: Oxford University Press, 1983) p. 150.
19. M. J. Peterson, *The General Assembly in World Politics* (Boston: Allen & Unwin, 1986) p. 256.
20. R. Rothstein, 'On the Problems of Being Small and Poor', in Olson *et al.*, *International Relations*, pp. 38–9.
21. Peterson, *The General Assembly in World Politics*, p. 293.
22. M. Marin-Bosch, 'How Nations Vote in the General Assembly of the United Nations', *International Organization*, vol. 41 (Autumn 1987) no. 4, pp. 705–24, see esp. p. 707.
23. W. Wallace, *Foreign Policy and the Political Process* (London: Macmillan, 1971) p. 19, groups social restraints emanating from the international system under three headings: international opinion, international mores and international law.
24. Peterson, *The General Assembly in World Politics*, p. 293.
25. For definitions and analyses of the term, see B. Urquabart, 'The Limits of Unilateralism', *Foreign Policy*, vol. 65 (Winter 1986–7) pp. 39–42; A. Schlesinger, 'A Democrat Looks at Foreign Policy', *Foreign Affairs*, vol. 66 (Winter 1987–8) pp. 263–83; L. Hamilton, 'Power without Purpose', *Foreign Policy*, vol. 65 (Winter 1986–7) pp. 29–33; see also D. Constas, 'Reaganism and Greece', *Athena Magazine*, no. 28 (November 1988) pp. 230–1.
26. P. Taylor, *The United Nations System in the 1980s: Playing the Numbers Game*, paper presented at the 30th Annual Convention, International Studies Association, London (28 March–1 April 1989) p. 3.
27. R. Gregg, *Congress and the US Assessment for the United Nations*, paper presented at the 30th Annual Convention, International Studies Association, London (28 March–1 April 1989) pp. 6 and 19.
28. See *New Opportunities for US Policy in the Eastern Mediterranean*, a staff report of the Committee on Foreign Relations, United States Senate, released on 17 March 1989.

10 Greece, Turkey and the Improvement of US–Soviet Relations
MATTHEW EVANGELISTA

The second half of the 1980s witnessed a considerable improvement in East–West relations. It was attributable in large measure to the advent to power of Mikhail Gorbachev in the Soviet Union and an eventual receptiveness to his policies on the part of the Reagan administration in the United States. If the trend continues, what effect will improved relations between the dominant powers in the two alliances have on their respective members? Will the atmosphere of reduced tension between the blocs contribute to the resolution of intra-alliance conflicts as well? This question is particularly important for the two countries in the NATO alliance whose relations have been most conflictual over the years: Greece and Turkey.

There are two potential sources of insight into the effect of superpower relations on intra-alliance conflict: the theoretical literature in international relations and past experience of US–Soviet relations. Neither source would necessarily predict that reduction in East–West tensions will lead to an improvement in Greek–Turkish relations. On the other hand, one possible by-product of the current US–Soviet *détente*, the talks on conventional armed forces in Europe, could contribute to reducing tensions between Greece and Turkey if they lead to a major restructuring of national armed forces within each alliance. If the forces of Greece and Turkey were configured to reduce their offensive capabilities and were oriented unambiguously toward territorial defence, they would not appear as threatening to each other and would be less likely to contribute to the outbreak of war during a crisis. This structural change in the military situation would make it easier for domestic forces in each country to argue in favour of improving relations because the 'enemy image' of the other side would be diminished.

INTERNATIONAL RELATIONS THEORY AND RECENT EXPERIENCE

International relations theory suggests that we should not expect improvements in East–West relations to lead to a greater cohesiveness within the alliances and a reduction in intra-alliance conflict. The opposite is more likely. Systemic theories of international relations, represented for example in the work of Kenneth Waltz, maintain that states in an anarchic international system engage in 'balancing behaviour', of which two forms are typically cited: building up military forces ('internal balancing') or forming and expanding alliances ('external balancing').[1] Waltz has very little to say about the prospects for improving relations between two dominant powers in a bipolar system, let alone what the effect might be within the two alliances. One assumes, however, that if conflict between the major powers leads to the formation of alliances, then co-operation would lead to the loosening and perhaps even disbanding of those alliances. This generalisation makes intuitive sense as well: one would expect that as the perception of external threat wanes, the degree of cohesion between allies would diminish and conflict would come to the fore.

Recent history appears to support in some respects the theoretical generalisation that suggests a positive relationship between superpower conflict and alliance cohesion. In particular, relations between the dominant power and the subordinate allies often deteriorate as relations between the alliance leaders improve. This was the case, for example, during the mid-1970s when the *détente* relationship between the United States and the Soviet Union allowed a number of festering problems (particularly economic ones) between the United States and the Federal Republic of Germany to erupt, whereas in an atmosphere of superpower tension they might have been suppressed. On the other hand, the worsening of superpower relations at the end of the Carter administration did not put an end to intra-alliance conflict between the United States and its allies. Even during the 'new Cold War' atmosphere of the early 1980s, the allies continued to come into conflict over such issues as arms control and the deployment of new US missiles to Europe.

An important comparative study of the security policies of small states suggests that the most important influence on the nature of intra-alliance relations may be found not at the international level of analysis – in the relationship between the two alliance leaders – but rather at the domestic level. Relations between two allies are heavily influenced by domestic political forces within each country. An examination of Greek security policy, for example, found that the nature of the relationship between Greece and the United States did not correlate with the level of US–Soviet tension. During the *détente* period of the late 1960s to mid-1970s, for example, the two allies were quite close even though the perception of a diminished Soviet threat should have seen them drift apart. By the same token, the heightened superpower tensions of the early 1980s did not bring the two allies closer together but, on the contrary, saw a sharp deterioration in their relations. Factors at the domestic level of analysis (in this case, the character of the Greek government) seem to explain the shifts in alliance relations better than the external environment.[2]

The postwar history of Greek–Turkish relations also casts doubt on the notion that improvements in the East–West atmosphere should contribute to *détente* between the two NATO allies. Some of the most conflictual events between the two countries occurred during periods of superpower *détente*: the 1974 invasion of Cyprus and the crisis of March 1987 come immediately to mind. There seems, then, to be little theoretical or empirical support for the hypothesis that relaxation of US–Soviet tensions will lead to improvements in Greek–Turkish relations.

THE OFFENCE–DEFENCE BALANCE AND THE SECURITY DILEMMA

Students of international relations have argued that one of the main determinants of conflict between states in an anarchic international environment is the perception of the offence–defence balance.[3] At times, the nature of military technology and strategy may appear to give an advantage to the side striking first or to make offensive action and territorial conquest seem easier than defence. Under those conditions war is more likely to break out during times of crisis because each side feels insecure for fear that the other side will gain an advantage from initiating an attack. This fear creates pressures for pre-emption and thus increases the risk of war by accident or miscalculation. Even if both parties to a conflict are *status quo* powers they will face this security dilemma: their efforts to arm in self-defence could appear threatening to their opponent, who in turn would arm in self-defence but appear threatening.

One way to dampen this spiral of mutual misperceptions of inter

tion is to deploy weapons systems that are unambiguously oriented toward territorial defence and could not easily be used for aggression. While it may be difficult to categorise weapons *per se* as defensive or offensive, it is less difficult to think in terms of weapons *systems*. A system that includes highly mobile armoured forces, self-propelled artillery and long-range fighter-bomber aircraft, for example, is clearly better suited to offensive operations for gaining and holding territory than is a system composed of short-range air-defence interceptors, fixed anti-aircraft guns, fortifications and so forth. In the naval realm, as well, a force of small craft oriented toward coastal defence, in combination with coastal artillery forces, is more clearly defensive than a force of large amphibious assault ships, airborne forces and marines.[4] Even if there is aggressive intent on the part of one or both parties to a conflict (that is at least one side challenges the status quo), a restructuring of forces toward limiting their offensive capabilities could still serve to dampen conflict, especially during times of crisis.

DEFENSIVE RESTRUCTURING

The notion of restructuring forces in order to favour the defence over the offence has mainly academic roots in western European peace research institutes and US work on crisis stability (which originally evolved from the study of nuclear strategy). It was later picked up by peace movements and governments in western Europe. In the Federal Republic of Germany, for example, advocacy of *strukturelle Nichtangriffsfähigkeit* (the structural inability to attack) has become the official policy of the Social Democratic Party.[5]

Interest on the part of the Soviet Union in alternative or non-provocative defence evolved gradually, starting in about 1984, and mainly in academic research institutes; civilian proponents of the new concepts eventually came to influence government policy.[6] It has now become the avowed goal of the Warsaw Pact to restructure its armed forces jointly with those of NATO to make the two alliances incapable of surprise attack against each other. The unilateral Soviet reductions announced by Mikhail Gorbachev in December 1988 also entail reduction in offensive capability, owing to the removal of bridge-laying equipment and a disproportionately large number of tanks relative to personnel. In the United States advocacy of alternative defence is largely limited to non-governmental circles, although there have been attempts to interest politicians and military officials in the ideas.[7]

'Ideal-Type' Alternative Defence Structures

Before considering the many political and military barriers to achieving such an outcome, we should describe what an alternative defence structure in the Warsaw Pact and NATO would entail. In principle there are two basic options. In the first, the two alliances would retain an integrated multinational command structure, dominated by the alliance leader, and would restructure their forces as an alliance to favour a strictly defensive posture. In the second option, the individual countries within each alliance would restructure their forces for territorial defence and would not participate in an integrated multinational command structure. Presumably, foreign troops would be withdrawn from allied territory unless they were to be retained permanently as part of the national territorial defence structure, and the superpowers' nuclear weapons would be withdrawn with them. This second option would diminish the *raison d'être* of the military alliances, not least because the forces of each country would be severely limited in their capability for offence, which would presumably include the capability for large-scale and rapid transport of forces to assist an ally.

Implications for the Warsaw Pact

One of the consequences of the Warsaw Pact's integrated command structure – and, some would argue, its main purpose – is to limit the independence of its member-states. Those countries that succeeded in establishing national territorial defence systems before the Warsaw Pact was formed (Yugoslavia) or before its integrated command structure was firmly established (Romania) have been able to maintain more independence from the Soviet Union in their foreign and domestic policies than those that became subordinated to Soviet military strategy and the Moscow-dominated alliance. Countries that tried to develop a more independent national military command such as Czechoslovakia in 1968, were prevented from doing so.[8]

The first 'ideal-type' alternative defence structure, the one that retained the existing integration of alliance forces, would perpetuate the Soviet Union's political and military dominance of its allies. The second option would allow for considerable autonomy for the member-states and might even entail disbanding the alliance. Indeed some Soviet republics, most notably Estonia, have argued for a national defence force independent of the Soviet Army precisely for reasons of increased autonomy. So far Moscow's interest in defensive restructuring applies only to efforts undertaken by the alliances as a whole.[9] If historical precedent is maintained, the Soviet Union would be unwilling to grant its allies autonomy in their security affairs. On the other hand, Gorbachev has already broken a remarkable number of historical precedents, so one should be cautious of any such definite predictions.

In principle, defensive restructuring by individual country in the Warsaw Pact should appeal to NATO for three reasons: (1) it would be consistent with NATO's history of rhetorical support for greater autonomy for the countries of eastern and central Europe; (2) it would be a way of reducing Soviet influence while inhibiting regional hostilities from finding offensive military expression – the function that Soviet dominance now fulfils (for example in containing conflict between Hungary and Romania over Romanian treatment of its ethnic Hungarian population); and (3) it would make defensive restructuring of Soviet and allied forces more difficult to reverse than if the Soviet Union maintained the dominant role in the alliance command structure.

Implications for NATO

Both options of defensive restructuring would raise problems for NATO, and, in particular, the United States. The question would arise, for example, of what to do about US naval forces in the Mediterranean and the North Atlantic, given that navies should be oriented only toward coastal defence. The disposition of nuclear weapons would also be a troublesome issue, considering that in addition to thousands of US-controlled nuclear weapons in Europe, Britain and France possess their own national nuclear forces. Finally, the prospect of a more independent *Bundeswehr* might be unsettling for West Germany's allies, even if it were configured strictly for territorial defence.

Defensive Restructuring and the Greek–Turkish Conflict

Greece and Turkey would probably benefit from defensive restructuring in that it would reduce the likelihood that crises between the two countries would erupt into war. Both countries' forces would be oriented toward territorial defence and would not be perceived as ready to strike first in the event of a crisis.

A defensive restructuring of Turkish forces would eliminate many of the components that the Greeks find most threatening. For example, in 1986 Yannis Kapsis, Greece's Deputy Minister for Foreign Affairs, in an interview with a Turkish journalist, described Turkey's Fourth Aegean Army as 'a tangible spearhead of the Turkish threat'. He called attention to its 147 landing craft, 'parachute forces, marine units and an airborne division with helicopters and a brigade of armoured forces'.[10] In a defensive restructuring, these forces would have to be replaced by systems more clearly oriented toward defence, such as coastal artillery, small missile-firing patrol boats and mines – thereby diminishing the Greek perception of threat and enhancing crisis stability.

Defensive restructuring of Greek forces would alleviate another Greek concern: NATO's historical unwillingness to provide the type of defence that Greece has deemed necessary. In the 1950s, for example, NATO authorities refused to adopt a 'forward defence' for the Balkans of the sort that West Germany enjoys in central Europe. Since the 1960s NATO has been unresponsive to Greek security concerns *vis-à-vis* Turkey.[11] If Greece adopted a system of national territorial defence, particularly one based on a citizens' militia, it could defend its entire territory without being constrained by the preferences of a multinational alliance.

Some of Turkey's concerns could also be alleviated if both sides adopted defensive postures. Turkey, for example, charges that the Greek island of Lemnos should be demilitarised, according to the Lausanne Treaty of 1923. Greece argues that the Lausanne Treaty was superseded by the Montreux Convention of 1936, which allowed the remilitarisation of the island. Perhaps a compromise could be struck on the basis of defensive restructuring of the Greek armed forces. The goal of demilitarising a territory is presumably to prevent it from being used for hostile purposes. If Greece had military forces on Lemnos that were purely defensive in nature (anti-aircraft systems, coastal artillery and so on) and incapable of posing an offensive threat against Turkey, that would appear to accomplish the same goal as demilitarisation of the island. At least two problems with this proposal are evident, however. First, it assumes that Turkey's concern with the demilitarisation of Lemnos stems from strictly defensive motives, whereas some analysts would question that view. Secondly, it disregards the extent to which the disposition of Greek military forces on Lemnos has become for Greece a political question going to the heart of the issue of Greek sovereignty over the island. On military grounds – for reasons of crisis stability – the proposal makes sense, but politically it may not be feasible.

Resolving the dispute over Greece's territorial waters would probably not be made any easier by adoption of defence-dominant military strategies. Such strategies might, however, help dampen a crisis of the sort that broke out in late March 1987. According to one Greek account, after the Turkish announcement of the sailing of the ship *Sismik 1* in the northern Aegean near Greek territorial waters, 'tension mounted both in Athens and Ankara, and troops and ships were being rushed toward the northern part of the frontiers of both countries'.[12] The notion of rushing toward the frontiers suggests the belief on both sides that there might be an advantage, in the event that war broke out, of striking first. Such pre-emptive incentives increase the likelihood that war would erupt during an intense crisis. If, however, each side were secure in its defensive preparations and knew that the other side's forces were also optimised for defence rather than offence, such pressure would be diminished. This is the contribution that defensive restructuring and a militia-based system might make to containing the Greek–Turkish conflict.

PROBLEMS OF IMPLEMENTING DEFENSIVE RESTRUCTURING

Agreeing on the merits of defensive restructuring is undoubtedly easier than implementing it. Yet after several years of discussion mainly among academics and activists, defensive restructuring is now on the agenda for East–West talks on conventional armed forces in Europe. In particular, both sides have advocated reducing the capability to engage in surprise attacks by limiting offensively oriented weapons, increasing 'transparency' of military activities, expanding 'confidence-building measures', such as advanced notification of military exercises, and so forth.[13] The negotiations are unlikely to reach any quick results, owing to the complicated subject matter, including the vast array of types of conventional weapons that must be taken into account.

It is not likely that the talks will yield anything very close to the two 'ideal-types' of alternative defence discussed above. The United States, for example, has been less than enthusiastic about the notion of restructuring NATO forces to eliminate offensive capability; indeed,

US doctrine has been shifting in the opposite direction. Thus, the Western position, dominated by US preferences, has focused on asymmetrical reductions in Soviet weapons and has eschewed such proposals as tank-free zones and heavy cuts in combat attack aircraft. Given the poor prospects for radical changes in the emphasis on defence over offence, one must pose the question whether compromise efforts in the direction of genuine defensive restructuring would still serve the interests of Greek–Turkish stability.

Background to the CFE Negotiations

The origins of the negotiations on CFE as they are formally entitled, lie in the failure of the previous set of negotiations, known in the West as the MBFR (Mutual and Balanced Force Reductions) talks. The suggestion to dispense with the unsuccessful MBFR forum came in Mikhail Gorbachev's proposal of 18 April 1986 to reduce conventional forces in Europe 'from the Atlantic to the Urals'. It was endorsed by the Warsaw Treaty Organisation in the 'Budapest Communiqué' of 11 June 1986. On 12 December 1986 NATO responded with the 'Brussels Declaration on Conventional Arms Control', which expressed willingness to open new discussions on conventional forces. Meetings between the members of the two alliances, known as the Group of Twenty-three (sixteen NATO members and seven Warsaw Pact members), began on 17 February 1987 in Vienna. The final details of the mandate were not completely worked out until mid-January 1989 in the last hours of the Reagan administration. The negotiations began in March.[14]

The mandate for the talks differs considerably from what Gorbachev originally had in mind. He wanted, for example, to include discussion of limiting operational-tactical nuclear systems deployed in Europe as well as 'dual-capable' systems such as aircraft that carry nuclear or conventional bombs and missiles or artillery that can fire nuclear or conventional (or chemical) rounds. NATO was unwilling to single out nuclear-capable systems for limitation as such, but would include discussion of dual-capable weapons. NATO also rejected Soviet proposals to include naval forces in the discussions, despite serious concern expressed by prominent Soviet military officers about the influence of US naval superiority on the conventional balance in Europe.[15] The exclusion of short-range nuclear forces and naval forces has important implications for the situation of Greece and Turkey.

The Special Case of Greece and Turkey

The Greek–Turkish conflict had played a special role in the new talks on conventional forces long before they had begun. Disagreements between the two countries delayed completion of the mandate even after the rest of the members of the two alliances had reached accord. Greece and Turkey are special cases in another, more important sense. They are the countries that could perhaps most benefit from limitations on the two types of forces the United States was unwilling to discuss: short-range nuclear forces and navies. The countries will not enjoy all of the potential advantages of adopting defence-dominant military strategies if nuclear and naval forces remain unrestricted.

Disagreements about Turkish territory
One of the issues that bedevilled the NATO–Warsaw Pact discussions on a mandate for the conventional-force talks concerned Turkey's desire to have some of its territory excluded from consideration. The Soviet Union had proposed talks to cover Europe 'from the Atlantic to the Urals', and argued that all of Turkish territory fell under that geographic specification. Turkey maintained, however, that not only was part of its territory technically in Asia, but that it had security concerns *vis-à-vis* Iran and Syria that had nothing to do with the NATO–Warsaw Pact confrontation. The Soviet Union eventually conceded and an arrangement was worked out whereby part of Turkey's south-east territory was excluded from the mandate. A line was drawn from where the eastern border of Turkey meets the 39th parallel down to the sea.

As the two alliances (the Group of Twenty-three) prepared to initial the mandate with the Turkish–Soviet compromise included, Greece raised an objection. The line that had been agreed upon left out the port of Mersin from which the Turkish force on Cyprus was supplied. Greece insisted that Turkish forces in Mersin be restricted as part of any conventional force agreement, and proposed that the line be curved south a bit in order to cover Mersin. Turkey refused to include the port. The final wording of the mandate left the matter unresolved: each country decides for itself whether it believes that Mersin is included and the other members of the Group of Twenty-three voice no preferred interpretation.[16] One diplomat involved in the talks complained that 'this has ceased to be an East–West negotiation and become a 21 + 1 + 1 negotiation in the last week'.[17]

The impact of excluding nuclear and naval forces
Neither Greece nor Turkey is likely to be satisfied with the ambiguity concerning Turkish territory. In addition, they both have reason to be concerned about the exclusion of nuclear and naval forces from the mandate. Turkey had wanted to include some restrictions on naval forces in order to limit the threat it perceives from the Soviet Black Sea Fleet. The United States rejected the proposal, however, in order to make sure that the actions of the American Sixth Fleet would not be constrained.[18] Greece also might have benefited from including naval forces in the mandate, particularly if Turkish forces that Greece finds threatening would be limited. Furthermore, Greece has long supported proposals to ban foreign naval forces from the Mediterranean and to declare it a 'zone of peace'.[19] Greece would probably have preferred to see nuclear weapons included in the talks; it had been advocating a Balkan nuclear-weapon-free zone for many years.[20] Turkey, on the other hand, has not supported the proposal.

The exclusion of naval and nuclear forces limits the possibilities for using the conventional-force talks as a means of defensive restructuring of Greek and Turkish forces. For one thing, much of the conflict concerns islands in the Aegean and therefore involves naval forces. If the East–West talks limited airborne forces, those limitations might play some role in reducing the availability of forces for use in offensive operations in the Aegean. The main need, however, is to limit naval forces with offensive, 'power projection' capabilities.

Leaving nuclear weapons out of the talks limits the possibilities of defensive restructuring in two ways. First, neither country will be completely free to adopt its own territorial defence strategy because it will be constrained by NATO contingency plans for using nuclear weapons. Secondly, the Turkish Defence Ministry has evidently proposed taking on a greater nuclear role in the alliance,[21] a move that would likely cause concern in Athens and complicate – at least politically – efforts at defensive restructuring.

The Potential for Unilateral Restructuring

Many of the initiatives that could enhance stability in Greek–Turkish relations if undertaken bilaterally could also be carried out unilaterally with positive results. A restructuring of Turkish forces, for example, to emphasise defensive capabilities might contribute to avoiding the type of crisis that erupted in late March 1987. In comments to the Turkish press about the incident, Prime Minister

Turgut Ozal expressed displeasure at what he called Greek attempts 'to show Turkey as the aggressor; I am in a position to assure you that this was not the case'.[22] If Turkish naval forces were configured so as not to pose an offensive threat to Greek territory, then Greece would have difficulty showing Turkey as the aggressor, because Turkey would lack the capability for sustained aggression. Events such as the *Sismik* crisis would perhaps not appear as threatening if they were not implicitly backed up by the prospect of further offensive activity. Of course, one must take into consideration the possibility that Turkey's actions were *intended* to appear threatening, in which case a strictly defensive posture would not serve its political objectives. The continued influence of the military in Turkish politics also calls into question the extent to which the country would be willing to shift to a defensive orientation.

Greece could do much unilaterally to enhance stability and deterrence, particularly in regard to the nuclear and naval forces that are excluded from the East–West talks. A rejection of US nuclear 'protection', for example, would provide Greece considerable flexibility in devising its own most efficient strategy for defending its territory. In the naval realm as well, Greece could probably defend its islands more effectively if it emphasised coastal defence installations and small, fast missile-carrying patrol boats over larger and less versatile vessels. Both of these initiatives could be carried out regardless of the course of East–West negotiations or Turkey's position. Given the current turmoil in Greek politics, however, it is uncertain that the government would be able to embark on an ambitious program of unilateral initiatives.

Unilateral efforts by members of either alliance would probably benefit from the existence of an international forum (the CFE talks) that stresses the importance of defensive restructuring for the prevention of surprise attack and the improvement of crisis stability. It is likely, for example, that countries such as Poland and Hungary, given the changes in their domestic political situations, will appeal to Soviet advocacy of defensive restructuring as they try to orient their armies toward national territorial defence. It is not inconceivable that some NATO countries would begin to think along these lines as well. Greece and Turkey would be prime candidates. One would hope that the superpowers would be interested in supporting such efforts to bring stability to the Greek–Turkish relationship. Such an approach would be consistent with the recent trend in Soviet diplomacy to pursue peaceful, compromise solutions to regional conflicts. One prominent US analyst, now a member of the Bush administration, expressed some urgency about the situation as well: 'The stakes are such, and the risks of an incident so high, that something must be done if the Aegean is not to trigger a confrontation between the two countries.'[23] That 'something' could be an effort to restructure regional forces toward a more defensive orientation.

CONCLUSION

Neither international relations theory nor past experience of US–Soviet relations provides any guarantee that an improvement in the East–West atmosphere will contribute to a Greek–Turkish *détente*. On the other hand, one of the practical products of the improvement in US–Soviet relations – the negotiations on conventional armed forces in Europe – may suggest a way to limit the danger that war could erupt from a Greek–Turkish crisis. The concept of defensive restructuring of forces is being increasingly recognised in both East and West as an important contributor to crisis stability. The mandate of the CFE talks unfortunately is not sufficiently broad to address all of the important aspects of defensive restructuring – such as limitations on offensive naval forces and nuclear weapons – but it could nevertheless lend impetus to unilateral initiatives that move beyond the mandate. Greek–Turkish relations could benefit from an international dialogue that emphasises the importance of defensive restructuring as a means of enhancing crisis stability, and, moreover, one that advocates 'common security' as an alternative to the zero-sum thinking that fosters crises in the first place.

NOTES

1. Kenneth Waltz, *Theory of International Politics* (Reading, Mass.: Addison-Wesley, 1979). See also Stephen M. Walt, *The Origins of Alliances* (Ithaca, NY: Cornell University Press, 1987).
2. Athanasios Platias, *High Politics in Small States* (Ithaca, NY: Cornell University Press, forthcoming).
3. Robert Jervis, *Perception and Misperception in International Politics* (Princeton, NJ: Princeton University Press, 1976) ch. 3; Jervis, 'Cooperation under the Security Dilemma', *World Politics*, vol. 30 (January

1978) no. 2; Stephen Van Evera, 'The Causes of War', Ph.D. dissertation, University of California, Berkeley (1983).
4. For a useful introduction to the subject of defensive restructuring, see the special issue of the *Bulletin of the Atomic Scientists*, vol. 44 (September 1988) no. 7.
5. Karsten D. Voigt, 'Konventionelle Stabilisierung und strukturelle Nichtangriffsfähigkeit', *Aus Politik und Zeitgeschichte*, vol. 18 (29 April 1988) pp. 21–34.
6. For a discussion of early Soviet (dis)interest, see Stephan Tiedtke, *Abschreckung und ihre Alternativen: Die sowjetische Sicht einer westlichen Debatte* (Heidelberg, 1986); for subsequent developments, see Gerard Holden, 'Alternative Defence and the WTO', in Michael Randle and Paul Rogers (eds), *Alternatives in European Security* (1988). For some important Soviet discussions, see A. Kokoshin, 'Razvitie voennogo dela i sokrashchenie vooruzhennykh sil i obychnykh voorushenii', *Mirovaia ekonomika i mezhdunarodnye otnosheniia (MEMO)* (1988) no. 1, pp. 20–31; A. Kokoshin and V. Larionov, 'Protivostoianie sil obshchego naznacheniia v kontekste obespecheniia strategicheskoi stabil'nosti', *MEMO* (1988) no. 6, pp. 23–31; and Vitaly Zhurkin, Sergei Karaganov and Andrei Kortunov, 'Reasonable Sufficiency – Or How to Break the Vicious Circle', *New Times* (12 October 1987) no. 40, pp. 13–15.
7. The best source for developments in this area is the newsletter *Defense and Disarmament Alternatives*, published by the Institute for Defense and Disarmament Studies in Brookline, Mass.
8. Christopher Jones, *Soviet Influence in Eastern Europe: Political Autonomy and the Warsaw Pact* (New York: Praeger, 1981).
9. One recent unofficial proposal, for a small professional army backed by a territorial militia, would seem to imply significant changes in the WTO. See Lt.-Col. Aleksandr Savinkin, 'What Kind of Armed Forces Do We Need?', *Moscow News* (1988) no. 45, p. 6.
10. Yannis Kapsis, 'Why We Feel Threatened', *Athena* (November 1986) p. 354.
11. Athanasios Platias, 'Evaluating the Costs and Benefits of American Military Bases in Greece', in *Europe after American Withdrawal: Myths and Realities* (London: Oxford University Press, 1989).
12. 'Almost a Tempest', *Athena* (April 1987) p. 121.
13. The most detailed coverage of the discussions leading to the new negotiations is found in the *Arms Control Reporter* (Brookline, Mass.: Institute for Defense and Disarmament Studies, monthly compendium).
14. Ibid., p. 407, A.1.
15. See, for example, the article by Marshal Sergei Akhromeev, then Chief of the Soviet General Staff, 'Voenno-morskie sily i vseobshchaia bezopasnost'' [Naval Forces and Common Security], *Pravda* (5 September 1988). For Western discussions of the naval balance in the Mediterranean, see the contributions by Michael McGwire, Gordon McCormick and Harry Train in *Prospects for Security in the Mediterranean*, part 1, Adelphi Paper no. 229 (London: International Institute for Strategic Studies, Spring 1988).

16. *This Week in Review* (23 January 1989) p. 2.
17. *Arms Control Reporter*, pp. 407, B.113–114.
18. Ibid., p. 407, B.14.
19. Ibid., section 405.
20. Athanasios Platias and Randy Rydell, 'The Balkans: A Weapon-Free Zone?', *Bulletin of the Atomic Scientists* (May 1982); Nikos Andrikos, 'Balkan Nuclear-Weapons-Free Zone', *Bulletin of the Atomic Scientists* (June–July 1985).
21. *Cumhuriyet* (4 January 1989), cited in the *Arms Control Reporter*, p. 408, B.1.
22. *Hurriet* (23 April 1987), quoted in *Athena* (April 1987) p. 121.
23. Richard Haass, 'Alliance Problems in the Eastern Mediterranean – Greece, Turkey and Cyprus: Part 1', in *Prospects for Security in the Mediterranean*, part 1, p. 69.

Part IV

Third Parties in Greek–Turkish Disputes

11 Third-party Involvement in Greek–Turkish Disputes
RONALD MEINARDUS

INTRODUCTION

It is commonplace in the field of international studies that in order to grasp the complexities of political disputes one must identify the levels of analysis. As in other international conflicts so too in the Greek–Turkish situation at least three – geographical – levels of analysis are distinguishable: local, regional and international. Let us take the Cyprus issue, which is at the core of the Greek–Turkish problem. First, the Cyprus issue is an intercommunal problem, where a Greek majority is at odds with a Turkish minority (local level). Secondly, the issue is a problem of Greek–Turkish relations, a problem between Athens and Ankara. This is the regional level. And finally the Cyprus issue is an international problem, affecting not only the United Nations, but also – as we will see – NATO, the European Community and the United States, to name but the most important actors.

The Cyprus issue, but also the Greek–Turkish conflict in general, is a clear example of the internationalisation of a local and/or regional problem. Third-party involvement or internationalisation – to use but another word – has two main causes. The first cause is the involvement of extra-regional powers on their own behalf and for their own interests. The second cause is pressure on these powers by the regional or local actors to get involved on their behalf.

Some analysts concentrate their studies regarding third-party involvement in Greek–Turkish disputes almost exclusively on the extra-regional actors' initiatives to gain influence. However, in this chapter emphasis will be put on the activities of the regional actors – that is Greece and Turkey – to invite third-party involvement in their disputes. The thesis is that both Athens and Ankara have in past decades internationalised their bilateral disputes, hoping to mobilise in the international community support for their respective causes in the bilateral conflict.

THE CASE OF NATO

The Cyprus war of 1974 brought to an all-time low the relations between Greece and Turkey. At the same time in the summer of 1974 Greece's relations with NATO had also reached a low point. In reaction to NATO'S conduct in the Cyprus issue, Athens left the military wing of the alliance in August 1974, as the second Turkish invasion reached its peak. By leaving the military integration, the ideologically pro-Western government of Constantinos Karamanlis demonstrated its disappointment at the passivity of NATO in the wake of Turkish aggression. In parliament Karamanlis stated that:

> Greece did not depart from the military command of NATO, because it is against the alliance. To the contrary. Under certain conditions we are for the alliance . . . Greece left in order to protest against the Turkish invasion in Cyprus.[1]

It is recorded that the Athens government had asked the alliance to intervene in Cyprus both politically and militarily in order to avert Turkish occupation of nearly two-fifths of the Republic of Cyprus.

However, Greece's efforts at 'NATOising' the Cyprus war in summer 1974 failed. The alliance did next to nothing to stop the Turkish invasion. NATO was so passive that some observers even expressed the view that the Western alliance was indirectly supporting or protecting Turkish aggression. This view has additionally been nourished by well-recorded US initiatives in the 1960s that aimed at destroying the Republic of Cyprus and dividing the island (the Acheson Plan).

The aim of gaining national advantages in the Greek-Turkish dispute by involving NATO was not only pursued by the Athens government. During the second half of the 1970s – after Greece's departure from the military command of NATO in 1974 – Ankara too tried, via NATO, to gain strategic influence in the Aegean. Athens soon desired to re-enter the alliance. But this plan was not supported by Ankara, which repeatedly blocked the Greek re-entry, making it dependent upon a reshaping of the operational military responsibility in the Aegean Sea. Ankara made it clear that it would thwart Greek entry with its veto until Turkey was granted more rights in the Aegean – rights that until then had clearly belonged to the Greeks. It is interesting that the Turkish policy of vetoing Greece's re-entry into NATO in the 1970s (and making it dependent on concessions in bilateral issues) is reminiscent of Greece's present policy of vetoing Turkey's entry into the European Community, at least as long as Ankara fails to call back its soldiers from Cyprus!

The solution to the problem of Greece's re-entry into NATO can hardly be called a brilliant diplomatic achievement. Athens re-entered NATO's military wing in 1980 on the basis of the so-called Rogers' Agreement. According to Papandreou's government this is defunct, as it does not clearly identify the disputed operational zones between Greece and Turkey in the Aegean. In this respect Turkey's strategy to increase her influence in the Aegean by asking NATO to support her claims has not succeeded. On the other hand, the Greek government and the military leadership are enraged as the Western alliance rejects their claim that only the pre-1974 zoning (status quo ante) is acceptable.

These are only two – but the two most important – examples of NATO's involvement in Greek–Turkish issues in the second half of the 1970s. I shall now add two more recent examples of NATO's involvement in Greek–Turkish disputes.

In October 1981, Andreas Papandreou came to power after having warned the Greek electorate in numerous speeches of what he called the 'Turkish threat'. The search for allies against 'Turkish expansionism' became the prime goal of Greek foreign policy. In December 1981 – only a few weeks after his triumphant election victory – Papandreou attended a NATO defence ministers' meeting, where he stubbornly insisted on a guarantee by the alliance to shield Greece from aggression by Turkey. As the NATO members were not willing to agree to this demand, the entire meeting ended in failure. For the first time in NATO's thirty-two year history no joint communiqué was issued. This was the most spectacular example of Papandreou's internationalisation strategy in NATO. The Greek demand for border guarantees was repeated for some years, but then shelved, as neither Washington nor NATO (let alone Turkey) were inclined to accept this kind of arrangement.

Turkey, too, tried to forward her position in the bilateral dispute via NATO. The single most important issue at stake was the 'Lemnos problem'. To this day Athens maintains that this strategically located island close to the Dardanelles may be militarised, thus stationing airforce and army units on the island. Turkey on the other hand quotes the Treaty of Lausanne (1923) and argues that this island must be demilitarised. (The Greeks point out that all demilitarisation claims are invalid since the Montreux Convention of 1936.) The

'Lemnos problem' is but a part of the overall Greek–Turkish dispute pertaining to the military status of the (Greek) islands of the eastern Aegean.

Ankara has successfully internationalised and NATOised this bilateral question by preventing – to the dislike of the Greeks – an inclusion of Lemnos in all NATO exercises. Ankara's argument is that since the island should be demilitarised, it should not be included in military manoeuvres. Greece, on the other hand, has reacted by boycotting all exercises that do not include Lemnos. Thus for all practical purposes no joint military exercises have taken place in the Aegean in the past couple of years. Turkey's internationalisation strategy in the Lemnos question has thus effectively paralysed the Western defence alliance's south-eastern flank.

THE ROLE OF THE UNITED STATES

There can be no doubt that the Cyprus war in 1974 and the violent partition of the island were also in part a result of a total failure of US crisis management. In the years following the Cypriot tragedy of 1974 the Greek government tried to move the US government to exert pressure upon Ankara, to force Turkey to withdraw its forces from the island or to make other concessions in Cyprus. This Greek policy of trying to exert pressure on Ankara via the United States may be called 'indirect strategy'. In the years after 1974 the United States was clearly in the centre of Greece's indirect strategy, as Washington had the means to exert political pressure on Ankara with its enormous financial and military aid. Former Greek Prime Minister Georgios Rallis in his memoirs writes that the United States is 'of all countries probably the only one that has interest and the capability, to help us effectively [in the Cyprus issue].[2]

Although the Greeks did not achieve their final aim, namely reunification of Cyprus and termination of Turkish occupation, their effort of mobilising political support against Ankara in the United States was not a total failure. In this context mention should be made of the US arms embargo (1975–8), with which the US Congress 'punished' Turkey for its invasion of Cyprus. Despite its loopholes and half-heartedness, the US embargo was and remains the only practical international sanction applied on Turkey after its invasion of Cyprus.

In the second half of the 1970s the centre of the Greek–Turkish conflict shifted from Cyprus to the Aegean. In the light of the Cypriot experience the Athens government was afraid that Ankara might be tempted to employ military force in this area as well. In order to avert this, Greek diplomacy sought political and military assistance from the United States. In this context a statement by Papandreou is revealing: 'If we speak about US–Greek talks or negotiations, these deal basically with the Turkish threat of our borders in the Aegean.'[3] The aim of the Greek strategy was twofold. Washington should (1) guarantee the territorial status quo in the Aegean; and (2) allocate its military aid to Greece and Turkey in a manner that would not disrupt the regional balance of power.

Regarding the maintenance of the regional balance the Greeks have been remarkably successful. Since 1978 it has been accepted practice for the US Congress to allocate military aid for Greece and Turkey in the ratio of 7:10. In other words, the United States has given to the Greeks 70 per cent of the military assistance attributed to the considerably larger Turkish armed forces, in spite of Turkish protests and the occasional unwillingness of the administration.

As to US guarantees for the territorial status quo, that is the present borders in the Aegean, Greek diplomatic efforts have not been quite so effective. Nevertheless, in 1976 the Karamanlis government (1974–81) obtained an official commitment from US Secretary of State Henry Kissinger, 'that the United States would actively and unequivocally oppose either side seeking a military solution and will make major efforts to prevent such a course of action'.[4] This was the closest the Greeks ever got to an official US guarantee for their country's borders with Turkey. In 1983 Papandreou, who in that year renewed the bilateral military agreement with Washington, shelved the issue of border guarantees. The emphasis since then has been on the question of balanced military aid and the 7:10 ratio.

THE ROLE OF THE EUROPEAN COMMUNITY

The decline of US influence and the increase of EC influence in the eastern Mediterranean are important developments affecting Greek–Turkish relations. The European Community by 1993 will not only be an economic 'superpower', it is bound to increase also its political weight in the world, and especially in the neighbouring regions, for example the Mediterranean.

For many years the European Community has quite effectively

kept out of Greek–Turkish disputes, leaving Western interventions either to NATO, the United States or isolated diplomatic activities by some of its member countries – the United Kingdom, France or the Federal Republic of Germany. But the Community has had – *nolens volens* – to reverse this passivity. Since Greece attained the status of a full member in 1981, the bilateral Greek–Turkish problems in one way or the other automatically affect the Community *in toto* too. Furthermore, all parties engaged directly in the Greek–Turkish dispute have relations with the Community: Greece is a full member; Turkey is an associate member and has applied for full membership; the Republic of Cyprus is also an associate member.

Despite this constellation, special EC mediation efforts in the Greek–Turkish conflict have not been developed – and this pertains to the Cyprus issue, as well as to Aegean matters. Nevertheless, the EC governments have in the context of their EPC dealt with the Cyprus issue, for instance after the Turkish invasion in 1974 or after the unilateral declaration of independence of the TRNC in November 1983. In both cases the Community rejected the Turkish *faits accomplis* and emphasised its support for a unified Cypriot Republic.

It is only rather recently that the Cyprus problem has begun to affect EC–Turkish relations directly. In April 1988 the meeting of the EC/Turkey Association Council was postponed at the last minute, after the Turkish side had been informed that the Twelve had included in their joint declaration a phrase stating that the Cyprus issue 'affects the relations of Turkey with the EC'.[5] Shortly thereafter, on 20 May 1988, the European Parliament – to the great dismay of the Turkish government – adopted a resolution on Cyprus that was worded much more strongly: *inter alia* the Strasbourg chamber noted that 'the unlawful occupation of part of the territory of a country associated with the community (i.e. the Republic of Cyprus) by the military forces of another country, also associated with the Community (i.e. Turkey), presents a major stumbling block to the normalization of relations with the latter, viz. Turkey'.[6]

Both declarations – the ministers' declaration and the European Parliament's resolution – were celebrated in Greece as major diplomatic victories. The documents are but two examples that for Athens the European Community has become an important arena of Greek–Turkish dispute. On more than one occasion the Greek government brought its differences with Ankara onto the agenda of EC meetings, hoping to mobilise in this exclusive setting political support in the bilateral conflict. Furthermore the Greek government has made it clear that it considers its vote in the European Community as an important leverage in its dealings with Turkey. Athens has demonstrated in words and in practice that it regards its approval on the further development of EC–Turkey relations as being dependent on Ankara's concessions in bilateral Greek–Turkish issues. We find an example of this strategy in the political '*quid pro quo*' Athens and Ankara agreed upon in the spring of 1988: only after prime minister Ozal assured the repeal of discriminatory measures against Greek nationals in Istanbul included in a secret decree of 1964 did Athens agree to accept the so-called Adaptation Protocol to the Ankara Agreement of 1964. This is but one example of the Greek strategy to 'Europeanise' her conflicts with Turkey.

Greece will continue to use its right of veto in the European Community as a political leverage against Turkey. The 'Greek factor' must therefore be considered seriously by Ankara, which wishes to attain full membership in the Community as soon as possible.

I want to conclude with two personal remarks. Sooner or later the European Community will have to play an even more active role in the Greek–Turkish disputes than it has done so far. And secondly, the Community must play – and this is a lesson of third-party involvement so far – a more constructive role than the United States and NATO have played. For Western involvement to this day has done little – if at all – to help Greeks and Turks find lasting and just solutions to their disputes.

NOTES

1. *Praktika tis Voulis ton Ellinon* [Record of the Parliament of Greece] period A, session C, vol. V, p. 5389.
2. G. Rallis, *Ores Efthinis* [Hours of Responsibility] (Athens, 1983) p. 317.
3. *To Vima*, Athens (13 December 1981).
4. Henry Kissinger's letter of 10 April 1976 to Greek Foreign Minister Dimitrios Bitsios, in Dimitrios Bitsios, *Pera apo ta synora, 1974–1977* [Beyond the Borders] (Athens, 1982) pp. 253–4.
5. See C. Stephanou and Ch. Tsardanides, 'The EC Factor in the Greece–Turkey–Cyprus Triangle', ch. 14 in this volume.
6. European Parliament, *Resolution on the Situation in Cyprus*, doc. A2–317/87.

12 US Policy towards Greece and Turkey since 1974

HELEN LAIPSON

The year 1974 was a turning-point for US policy towards the two NATO allies that form the south-eastern flank of the alliance. It was a year of extraordinary change and turbulence in the two countries and in their common cousin, Cyprus. All of the three countries' major Western partners and allies faced the same challenge of responding to the new situation and trying to restore order to the region. The crisis on Cyprus, the subsequent fall of the military junta in Greece and sharp downturn in US–Turkish relations resulting from US reactions to the Turkish response to the Cyprus crisis, all shaped US policy in the years that followed.

The turning-point is equally defined by changes in Washington. The fall of the Nixon presidency and the resulting surge in congressional activism in foreign policy, the catalytic effect of the Cyprus crisis on the Greek-American community, and the trends in US–Soviet *détente* and in post-Vietnam US foreign policy are equally part of the landscape in which US policy must be viewed.

This analysis of US policy towards Greece and Turkey addresses, like the other chapters in this volume, the domestic and external pressures that shape policy. In the case of US policy, this framework tells much of the story. It has been the conventional wisdom, and nearly a cliché, to explain US policy towards Greece and Turkey as a struggle between two competing policy impulses: one driven by the legislative branch, by domestic ethnic interests and by those who advocate a morality-based policy; and another driven by the executive branch and by strategic interests, that is the overriding importance of maintaining good relations with Turkey, a key NATO player in resisting Soviet expansion. One theme argued in this chapter is that the struggle has no end, and as a result neither of the rival poles for dominance of US policy ever achieves enough of what it wants. US policy-makers make efforts in good faith to refine and retool policies, yet face relentless criticism from the two allies. The policy never achieves the needed resilience and receptivity, and there is dissatisfaction all around.

This chapter examines the development of US policy (or policies) towards Greece and Turkey since 1974, that important year. The subject is treated both chronologically and thematically. It outlines six phases of US policy, defined primarily by changes in presidential administrations. It then identifies factors and themes relating to both US foreign and domestic policy that affect, directly or indirectly, policy toward Greece and Turkey. It is by examining where policy to Greece and Turkey fits in to larger trends in US politics and foreign policy that we can look to the future, and try to anticipate how policy may be affected by the recent dramatic changes in the European environment and in East–West relations.

PHASES OF US POLICY TOWARDS GREECE AND TURKEY

US Policy Towards the 1974 Cyprus Crisis

It is difficult to overestimate the impact that events in the small non-aligned island nation of Cyprus have had on US policy towards NATO allies Greece and Turkey. While US policy towards the two allies from their accession to NATO in 1952 had been subject to the sensitivities of their bilateral problems and to tensions relating to Cyprus, the 1974 crisis had a more profound effect for three reasons. First, the United States was perceived as complicit in the decision of the failing Greek junta to try and oust the troublesome (from their view) Cypriot president, Archbishop Makarios. US signals (or silences) during a period of close US–Greek relations were interpreted as signs of encouragement, in light of Secretary of State Kissinger's reported views on Makarios, and his strategic approach to regional conflicts.[1] Secondly, the failure of US crisis mediation either to prevent the Turkish military action or to bring about its quick withdrawal after a civilian government was restored in Nicosia is deeply imprinted in Greek and Greek-Cypriot political consciousness as evidence of US approval of Turkey's actions, or, as some more reluctantly concede, US impotence to alter Turkey's policy. Lastly, the resultant US decision (imposed on a disgruntled Ford administration by the US Congress) to cease all military aid to Turkey in 1975 has changed the tone and nature of US–Turkish relations for the foreseeable future.² Kissinger, often portrayed as one of the villains of the policy *débâcle* of 1974, wrote in his memoirs that Cyprus was one of his greatest failures, and the bureaucracy's handling of the crisis became a target of Congressional investigation and considerable criticism in the policy community.

The crisis atmosphere profoundly affected US relations wtih the two motherlands, Greece and Turkey. It was difficult to conduct bilateral relations on a host of other issues while the recriminations and political fall-out of the crisis lingered.

The Ford Administration: Recovery Efforts

As a result of the multiple crises of 1974, US relations with each of the three countries suffered, and a period of US retrenchment from the region set in. Policy-makers were reluctant to pursue activist or high-profile initiatives both because of continued hostility to the United States in each country, and because of the lack of domestic consensus as to what policies would be desirable. One exception technically beyond the scope of this chapter was US involvement in humanitarian and refugee relief on the island, including a major US role in financing the resettlement of refugees. US aid in support of refugee resettlement and relief was over $50 million in the period 1974–6.

One delicate challenge for the Ford administration was restoring relations with a new civilian government in Athens, where long-pent-up rage against US–Greek co-operation during the junta years was being vented on a daily basis. The official US policy was to maintain a low profile, and included a voluntary end to Sixth Fleet port visits in Athens, instructions for US military personnel serving in Greece to dress in civilian clothes off-base, and a reduction in overall US military presence in the country. By 1977, anti-American demonstrations had taken on a 'ritualistic' style, and an air of normalcy in bilateral relations was restored.³

One contributing factor to this mellowing of relations was the public debate in the US Congress over the shortcomings of US policy toward the junta, viewed as a kind of semi-official *mea culpa*, led in large measure by liberal Democrats. In addition, the legislative branch insistence on punishing Turkey for its actions on Cyprus by means of the arms embargo increased understanding among informed Greeks that there were multiple opinion and power centres in the US system, and that some could be influenced to support pro-Greek positions.

US relations with Turkey in the 1975–7 period went in the opposite direction: initially satisfied with the administration's hands-off reaction to events in Cyprus, the Turks were shocked by the imposition of the embargo, which in their view gravely undermined the alliance relationship and set back Turkey's ability to fulfil its military obligations to NATO. The embargo also had a different political impact on informed Turks: it exposed the weakness or inability of the US administration to conduct its own foreign policy. For Turkey, the embargo was a rude awakening that shook the premises of the 1950s commitment to partnership with the United States.

The Ford administration saw the need to return US relations with the eastern Mediterranean states on a surer footing, but its policy efforts fluctuated between exasperated expressions of harm to US and NATO interests and quiet acceptance of the need to pull back from status quo ante relations with the two principal parties.

Renewal of agreements governing US use of military facilities in both countries proved politically impossible, particularly in light of Greece's withdrawal from the military command of NATO to protest at what it viewed as the alliance's failure on Cyprus, and in light of Turkey's downgrading of bilateral co-operation after the embargo. The bases continued to operate on an *ad hoc* basis, but the arrangement was less than satisfactory from a US point of view. In general the administration set modest goals and sought to avoid raising expectations of policy success in this troubled region. In the final analysis, Ford fell short of his own objectives in the eastern Mediterranean.

Carter Administration Activism

The Carter administration, elected in part because of a popular groundswell for a more moralistic, idealistic leadership in the White House, promised Greek-American voters that it would uphold the embargo, and work to remove Turkish troops from Cyprus. During his campaign, Carter also pledged non-interference in the affairs of Cyprus. As a consequence, Greeks welcomed Carter's election, and Turks anticipated that relations with Washington would continue to be strained.

Once in office, however, the Carter administration viewed the eastern Mediterranean situation in different terms. The new administration found considerable interest in Congress in a more activist American policy towards Cyprus, which appeared to be a shift away from the hands-off policy initially preferred by friends of Greece and

Greek Cypriots. This led to a short-lived US initiative to develop a settlement plan with the British and Canadians. (The plan called for a bizonal federal solution.) More dramatically, in early 1978, a little more than a year after the election, Carter changed his position on the utility of the embargo, and worked vigorously – and eventually successfully – to have it lifted.

The change in strategic view was affected by important developments in the region, most notably the signs of imminent collapse in the Shah's Iran. Carter and his conservative National Security Advisor, Zbigniew Brzezinski, took a hard-nosed look at the threats to US interests in the Middle East, and a more strategically driven policy was developed, as compared to the earlier, more idealistic and human rights-oriented Carter foreign policy. In this newly developed world view, Turkey played an important role. Carter became convinced that the embargo had both failed to achieve its stated goal, and was a self-defeating policy, in the larger sense. Turkey was too important, in his view, to be treated shabbily by its major partner in security and defence matters. Carter worked with his typical intense and detail-oriented concentration, and lobbied individual members of Congress throughout the spring and summer of 1978. On 26 September 1978, legislation was presented to the president that enabled him to certify that Turkey was acting in good faith to achieve a just and peaceful settlement on Cyprus. With his certification, the embargo was lifted.

The end of the embargo did not, in fact, represent a clear change of direction in US policy toward Turkey. First, the Cyprus settlement initiative (the so-called ABC – American–British–Canadian plan) was intended to address expected opposition to lifting the embargo, and to couple restoration of normal defence relations with Turkey with a renewed effort to end the division of Cyprus and the Turkish troop presence there. Secondly, and beyond the control of the administration, was the congressional compromise forged at the time the embargo was lifted. The new statement of US policy toward the eastern Mediterranean[4] reiterated congressional concern about a just and lasting Cyprus settlement and articulated the principles governing US policy towards the region as including 'security assistance for Greece and Turkey . . . shall be designed to ensure that the present balance of military strength among countries of the region, including Greece and Turkey, is preserved'. This evolved into what has become a constraint on successive administrations in expanding security relations with Turkey on their own terms. The linkage of military aid to the two countries is now known as the 7:10 ratio, and can be considered the political trade-off or compromise made in the Carter era to achieve the lifting of the embargo.[5]

More normal functioning of the two base arrangements was achieved during the Carter administration. The Karamanlis and Rallis governments in Athens were firmly committed to restoring Greece's credibility in the Western camp, including becoming a full member of the European Community, and returning to the military command of NATO. In effect, this pro-Western policy gave the Greek government considerable leverage in its relations with Washington, and there were pressures on US policy to facilitate Greek re-entry, in order to complete a new base agreement. Thus the United States and the NATO commanders, US generals Alexander Haig and Bernard Rogers, became involved in trying to mediate Greco-Turkish Aegean problems, resolution of which had become a Greek condition for re-entry into NATO. Efforts to solve the Aegean command problem faltered; none the less, the Rallis government agreed to return to the NATO Council in 1980, but base talks with the United States were not completed until governments changed in both Athens and Washington.

In Ankara, the lifting of the embargo allowed base talks to proceed. In March 1980, the two governments signed a Defense and Economic Co-operation Agreement, which included US government 'best efforts' pledges to help finance a multi-year weapons modernisation program. For Turkey this may have been seen as an effort to compensate for the defence deterioration of the embargo years, although in the US community, there continued to be disagreement about the extent to which the embargo could be blamed for the sorry state of Turkish military equipment.[6] In the US defence establishment, there was widespread relief at the restoration of defence relations, coloured dramatically by the fall of the Shah of Iran, and its related loss of US access and influence in Turkey's eastern neighbour.

Reagan Era: Tilt towards Turkey

The decade of the 1980s provides graphic examples of ideologically driven policies, both in the eastern Mediterranean and in Washington. The election of the Soviet-bashing Republican Ronald Reagan led naturally to ever more cordial ties between Washington and Ankara. The military government that ruled Turkey from September

1980 until elections in 1983 won favour in Reagan's camp, both because of its anti-Soviet stance and because it came to power in a life-and-death struggle against terrorism. The 1983 election of Turgut Ozal to the premiership further strengthened the bonds, based on shared strategic and economic philosophies.

Across the Aegean, an opposite set of dynamics was in place, and this led, also understandably, to friction with Washington. The election of PASOK leader Andreas Papandreou in 1981 did not make for harmonious relations with the new American president. Papandreou's official positions on NATO, US bases and East–West relations in general, even if best understood as rhetoric or hyperbolic abstractions, were taken more literally by many Reagan ideologues. The relationship underwent serious strains, although there are some differences in perception of how bad things were. People closely involved in day-to-day relations, both in Athens and Washington, continue to maintain that the degree of friction has been exaggerated, and it is correct that mid-level officials of the Reagan era worked to maintain normalcy in US–Greek relations. But at a macro level, in Washington perhaps more than in Athens, one cannot escape the perception of two ostensibly friendly governments whose world views and reactions to events were seriously at odds.

This striking dichotomy in Reagan era official views of Greece and Turkey underscores another point: during the Reagan years, policy to the two countries was seen essentially as two discrete and separate policies. There was an intentional downgrading of the linkage in US policy to the two regional adversaries, and an articulated desire to move US policy away from the limits of a regional policy, which had been hampered by a zero-sum mentality. Instead, US interests and policy options were clearer and more positively expressed if the two countries were viewed as distinct, with separate needs and separate bilateral relationships. This effort to delink the regional and bilateral problems was a source of some friction between the Reagan administration and Congress.

Yet Greece's friends in the United States could not dispute the difficulty they were having in maintaining cordial bilateral ties. Greek opposition to allied sanctions against Poland in early 1982, reaction to the 1983 Korean airliner incident, a Papandreou speech to PASOK in 1984 in which he called the United States the 'metropoli of imperialism', and other events helped create a constituency in the US government for a new and cooler policy toward Greece. Terrorist incidents against US servicemen in Greece mounted, and while no one has suggested that the perpetrators were PASOK followers, the failure of the security apparatus under PASOK to make arrests or to prosecute the cases led to an erosion of confidence in the government in Athens. Coupled with increased activity by and support for Palestinian militants in Greece, the gap between the Greek and US governments loomed large through 1984.

Papandreou made efforts to clear the air in his spring 1985 campaign, when he called for 'calmer seas' between the two countries, a sentiment seconded in Reagan's congratulatory telegram to the Greek premier upon his re-election. But within days, new troubles arose with the hijacking of TWA flight 847 and US allegations of lax conditions at Athens airport. In June 1985, the United States issued a travel advisory, warning US citizens essentially that it no longer had faith in the Greek government's anti-terrorist efforts, and could not declare the Athens airport safe for travellers. This was a shock to Greeks, and was considered a particularly hurtful economic sanction, due to the relatively high importance of tourism from the United States as a source of revenue. In some senses, the travel advisory proved to have a catalytic effect on US–Greek relations; Greece and its supporters in the US system worked to improve Greece's image, as well as to improve security conditions in Athens. (The travel advisory was lifted in July.)

The first Reagan term witnessed a blossoming of US–Turkish relations, although the US Congress took some steps to curb the growth in ties. Even before the restoration of a civilian government in Ankara, the Reagan team's able Assistant Secretary of Defense, Richard Perle, began an energetic campaign to expand co-operation with Turkey. In 1983, the administration's request for military aid to Turkey rocketed to $755 million (the previous year was $465 million). Congress approved aid of $715 million, which, due to congressional linkage of aid to the two countries, also meant that Greece enjoyed a similar increase. The administration's expressed goal was to reach $1 billion annual levels of military aid for Turkey, and US and Turkish defence officials worked closely in developing a comprehensive modernisation programme for all branches of the Turkish armed forces.

Congress resisted this dramatic policy initiative, and sought to temper the new enthusiasm for relations with Ankara with some sober warnings about human rights conditions and Turkey's full return to democracy. There was some debate about whether Turkey had fulfilled the latter goal in the 1983 elections, in light of the military's role in approving the political parties eligible to run, and the way in which General Evren's presidential term was written into the constitution. Human rights performance did not become a formal condition for aid, despite some congressional efforts, and there were also several close calls on legislation that would have linked Turkey's military aid to removal of troops from Cyprus and other unilateral measures on the island.

In light of the continued gap in perceptions of Turkey within the US government, the Reagan administration sought, by the end of its first term, to move bilateral relations away from such heavy reliance on defence issues. State Department official Richard Haass, a Deputy Assistant Secretary responsible for the eastern Mediterranean, spoke of the need to diversify relations, to protect ties from what he called the unpredictable 'domestic political winds' in both countries. Trade with Turkey was a natural focus of these efforts; US officials had only praise for Turkey's economic policies and wanted to support the clear need to expand exports to stimulate growth there. The value of trade in both directions trebled in the first half of the 1980s, and Turkey had the dubious distinction of being one of the few countries with which the United States enjoyed a trade surplus.

Second Reagan Term

The second term of the Reagan administration can be distinguished from the first with respect to Greece and Turkey in some modest ways. What some would consider the polarity of close ties with Turkey and just correct ties with Greece was softened. Relations with Turkey had settled into a more mixed pattern of positive rhetoric tempered by Turkish disappointments. The policies of the second Papandreou term created fewer opportunities for bilateral disputes, although concerns mounted on the US side regarding the renewal of a base agreement, and the scandals and political uncertainty that plagued Greece after 1988 led to a reduced level of foreign policy activity. A number of bilateral issues were simply put on hold.

It was perhaps inevitable that the momentum of building new and expanded US-Turkish relations could not be sustained in the second Reagan term. Turkey faced internal problems, such as a downturn in economic performance and violent Kurdish separatist activities in the south-east. These issues were largely beyond the scope or interest of Washington. In addition, as Reagan's policy responded to new opportunities presented by the new Soviet leader, the relative importance of the Perle–Turkey alliance faded. Turkey also found it had to lower its expectations of having the promises of the early 1980s fulfilled; traditional congressional attitudes toward Turkey coupled with the mounting US deficit crisis combined to make virtually certain that aid levels would never reach the goals envisioned for the modernisation programme. Even in trade there were mild disappointments for Turkey; Turkish trade officials hoped for special treatment on imports of textiles, steel and cement, and found another form of entrenched American parochialism. Mounting trade protectionist sentiment, largely driven by Japan-related problems, made it difficult for Turkey to make headway on its trade requests. US officials also chafed at what they viewed as Turkey's inability to adjust its exports to the opportunities in the US market, and to learn to cope with the arcana of US trade regulations.

For US–Greek relations, the late 1980s represented a slight relaxation of tensions, although a number of contentious issues remained unresolved. Even in the legislative branch, there were misgivings about Greece's efforts to prevent terrorism and its intentions regarding the US bases. Debated but not approved were several pieces of legislation for which Greece was one of the unnamed targets: one addressed a cut-off of aid to countries that ceased military co-operation with the United States, and another authorised the president to reduce aid to countries that had not yet spent previous years' aid.

Yet in other ways, the mood in US–Greek relations seemed to lighten in the late 1980s. The Greek government began to focus on its European responsibilities, in light of the 1992 EC integration deadlines, and this relieved some of the pressure from US–Greek relations. By 1988, the PASOK government was preoccupied with internal problems. A scandal involving embezzlement and illegal financial transactions was alleged to be directly linked to PASOK officials, including the prime minister, and this had the effect of delaying or putting aside contentious bilateral issues with the United States. Some sparks did fly, however, over the issue of extradition of the banker at the heart of the scandal, George Koskotas, who was being held in a US jail. In addition, one terrorist case remained unresolved at the end of the Reagan term. The US requested extradition of Mohammed Rachid, a Palestinian charged for his role in a 1982 Pan Am bombing. Greek legal deliberations proceeded, with some delays due to political change, but public discussion refocused attention on the gap between PASOK's support for some Palestinian incidents as acts of national liberation, and the activist anti-terrorist policies of the Reagan administration.

The Bush Administration

The foreign policy of the Bush administration has diverged from that of the Reagan era in its lower degree of fervour, rather than the substance of policy. There is a less ideological underpinning to Bush's world view, and the president's extensive past government experience generally means that he is well informed on foreign policy developments. Visitors from the eastern Mediterranean have been struck with his command of details and history, which does not necessarily translate into new policy initiatives or activism in the region. Although Bush's foreign policy has been Europe-oriented, there has been little eastern Mediterranean focus to it. A minor exception is increased attention to the Cyprus problem, with the naming of an activist Special Cyprus Co-ordinator, Nelson Ledsky, and a short-lived spurt of optimism that the UN settlement effort might yield results.

The Bush administration, as of early 1990, has had little opportunity for high-level dealings with Greece, in part due to the unusual electoral uncertainty there. The transitional governments elected in June 1989 and again in November 1989 essentially held in abeyance any new bilateral business, although the apparent intention of the national unity parliament in Athens to extend the base agreement until November 1990 is expected to enhance satisfactory conclusion of a new base agreement, one premised on a reduced US presence in Greece.

Relations with Turkey were rocky in the first year of the Bush administration, due to a series of issues that made Turkey uneasy. Turkey has been dissatisfied with its aid and trade relations with Washington, although US officials have resisted seeing such chronic complaints as an acute situation. Of greater concern was the prospect for a dramatic downturn in relations that could occur if the US Congress should approve a resolution essentially calling the treatment of Armenians by Ottoman authorities in the World War One period genocide. Similar legislative efforts in the early 1980s were thwarted by the Reagan administration. In late 1989, the sponsor of the initiative was Republican Senator Robert Dole, and Bush pronouncements on the issue during his election campaign leave open the possibility that he would sign such a measure into law. This has cast a shadow on US–Turkish relations, in a time when Turkey is struggling to adjust to a dramatically changing world environment. Turkey's supporters in the United States have not been able to shift the focus of relations to more positive topics.

THE LARGER CONTEXT OF US POLICY TOWARD GREECE AND TURKEY

Having surveyed the incremental steps in official US policy toward the two eastern Mediterranean allies, it is now possible to examine this policy history from a more thematic perspective. It is useful to consider the larger context of trends in US foreign policy since 1974, as well as important domestic factors that came into play in the formulation of US policy.

The United States has been and remains today a global power, and maintains a presence and an interest in virtually all the countries in the world. Yet an important distinction can be made in identifying the countries, regions and issues that dominate US foreign policy versus those that are merely monitored and managed by the working-level policy apparatus. Some issues acquire a salience that goes beyond the group of specialists and diplomats who are given the task of tracking the particular country and issue. These high salience issues are sometimes thrust upon US policy-makers, as was the case when Iran seized the US embassy in Tehran and took US diplomats hostage. In other cases, an administration sets an objective, and raises the profile and the stakes, so that interest in the issue transcends the usual inner circle of experts. Examples of this would be Reagan's focus on Central America or on the international drug problem. Most other issues remain on a second tier, where US experts and diplomats monitor developments and pursue normal relations, but cannot expect to have the attention of the president or even the secretary of state on a regular basis.

There is little evidence to suggest that, with the exception of the summer of 1974, and possibly the autumn 1978 debate over the arms embargo, US policy toward Greece and Turkey ever achieved that higher salience category. Instead, one can argue that policy was driven primarily by a narrow set of factors that remained fairly constant during the period under consideration. This state of affairs has not always been satisfactory to Greece and Turkey, or to their supporters in the United States, who have sometimes bemoaned the low level of attention given to the regional tensions and to bilateral US relations with each country.

East–West Relations

The overarching theme of US foreign policy in the post-war period has been the challenge of East–West relations, and US leadership of the Western alliance's efforts to contain the Soviet threat. Historically, there is no doubt that US policy towards Greece and Turkey, from the 1947 Truman Doctrine, the subsequent US support for Greek and Turkish entry into NATO and establishment of close security ties to both countries, was shaped by US perceptions of the Soviet threat. Initially, Greece was seen as more vulnerable to communist influence, although the later debate over Soviet designs on the Turkish straits gave both countries different but powerful claims on the need for the West to help them defend against the Soviet Union.

In the period since 1974, the Soviet factor has been cited intermittently as the driving force behind US policy, but has competed with other more immediate and local US concerns. In large measure because of the Cyprus crisis, the period from 1974 to 1980 was focused nearly exclusively on the immediate regional environment. Although the embargo debate prominently featured arguments about Turkey's strategic value *vis-à-vis* the Soviets, few considered direct Soviet attacks on Turkey a plausible scenario. The immediacy of the threat had diminished, although US commitment to the two states and policy responses during the crisis were indirectly linked to the East–West factor, through the alliance concept.

After the Soviet invasion of Afghanistan, the Soviet factor resurfaced, and did not affect US policy toward the two eastern Mediterranean states in the same way. Turkey loomed large in the strategic picture, part of the 'arc of crisis' that preoccupied the late Carter years and made more possible the election of a conservative president. Turkey's stock in Washington rose dramatically: security co-operation with Turkey took on new value after the loss of intelligence facilities in Iran, and for those who saw in Afghanistan the nightmare of Soviet southward expansion, Turkey's ability to control the Caucasus and the Straits seemed more significant. Greece, on the other hand, with the neutralist yearnings of PASOK, was viewed by administration ideologues as part of the problem of Western complacency *vis-à-vis* the Soviet threat.

Since the arrival of Gorbachev and the remarkable warming in US–Soviet relations at the end of the Reagan presidency, and the extraordinary collapse of communist regimes in eastern Europe, the East–West dimension of all of US foreign policy has been under constant scrutiny, and has not yet found a new equilibrium. It is clear that relations with Greece and Turkey, as with other Western allies, are moving toward a new concept of power-sharing and burden sharing in a post-Cold War world. This is likely to include a reduction in the US presence in Europe, achieved probably through multilateral arms control agreements, but conceivably through new West-–West understandings. The announcement in January 1990, for example, that the United States is proposing to leave two of its four major installations in Greece as part of its base renegotiation is the first sign of unilateral pull-backs in the Western camp comparable to what the Soviets have been proposing to their allies.

Regional Settlement Efforts

A second prism through which US policy towards Greece and Turkey can be examined is the prism of regional conflict policy. Although their common membership in NATO has inhibited allies of Greece and Turkey from relegating their problems to the 'regional conflict' category, the chronic tensions in Greek–Turkish relations over Cyprus and the Aegean in the post-1974 period have placed the region on the list of diplomatic headaches, alongside the Arab–Israeli conflict, Indo-Pakistani problems and Central America, that are often the subject of conferences and symposia in Western capitals. This is understandable if one takes into account Cyprus's status as a small non-aligned country, but is often not the context in which Greeks and Turks want their problems debated.

US policy toward regional conflicts has changed over time. With respect to Greece and Turkey, the US policy establishment's willingness to consider conflict-resolution efforts has often reflected Washington's sense of whether the parties would be receptive to such mediation. For much of the period since 1974, the United States has concluded that such efforts would bear little fruit. During acute periods, however, it becomes an article of faith to debate how and whether the United States can become more actively involved. A recent example was the March 1987 flare-up over Aegean oil drilling. The Ozal and Papandreou governments declined both US and NATO mediation offers, and were able to back away from the brink.

In the immediate aftermath of 1974, the United States was not a credible outside mediator, because of suspicions on the Greek side in particular that Washington had encouraged or acquiesced to Turkey's action on Cyprus. In addition, the post-junta climate in Greece required both governments to move gingerly in bilateral relations. Even NATO was an implausible dispute mediator after Greece withdrew from the military command. The United Nations became the lead player in Cyprus settlement efforts, but this left the Greco-Turkish dimension unattended, and has never been completely satisfactory from Turkey's point of view.

In 1978, after a cooling-off period of several years, the Carter administration launched a Cyprus settlement initiative with Canada and the United Kingdom. The plan was coolly received in Turkey and Cyprus, and was set aside. Its existence may best be viewed as a tactical requirement, complementing the policy initiative to lift the embargo. Despite continued Cyprus troubles, the governments in Athens and Ankara tried to improve bilateral relations, and pursued a ministerial-level dialogue. There were also two high-level meetings, including one in Washington between premiers Karamanlis and Ecevit. The Carter administration offered its good offices, which were later to prove useful to Egypt and Israel, but Greece and Turkey were either still resistant to a US-brokered settlement of their differences, or, more likely, simply not ready to address their deep-seated problems and work for solutions.

The United States has been indirectly involved in the NATO-sponsored efforts to solve the Aegean command issue. Washington was engaged more than most NATO countries when two successive SACEURs, generals Haig and Rogers, tried to develop plans to solve the problem. Yet occasional US probings to see if the myriad of Aegean issues could be linked, or the Cyprus and Aegean issues considered together in confidence-building efforts, have run into resistance from Greece and Turkey, who had entrenched their respective Aegean positions in what appear to be mutually exclusive concepts.

It has generally been the view of the Turkish government in particular that direct talks rather than multi-party formulas best suit the needs of Greece and Turkey. The State Department and White House have usually been content with offers of help, but show preference for direct initiatives of the parties themselves. This was the case in the short-lived Davos process, a series of meetings between then-premiers Papandreou and Ozal in 1988. The *rapprochement*, encouraged by various European states with little apparent US involvement, stalled in autumn 1988 due to Papandreou's illness and political difficulties at home. Should there be new momentum in that effort, it is likely that the United States would not be called on for a direct role.

The Reagan administration's activism in regional conflicts through the policy popularly known as the Reagan Doctrine did not address the eastern Mediterranean. Reagan Doctrine aid recipients were Third World movements fighting Soviet-backed governments in Angola, Nicaragua, Afghanistan and Cambodia. This US activism was directed at conflicts with a clear East-West dimension, which did not pertain to Greek-Turkish disputes or to Cyprus.

With the diminution of regional conflicts that were indisputably exacerbated by superpower rivalry, some analysts see promising prospects for many regional conflicts winding down. Yet the opposite view appears equally valid: absent the simple symmetry of a bipolar world, long-festering ethnic and religious conflicts can flare up. Azerbaijan and Armenia, Bulgarians and Turks, Baltic and Slavic tensions have already emerged. This may reinforce the ethnic and cultural overtones of Greco-Turkish differences. Both Greece and Turkey are faced with domestic repercussions of the Soviet and eastern European upheavals, and these new pressures may make it difficult for either government to take the high road on their bilateral disputes.[7]

One result of the Reagan administration's activism in regional conflicts was Soviet agreement to conduct a regular dialogue, among regional experts in both governments, on specific conflicts. It was notable that in the late 1980s, Greek Cypriots expressed their desire to be on the US-Soviet agenda, but the United States was loath to address at the superpower level a conflict that was essentially within the Western camp. Reagan administration officials were also of the view that Greek-Turkish problems were manageable, and not in an acute crisis phase. Although some in Congress continued to argue that the region deserved more attention, there was little movement to place the eastern Mediterranean higher on the regional conflict agenda.

Congressional-Executive Relations

It is by now clear that participants in the US policy process have not been in easy agreement on the relative and absolute importance of Greece and Turkey throughout the period since 1974. The lack of consensus as to the nature of the problem and the desired US policy response has kept the region a source of chronic inter-branch friction. The Congress, motivated primarily by a core group of a dozen or more members who are active and interested in the region, has virtually consistently advocated greater US involvement in the area, in Cyprus in particular. Administration officials testifying before congressional committees face a now familiar ritual of trying to close the gap between executive branch bureaucracy that has wearied of new initiatives in the region and has other priorities, and a legislature that seems to favour greater US activism and more forceful policy efforts.

Congress has generally used its control of foreign aid funding to try and achieve its objectives in the region. In fact, measures aimed at curbing aid to Turkey until troops are removed from Cyprus, for example, can also been seen as punitive measures against the executive branch. Congress has signalled in many ways since 1974 its disapproval both of the continued stalemate on Cyprus and of administration ineffectiveness in creating conditions for change in the region.

In its aid deliberations since the lifting of the embargo, Congress has used the 7:10 ratio formula as a means of implementing its 'present balance' pledge; although it is rarely explained, the underlying premise appears to be that the balance in aid may make less likely aggressive Turkish moves against Greece. In fact, the Greek premier indirectly praised this US policy during the 1987 Aegean crisis when he said that for the first time since 1974 Greek forces were prepared to go to war with Turkey. Although many experts believe that the 'balance' in military might still greatly favours Turkey, it is an article of faith between Greece and its supporters in the United States that the ratio, and its resulting curb on what would otherwise be higher levels of aid to Turkey, has at least partly redressed the imbalance and insecurity that Greece perceived in the mid-1970s.[8]

Aid to the two countries peaked in 1984 at the levels of $715 million in military aid to Turkey, $500 million for Greece. Levels declined in subsequent years due to overall cuts, and were $500 million and $350 million respectively at decade's end. In early 1990, Senator Dole launced a long-awaited debate over aid and reallocating scarce aid dollars in light of the pressing challenges in eastern Europe and Panama. The sensitive part of this debate is expected to be cuts in aid to Egypt and Israel, which together have received over $5 billion annually since the early 1980s. But after that programme, viewed by many as a congressional sacred cow, Greece and Turkey figure prominently, and the prospects of aid cuts to the eastern Mediterranean states will have repercussions for overall US policy to the two states and to the congressional–executive interplay over that policy.

Aid has not been the only vehicle for Congress to play a role in the formulation of policy toward Greece and Turkey. In other legislation, Congress has expressed its concerns and reservations about a number of issues, ranging from Turkey's prison conditions and elections, to Greece's attitudes towards terrorism and bases. These public signals are sometimes helpful to administration policy. Over the years, there has been some tacit co-operation between the branches on Cyprus settlement efforts, human rights and terrorism. Again, since the dramatic and damaging stand-off of 1974-8, the inter-branch policy debate over Greece and Turkey has created some common ground. Friction remains over tactics, but by the late 1980s the differences between the two branches over interests and policy options had become as much stylistic as substantive.

One should be wary of concluding that there is a sustainable consensus within the United States over policy towards Greece and Turkey. What can be said is that supporters of Turkey and supporters of Greece within Congress are more even in number and more even in temper than they used to be; they can co-sponsor resolutions urging the parties in Cyprus to move more quickly on a UN plan. They can find compromise language on prodding Turkey on Cyprus, or Greece on terrorism or base talks. They use informal consultations with the executive to express their policy preferences, rather than more formal and contentious means. But the period ahead, during which the relative value of relations with Greece and Turkey may be revealed as being considerably less than it used to be, will be a test of their political clout and their ability to conceptualise the US stake in these two countries with a new vocabulary.

NOTES

Helen Laipson writes on US policy in the eastern Mediterranean and the Middle East at the Congressional Research Service of the Library of Congress. The views expressed here are her own.

1. Kissinger referred to the Cypriot president as the 'Castro of the Mediterranean'. For critical views of Kissinger's role in the Cyprus crisis, see Laurence Stern, *The Wrong Horse* (New York: Times Books, 1977); Harvey Starr, *Henry Kissinger: Perceptions of International Politics* (Lexington: University of Kentucky Press, 1984).
2. For more on US policy towards the Cyprus crisis and the Turkish arms embargo, see by this author 'A Quarter Century of US Policy toward

Cyprus', in J. T. A. Koumoulides (ed.), *Cyprus in Transition, 1960–1985* (London: Trigraph, 1986); and *Congressional Executive Relations and the Turkish Arms Embargo*, published by US House Foreign Affairs Committee (1981).
3. See Theodore Couloumbis, *The United States, Greece and Turkey: The Troubled Triangle* (New York: Praeger, 1983) p. 139.
4. Contained in Sec. 620C of the Foreign Assistance Act, 22 USC 2373.
5. For more discussion of the 7:10 ratio, see Helen Laipson, 'Greece and Turkey: The Seven-Ten Ratio in Military Aid', CRS Report 90–29F (26 December 1989).
6. Some US sources consider of equal consequence poor Turkish economic performance, internal US and Turkish defence management and decision-making. See, for example, US Senate, Committee on Foreign Relations, 'Turkey, Greece and NATO: Strained Alliance, A Staff Report' (Washington, DC: US Government Printing Office, March 1980) pp. 17–19.
7. On Cyprus, the two communities have reacted to a changing Europe in strikingly different ways: the Greek Cypriots want to be associated with the peace epidemic, and want the walls in Nicosia to come down. Turkish Cypriots, on the other hand, find validation of their separate status in the growth of nationalist movements in eastern Europe.
8. As the ratio has endured through many changes in the politics of foreign aid, some curious counter-arguments can be made. Aid to Turkey, for example, could conceivably have been *lower* without the ratio, since the ratio has earmarked, or protected aid in years when aid for non-earmarked countries suffered. It also appears that for the Greeks, the ratio as a symbol outweighs its actual monetary value. The Greeks have accepted aid cuts without complaint, so long as Turkey is also cut. This, and unspent aid balances, seem to undermine their argument for upgrading their defences *vis-à-vis* Turkey.

13 Soviet Relations with Greece and Turkey: A Systems Perspective*

ROBERT CUTLER

The geography of the Balkan/Asia Minor region conditions military thinking. Even advances in the military application of technology cannot alter this.[1] The political salience of the region's geography has only increased since the end of World War Two. The eastern Mediterranean is a potential choke-point interdicting oil supplies destined for NATO's European members. Turkey exerts pressure against the eastern flank of the Warsaw Pact, diminishing the latter's freedom to move against NATO in central Europe. Any conflict in central Europe would give Turkey an important role in maintaining freedom of the seas and in monitoring military deployments by both alliances.

The Dardanelles and the Bosphorus are the source of the region's sensitivity in a multiplicity of international contexts over time. The Turkish straits remain the only egress for the Soviet navy from the Black Sea to the Atlantic Ocean and, via Suez, the Indian Ocean. The straits and adjacent Thrace are one of the few regions in Europe where a *Blitzkrieg* manoeuvre by Warsaw Pact forces might seize appreciable territory before NATO reinforcements could arrive. Command-and-control targets in Bulgaria and the southern Soviet Union are vulnerable to tactical aircraft based in Turkey. Two dozen American military bases in Greece provide intelligence facilities and essential logistic support.[2]

The Balkan/Asia Minor region straddles the European and Middle Eastern subsystems of the general international system. In particular, the Balkan subregion of Europe and the south-west Asian subregion of the Middle East intersect in Greece and Turkey. The dispersal of peoples, cultures and states across the region changes, yet unchanging geography remains the framework of current political conditions

---

* I wish to thank Zachary T. Irwin for his comments on a draft of this chapter.

and constrains their evolution. Such continuities make an analytical summary of the region's history worthwhile. The first section of this chapter presents a theoretically informed overview of Greek and Turkish relations with Russia and the Soviet Union. In particular, a comparative survey of the Balkan/Asia Minor region under various international systems from 1713 to 1936 generates a set of propositions. These propositions associate specific changes in the international environment with specific changes in the behaviour of states in the region. The third section of the chapter examines in detail the period since 1974, in a comparative systems perspective. On this basis, the propositions derived from the historical record are again scrutinised. Nuances and corollaries introduced to the original propositions then permit an evaluation of current Greek and Turkish relations with the Soviet Union. The general course of these relations in the future is then projected.

FROM UTRECHT TO MONTREUX: THE HISTORICAL INHERITANCE

A Comparative International Systems Approach

The Treaty of Utrecht (1713) created the 'European State System [as] an indissoluble unity [where] all States, east and west, were involved in every contest between any of its members'.[3] Since then, six distinct international systems have occupied the European stage: the European balance, 1713–89; the concert of Europe, 1815–66; the Bismarckian system, 1871–1914; the inter-war league system, 1919–39; the nuclear superpower system, 1949–79; and multipolar interdependence, since 1979. To make the text more concise, the justification of these dates appears in relevant notes.[4]

This section surveys relations among Greece, Turkey and the Soviet Union/Russia[5] from 1713 up to the decline of the inter-war league system. The year inaugurating that decline (1936) is also that of the Montreux Convention governing the Turkish straits. The general propositions emerging from this history are therefore called 'lessons of pre-Montreux history'.[6] Some of them reflect constants transcending historical states and international systems in the region. Others establish that particular changes in the international environment account for particular changes in state behaviour in the region.

The European balance, 1713–89 (declined after the first partition of Poland, 1772)
The European balance was bipolar; Europe was continually divided into two antagonistic blocs. During all this time, Russia was not terribly concerned with the Greek nation. Catherine the Great's 'Greek project' in the 1760s sought only to use Greek Orthodox clergy as agents of Russian influence in the Balkans. Towards the end of the Napoleonic Wars, the tsar endorsed Ottoman suppression of the Greek national revolt. One reason was that the unrest worked against Russian interests. Another reason may have been the demographic analogy between the multinational Russian state and the multinational Turkish state. During the life of this international system, the Russian and Ottoman Empires were strong states in the system and *vis-à-vis* one another, and their mutual relations were conflictual.

The concert of Europe, 1815–66 (declined after the Crimean War, 1854)
The concert of Europe was a multipolar system founded by a coalition of states on the principle of public law and on the norm that diplomatic practice should follow legal precedent.[7] Greek affairs were marginal to Russia during the concert of Europe. Even Russia's qualified support for Greek independence in the 1820s was but a by-product of its desire 'to maintain Turkey as a weak power and to advance and expand Russian political and commercial interests' in the region.[8] Greece's internal problems after the Crimean War effectively prevented the country from playing any significant international role. During the concert of Europe, Russia was strong until its defeat in the Crimean War, whereas the Ottoman Empire was weak. Russia's loss of prestige during the concert's decline yielded a relative increase in Turkish strength. However, both states remained weak *vis-à-vis* the international system. Mitigated antagonism before the Crimean War, and unmitigated antagonism after it, characterised relations between Russia and Turkey.

The Bismarckian system, 1871–1914 (declined after Bismarck's resignation, 1890)
This was a unipolar but not hegemonic system. Germany as fulcrum did not value the Balkans greatly, and Bismarck as Chancellor mediated Austro-Russian disputes in the region. Russia's pan-Slav

impulses in the Balkans antagonised Greece. The establishment of a Bulgarian state, with all its implications for Greek Macedonia, formed the basis of Imperial Russian policy in the Balkans during the crucial years 1875–8.[9] Principally because of Bismarck's reinforcement of Russia's and Austria's positions in the Balkans at Turkey's expense, the Russian Empire was a strong state at the height of this system, while the Ottoman Empire was a weak one. However, Japan's defeat of Russia in the 1904–5 war and the 1905 Russian revolution greatly sapped Russia's power during this system's decline. Relations between Russia and Turkey were antagonistic throughout the life of the Bismarckian system.

The inter-war league system, 1919–39 (declined after Hitler's reoccupation of the Rhineland, 1936)
The inter-war league system was a multipolar system that attempted, like the concert of Europe, to found the practice of diplomacy upon public law and legal precedent. It did not abolish the practice of power politics, and this led to its demise. From 1920 to 1936 Turkey and the Soviet Union shared an interest in opposing the West in general and the United Kingdom in particular.[10] The Soviet Union supported Turkey at negotiations over a regime to regulate the straits (Treaty of Lausanne, 1923), and the two countries subsequently agreed on a series of bilateral protocols on naval tonnage (1931). After Hitler's rise to power Turkey became caught between Soviet and German imperatives, and Turkish–Soviet relations deteriorated. During the inter-war league system, the Soviet Union and the Turkish Republic were both very new and very weak states.[11] Their common weakness led them to co-operate on a series of bilateral and multilateral issues until the mid-1930s. In the 1930s, disputes over the Macedonian question erupted inside the Communist International among the Greek, Bulgarian and Yugoslav communist parties. When the Soviet Union forced a policy favouring Macedonian autonomy upon the Greek Communist Party, the latter split, losing domestic support.[12]

The Lessons of Pre-Montreux History

Five general propositions emerge from this survey of the history of international relations in the Balkan/Asia Minor region.

Proposition 1. A stable multipolar system (concert of Europe, inter-

war league system) mitigates conflict between the Russian and Turkish states more effectively than a bipolar (European balance, nuclear superpower system) or unipolar (Bismarckian) system.
Proposition 2. Russian/Soviet rulers consider Greek independence and autonomy secondary to their own preoccupations with Turkey and the Balkans.
Proposition 3. Russian strength and Turkish weakness produce a latent antagonism between the two states that fuels specific conflicts.
Proposition 4. Overt Russo-Turkish conflict is most likely when both countries are strong *vis-à-vis* the international system and one another.
Proposition 5. Co-operation between the Russian and Turkish states increases when both are weak *vis-à-vis* the international system.

The two international systems identified since the end of World War Two provide the framework for examining the post-war period. These were the nuclear superpower system (1949–79, declined after 1974)[13] and multipolar interdependence (1979 to the present). By way of introduction to the nuclear superpower system, however, it is necessary first to give special treatment to the years from 1936 to 1948. These years transformed the Soviet Union from a diffident semi-outsider in one international system, into a constitutive pillar of the successor system. More than that, they were the crucible out of which the post-war situation in the Balkan/Asia Minor region emerged. Since the imprint of these years upon international politics in the region is still evident, it would be negligent not to signal their salient features.

FROM MONTREUX TO NICOSIA: THE END OF THE INTER-WAR LEAGUE SYSTEM AND THE RISE OF THE NUCLEAR SUPERPOWER SYSTEM

The Transition from the Inter-war League System to the Nuclear Superpower System (1936–48)

Greek–Soviet relations
Soviet relations with Greece had been bad since before the war, as Stalin's instigation of the Greek communists to civil unrest facilitated General Metaxas's coup in 1936. Tito, who had designs on Macedonia, instigated a Greek communist insurgency immediately after the

conclusion of World War Two. Moscow did nothing to discourage Yugoslav or Bulgarian military pressure on Greek Macedonia, which remained the key problem between Greece and the Soviet bloc.

Throughout the late 1940s, the Soviet bloc maintained that external (that is British) interference in Greek domestic affairs endangered international security in the region. In early 1946 the Soviet Union presented to the United Nations a complaint against the UK military presence in Greece. Debates at the UN and the organisation's actions 'exerted serious pressure on the Soviet Union and the satellite countries'. They effectively 'delegitimiz[ed] the actions and statements of the Soviet Union, its satellites, and the guerrillas in Greece' and 'expos[ed] their actions *vis-à-vis* Greece and the guerrillas'.[14] In view of Stalin's concession of Western influence in Greece under the famous 'percentages agreement' with Churchill, the question remains why Stalin turned to the United Nations in this instance. In fact, he had no other diplomatic instrumentalities at his disposal. The various national Balkan communist parties (including the Greeks) did not heed his word, and he had no direct means for applying military pressure. Stalin 'could not afford to miss any opportunity for advantageous propaganda' even though he preferred a policy of 'open diplomatic action in the Balkans rather than subversion and revolution' at the time.[15]

Turkish–Soviet relations
The Western powers' failure to make good on guarantees to Turkey in the early and mid-1930s led to the convocation of a new conference on the straits.[16] At this conference, from which emerged the regime of the Montreux Convention (1936), the Soviets were able to assure passage for warships of Black Sea powers and to limit the movement of ships of other powers.[17] The Montreux Convention was the first step by the United Kingdom and France 'to encourage Turkey either to involve its war fleet in war against Germany or to maintain strict neutrality in the event of conflict between the Western Allies and Germany'.[18] These steps were ultimately successful.

In mid-1939 Stalin proposed to the United Kingdom and France a military assistance pact guaranteeing the integrity of all states from the Baltic to the Black Sea. When the United Kingdom and France declined, Stalin proposed to Turkey that it share sovereignty of the Straits jointly with the Soviet Union. When Turkey responded by signing a military alliance with the United Kingdom and France (October 1939), Stalin proposed joint Soviet–German sovereignty of the straits to Hitler. In 1940 his foreign minister, Molotov, publicly implicated Turkey in Allied designs on the Baku oilfields.

Germany's pressure on Turkey to join in a military alliance was not successful, but Turkey did sign a Treaty of Friendship that ensured Turkish neutrality towards Germany. This stance of neutrality, to which the Turks clung almost throughout the war, was not equivalent to passivity. As a senior Soviet historian has correctly pointed out, it was not always even equivalent to neutrality.[19] Turkey remained formally neutral but sought to enhance its regional influence by bargaining with various belligerents. If in the end it gained nothing, this was because 'every one of its demands came into conflict with the interests or the diplomatic tactics of the warring powers'.[20]

In late 1945 Stalin proposed to Turkey the joint Soviet–Turkish administration of the straits, plus a general prohibition on passage by ships of states not bordering on the Black Sea. Turkey replied that these provisions would infringe its own independence and security. (Rubinstein has aptly characterised this move as 'Stalin's grab for the Straits'.[21]) The United Kingdom and the United States strongly supported Turkey's position.[22] Stalin's additional claims to the Turkish districts of Ardahan and Kars, which the Russian Empire had ruled from 1878 to 1917, did little to mollify the Western powers. The Truman Doctrine, proclaimed in 1947, only reinforced Turkey's resolve in standing up to the Soviets. Turkish–Soviet relations did not improve until after Stalin's death in 1953, when the Soviet government began trying to win over the Turkish government instead of undermining it.[23]

The Rise of the Nuclear Superpower System (1949–74)

By the time Stalin died in 1953, he had succeeded in alienating both Greece and Turkey. Greece and Turkey each joined NATO in 1952. In 1954 they signed with Yugoslavia the Balkan Pact, which Khrushchev's visit to Belgrade subsequently obviated although it remains in force. Other events in the region deserve little note here until the late 1950s, when the Soviets deployed eight submarines to Valona, Albania.

The Soviet build-up in the Mediterranean
The apparent purpose of the Soviet deployment to Albania was to facilitate sealing the Turkish straits, through attack upon seaborne NATO reinforcements, in time of war. This deployment ended in 1961 when Albania became implicated in the Sino-Soviet dispute.

Increasing Soviet naval strength in the eastern Mediterranean remained the most striking feature of relations in the region during the 1960s and early 1970s. In the early 1960s the Soviet Union sought to enlarge its maritime defence perimeter, and a Mediterranean deployment fitted into this pattern. When President Kennedy withdrew the Jupiter missiles from Turkey (in the wake of the Cuban missile crisis) and President Johnson criticised Turkey's 1964 actions concerning Cyprus, the Soviets took advantage of the strain to deploy a cruiser and two destroyers through the straits. (The Montreux Convention, still in force, permits transit by capital ships of Black Sea powers escorted by no more than two destroyers.) By 1966 the Soviets had built up their Mediterranean force to an average daily strength of fifteen ships which were making port calls from Egypt to Gibraltar.[24]

Events in the Middle East impelled further build-ups of Soviet naval strength in the eastern Mediterranean. During the Six Day War (June 1967) the Soviets, seeking to counter the US Sixth Fleet, increased their force to seventy ships in a show of support for the Arab states. Soviet naval aircraft began operating in the region on a regular basis. The Soviet Union continued to increase its forces thereafter, augmenting them substantially at the height of the Jordanian crisis (September–October 1970). During the Yom Kippur War (October 1973) this force rose from fifty-two to ninety-five ships, including over a dozen destroyers and nearly two dozen submarines,[25] all protecting the sealift of Soviet arms to Egypt and Syria. However, the political benefits obtained by a similar show of force in 1967 did not repeat themselves. In 1976 President Sadat, having expelled Soviet advisors and air units from Egypt, closed Egyptian ports to the Soviet navy. Soviet naval forces in the Mediterranean have never regained the strength they enjoyed in the early 1970s.[26]

Greek–Soviet relations
Stalin had alienated Greece through his policy in the Balkans. It was not until the military junta of 1967–74 that any Greek regime even considered a diplomatic *rapprochement* with any communist government at all. The Greek colonels worked first through Albania, Romania and China, before establishing contact with the Soviet Union. The substance of these relations, however, did not amount to much at the time.

Turkish–Soviet relations
Turkey began acting more independently of American policy from

the mid-1960s to the mid-1970s, and reasserted its traditional regional interests. Improvement in relations with Moscow was part of this approach. At the same time Ankara maintained its fidelity to NATO and continued its military and economic co-operation with the United States. In 1965 Soviet President Podgornyi and Foreign Minister Gromyko both visited Ankara, followed in 1966 by Prime Minister Kosygin. In 1967 Turkish Prime Minister Demirel accepted a Soviet invitation to visit Moscow. There he signed an economic co-operation agreement under which Turkey developed huge public-sector projects with Soviet industrial and financial assistance. Trade soared and even the Turkish military coup in 1971 did not disrupt relations.[27]

The 'Lessons of Pre-Montreux History' Examined

Let us examine what light the experience of the years 1936–74 sheds on the 'lessons of pre-Montreux history' drawn earlier.

Proposition 1 cannot be evaluated. No stable multipolar system existed during the years 1936–74. Turkish–Soviet relations were equally conflictual during the breakdown of the (multipolar) interwar league system and the rise of the (bipolar) nuclear superpower system.

Proposition 2 is borne out. Soviet concern with Greece derived from how Greek policy could possibly benefit Soviet goals in the region and not from any genuine concern for Greek affairs. Like the rulers of the Empire of All the Russias, Soviet leaders from 1936 to 1974 considered Greek autonomy and independence quite secondary to their own preoccupations in the region.

Proposition 3 is borne out. When the Soviet Union was strong and Turkey was weak, then antagonism tended to result. The Soviets abandoned their antagonism towards Turkey during World War Two because the very survival of the Soviet Union was at stake. However, this antagonism reappeared after 1945 with a focus on the Turkish straits. The Soviet Union was then strong *vis-à-vis* the international system and Turkey was weak, but Turkey had the support of the major Western powers. Since the two countries had no common enemy, their antagonism worsened. After the mid-1960s Turkey increasingly asserted its autonomous regional interests and augmented its regional prestige. The Soviets accommodated this development, and the level of Turkish–Soviet antagonism diminished.

Proposition 4 is contradicted. Overt conflict was no longer automatic when both the Soviet Union and Turkey were strong states. Towards the end of the period 1936–74, Turkey's strength as a regional power began to rise. However, Turkey was hardly as strong as the Soviet Union *vis-à-vis* the international system. Although the United States supported Turkey against the Soviet Union, there was no overt Turkish–Soviet conflict. *Specific features of the nuclear superpower system account for the contradiction of this proposition.* Those features are the promotion of the Soviet Union to the rank of great power and the reduction of Turkey to the rank of regional power.

Proposition 5 is contradicted. When both the Turkish and Russian states were weak, mutual antagonism was absent. From 1920 to 1936, Turkey and the Soviet Union were weak states in a multipolar international environment and they enjoyed a high degree of co-operation. Between 1936 and 1948 that international environment was disintegrating and its collapse affected the Balkan/Asia Minor region. Consequently, Turkish–Soviet co-operation was negligible even though both countries were weak *vis-à-vis* the international system. Under the nuclear superpower system, bilateral Turkish–Soviet co-operation was nil until the late 1960s. As with the fourth proposition, *specific features of the nuclear superpower system account for the contradiction of this proposition.* In this instance, those features are the system's bipolarity and the peripheralisation of the Balkan/Asia Minor region, within the international hierarchy, by the emerging Third World and the appearance of the latter on the international agenda.

The second and third propositions illustrate that certain constants transcend historical states and international systems in the region. The fourth and fifth propositions illustrate that changes in the international environment can account for some changes in state behaviour in the region. It will therefore be instructive to examine all five propositions also in relation to the period since 1974, which has seen fundamental shifts in the organisation of the international system. Following that second round of verification, it will be possible to project the future course of Greek and Turkish relations with the Soviet Union.

FROM NICOSIA TO THE PRESENT: THE DECLINE OF THE NUCLEAR SUPERPOWER SYSTEM AND THE RISE OF MULTIPOLAR INTERDEPENDENCE

The Decline of the Nuclear Superpower System (1974–9)

The year 1974 marked the beginning of the decline of the international system we have called the nuclear superpower system.[28] Also in 1974 the Greek contingent of the Cypriot National Guard staged a coup ousting President Makarios. This action led Turkish troops to occupy the northern third of Cyprus and precipitated the fall of the Greek junta. The events surrounding Cyprus in 1974 did not just affect both Greek and Turkish foreign policy, they also transformed Moscow's approach to the region.[29]

The Cyprus conflict
The Soviet government accepted the original Turkish justification for landing its troops, namely that no peaceful settlement of the conflict on Cyprus was possible. In Moscow, international-affairs specialists were divided in their evaluation of events. One school of analysis saw the coup against Makarios as a NATO plot to overthrow a non-aligned government and transform the island into an 'unsinkable aircraft carrier'. Another school of analysis in Moscow, emphasising Greek–Turkish confrontation rather than East–West conflict, saw the conflict's regional aspect as primary. When it became evident that US, UK and NATO policies were not the same, the second school of analysis gained the upper hand in Moscow. Greece's withdrawal from NATO's military command further undermined the school of analysis in Moscow which saw events on Cyprus as a straightforward NATO plot.

In August, the second Turkish landing on Cyprus made partition of the island likely. Since this development made the restoration of Makarios's independent non-aligned government more difficult, it was not in Moscow's interest. However, Moscow's desire for a role in whatever settlement emerged was greater than its desire for Makarios's restoration. The Soviet Union decided to improve ties with Turkey and reinvigorated its economic aid programme to Ankara. Retreating from overt advocacy of Makarios's cause, the Soviets reoriented their policy regarding Cyprus. They turned to the United Nations, sending an observer to the intercommunal talks in Geneva that the UN Security Council had authorised. The Soviets proposed that, to verify the ceasefire, the Council should send to Cyprus a mission comprising representatives of the Soviet Union and two non-aligned countries. Although this suggestion was quickly forgotten, the salient development was the Soviet turn towards the United Nations as the diplomatic instrumentality of choice. The reason for this was the same as for Stalin's approach to the United Nations over the Greek question immediately after World War Two. The Soviets had no other significant means through which to influence either the military or the diplomatic outcome of the situation.

Greek policy in the late 1970s

The reorientation of Greek foreign policy after the 1974 Cyprus conflict concentrated at first on the Balkans. Prime Minister Karamanlis of the New Democracy government visited Romania, Yugoslavia and Bulgaria in 1975, and he played host to an inter-Balkan meeting in early 1978. Greece and the Soviet Union signed a series of agreements on economic and technical co-operation during these years, and trade increased significantly. However, it took four years for the two countries' foreign ministers to meet, and the only result of the meeting was another accord on cultural and technical co-operation. NATO circles began to worry when the merchant-marine aspect of that accord led a Greek company to offer shipping repair services to the Soviets. They were afraid this might entail servicing support vessels of the Soviet Mediterranean squadron.[30] Greece's relations with the Soviet Union deteriorated following the invasion of Afghanistan. By then, however, contracts were in place for the purchase of Soviet oil and electricity, and for Soviet aid in building two power plants.[31] Greece rejoined the NATO military command in late 1980.

Turkish policy in the late 1970s

Turkey, like Greece, turned after 1974 towards expanding its Balkan relations.[32] It had diplomatic exchanges with all the Warsaw Pact members in the Balkan region, plus Yugoslavia and Albania. Turkish–Bulgarian relations in particular improved remarkably.[33] Turkish–Soviet economic co-operation focused on energy-production projects and raw-materials extraction and processing, and relations expanded hugely.[34] When Kosygin visited Ankara in 1978, he signed an agreement on Principles of Good-Neighbourly and Friendly Co-operation with the Turkish prime minister, Ecevit. However, the most significant result of the meeting was the agreement on economic co-operation.[35] A 1979 protocol to the 1978 agreement foresaw nearly four billion dollars' worth of projects in these fields.

The Soviets have little to show politically for the vast increase in economic ties with Turkey. Ankara accepted a Soviet invitation to observe military manoeuvres in the Caucasus in the mid and late 1970s, it permitted the aircraft carrier *Kiev* through the straits,[36] and it refused Washington's request to use Turkish territory to replace monitoring stations lost after the revolution in Iran. Yet a strengthening of Atlanticism was, in the words of a senior Soviet scholar, 'the chief trait characterizing Turkey's foreign policy' in the late 1970s and early 1980s.[37] The principle result of closer Turkish economic ties with the socialist countries of eastern Europe was the creation of an atmosphere more sympathetic to all-Balkan co-operation.[38]

The Rise of Multipolar Interdependence (1979–Present)

Greek–Soviet relations
Andreas Papandreou, after his election in 1981 at the head of a PASOK government in Athens, reversed the decision against offering shipping repair services to the Soviet Union. He signed a declaration with the Romanian leader Ceaucescu calling for a nuclear-free zone in the Balkans. Greece was the only EC member not to impose sanctions on Poland in the early 1980s after the introduction of martial law there. It was the only NATO member not to approve deployment of Pershing II and Cruise missiles in Europe. As time went on, however, it became clear to all observers, including the Soviets, that fundamental change Greece's international relations was minimal. The Diplomatic Academy in Moscow (a research and training institute under the Soviet Foreign Ministry) accepted *Le Monde*'s conclusion that 'the chief aim of Athens's new diplomatic line is "to secure for Greece a significant international rank [by] . . . playing an original role in relations between East and West"'.[39] Papandreou's signature of a new Defence Co-operation Agreement with the United States in late 1983 underlined the limits of his deviation from longstanding Greek foreign policy.

Papandreou hosted a conference on Balkan co-operation in early 1984, but Greek relations with its Balkan neighbours have lost their dynamism since 1985. A visit to Moscow in early 1985 yielded little more than a few economic agreements, and Greek relations with the

Soviet Union have shown little progress since then. Greek–Soviet relations soured in particular following the exposure by a Soviet defector of Moscow's operations in Athens, including disinformation activities and subversion of local peace movements and mass media. The level of Greek–Soviet trade has actually declined in recent years. The Greek trade deficit with the Soviet Union has increased, partly because the Soviets refuse to spend their foreign trade earnings on Greek goods. Industrial co-operation projects are at a standstill. A politically sensitive joint project to construct an alumina plant near Delphi is dormant.[40] Papandreou maintained his independent line by condemning SDI and by continuing to tout a Balkan nuclear-free zone. However, Greece's concern with internal problems over the last few years has not permitted sustained attention to either economic or political relations with the Soviet Union.

Turkish–Soviet relations
Even before the Turkish military took power in September 1980, Suleiman Demirel's Justice Party government signed a new Defence Co-operation Agreement with Washington. In 1982 General Evren visited Bulgaria, Romania and Yugoslavia; Moscow cordially received his foreign minister later that year. By the time Soviet Prime Minister Tikhonov visited Ankara in late 1984, Turgut Ozal had formed a civilian government. The principal results of this visit were yet another important series of long-term accords on trade, economic, scientific and cultural co-operation. Yet better political relations between the two countries did not follow the improvement in economic ties. Bilateral disputes soured Turkish–Soviet relations, and these did not improve when Ozal was snubbed during his visit to Moscow in mid-1986. Nor was a trade accord signed during that visit.

Turkey's decision to participate in SDI triggered a rash of complaints in the Soviet press about Turkish conventional military co-operation with the United States. In early 1986 General Secretary Gorbachev restated Soviet support for UN efforts to settle the Cyprus conflict, including an international conference leading to the island's demilitarisation. Soviet policy towards the Cyprus conflict has since favoured Greece. In mid-1988 Soviet Foreign Minister Shevardnadze met with the newly elected President Vassiliou of Cyprus and emphasised Soviet support for the island's 'independence, sovereignty, unity and territorial integrity'. Subsequent Soviet statements have stressed this theme and continued to advocate the United Nations as a means for settling the Cyprus conflict.[41]

The 'Lessons of Pre-Montreux History' Re-examined

From the recent historical record we arrive at the following evaluations of the propositions generated earlier.

Proposition 1 holds true with one amendment. The absence of Turkish–Soviet warfare under multipolar interdependence appears to verify this proposition, but neither was there any conflict under the nuclear superpower system. This proposition could not be evaluated by the record of the years 1936–74, because no stable multipolar system then existed. However, the long perspective from 1713 to the present, including the concert of Europe and the inter-war league system, permits the emergence of:

Corollary 1. The intensity of conflicts between the Russian and Turkish states is mitigated not by multipolar systems per se but by a secular trend toward international co-operation that multipolar systems permit more clearly to manifest.

Proposition 2 remains valid. Soviet relations with Greece are governed by the utility of Greek policy for Soviet goals. However, the first four systems also generate, and events during the last two international systems confirm:

Corollary 2. The salience of Greece to Russian/Soviet policy increases when the Russian state is a maritime and commercial player in the eastern Mediterranean.

Proposition 3 must be modified. It is no longer Soviet strength and Turkish weakness that fuel conflicts between the two countries. The recent worsening of Turkish–Soviet relations is due to Soviet intolerance of Turkey's increased regional strength and autonomy. (Nor are Turkey's regional strength and autonomy likely to decrease in the future.) Moscow accommodated Turkey's rising regional prestige in the region from the mid-1960s to the late 1970s but has become more negative towards it since the late 1970s. Soviet relations with Turkey have deteriorated as a result. These developments, taken together with the course of events from 1713 to 1936, generate two further insights:

Corollary 3(a). The peripheralisation of the Balkan/Asia Minor region in world politics, resulting from the rise of the Third World, has permitted the rebirth of Turkey as a regional power.

Corollary 3(b). Multipolar systems have historically enhanced the salience of Turkey's regional role.

Proposition 4 is valid if revised. It must take the changed international system into account. In the late 1930s the Soviet Union and Turkey had a common enemy, and this proposition was not valid. The elevation of the Soviet Union to the rank of great power accounts for the proposition's lack of validity from 1949 to 1974. The system of multipolar interdependence has important similarities with the two systems that originally generated this proposition, the concert of Europe and inter-war league systems. Under present conditions, including the peripheralisation of the Balkan/Asia Minor region in world politics, this proposition should be restated as:

Corollary 4. Overt conflict between the Soviet Union and Turkey is most likely when both are strong vis-à-vis the Balkan/Asia Minor regional system and one another.

Proposition 5 does not apply. In the period since 1974, neither the Soviet Union nor Turkey has been a weak state, either *vis-à-vis* the international system or *vis-à-vis* the regional system.

CONCLUSION: THE SOVIET UNION AND THE BALKAN/ASIA MINOR REGION

Looking Outward from the Region

In the 1970s an important justification for East–West *détente* in Soviet eyes was the favour to be gained in Western political circles that were tied to economic circles profiting from trade with the Soviet Union.[42] Yet the increase in Soviet trade with Turkey and Greece had this effect on neither of these two countries. Greek and Turkish relations with eastern Europe improved noticeably during the mid and late 1970s. However, this development was an integral part of the two countries' autonomous foreign policy reorientations and had no direct connection with their respective relations with the Soviet Union. Although Greece's foreign policy reorientation was not systematised as doctrine until the 1970s, its origins can be traced to the late 1960s. Turkey's reorientation had begun as far back as the mid-1960s. Soviet *détente* policy was not the motive force in either instance. The Soviet Union may be a Balkan power but it is not a Balkan state; the Balkan states include Yugoslavia and Albania, which are not members of the Soviet bloc. *For both Greece and Turkey, eastern Europe is first and foremost south-eastern Europe, that is the Balkans.* Because of the Balkan connection, eastern Europe and the Soviet Union are linked together less organically in both Greek and Turkish foreign policy than in the foreign policies of other NATO members.

The division of labour in the USSR Academy of Sciences reflects the multifaceted nature of the Balkan/Asia Minor region. Turkey falls within the purview of the Institute of Eastern Studies, while the Institute of the USA and Canada has responsibility for studying Greece's relations with the NATO countries. In the past, Greek affairs have been the province of the Institute of World Economy and International Relations. The new Institute of European Studies probably now assumes this responsibility. The Russian state has always viewed Turkey as a state more implicated in 'eastern' than in European questions. Turkey's Muslim population is another reason the Soviets consider it principally an eastern rather than a European country. The Soviet emphasis on a 'common European house' reinforces the separation of Greece and Turkey in Soviet studies of world politics; Greece and Turkey are the responsibility of different departments of the Soviet Foreign Ministry. It remains to be seen how the Soviet Union's approach to Turkey will be affected by the latter's bid to join the European Community and its eventually success or failure.

The Cyprus Question

Despite improved economic relations between the Soviet Union and Turkey, the Cyprus conflict has troubled *political* relations between the two countries.[43] In their foreign propaganda, the Soviets still criticise NATO's supposed role in the island's problems. Moreover, they have motivated a change in the tactics of the Cypriot AKEL, one of the largest political parties on the island. Since the retirement in 1988 of Ezekias Papaioannou, its eighty-year-old general secretary who had held the post since 1949, AKEL has supported President Vassiliou, a businessman with little political experience. His government proposes a 'federal' solution to the Cyprus problem as against the 'confederal' solution, with only nominal central power, advocated by Rauf Denktash, the leader of the Turkish Cypriots.[44] (Moscow advocated a federal solution after the 1964 troubles but dropped this proposal when Greece expressed its irritation.)

If Greece and Turkey constitute the 'intersection' of the Balkan subregion of Europe with the south-west Asian subregion of the Middle East, then Cyprus and the other bilateral disputes lie at the 'intersection' of Greece and Turkey. The Soviet Union's approach to the Cyprus problem expresses the principal diplomatic dilemma that it faces in the region. The international framework of treaties guaranteeing Cypriot independence since 1960 excludes the Soviet Union. The signatories – Greece, Turkey and the United Kingdom – are all NATO members. The island hosts various Western radio facilities and extra-territorial British bases. Since the Balkan/Asia Minor region is peripheral to both the European and Middle Eastern subsystems of the international system, the substantial Soviet influence in those two subsystems is only marginally useful in the region itself.

The Soviet Union does not dispose of exceptional diplomatic resources in either south-east Europe or south-west Asia. Nor have bilateral ties with either Greece or Turkey brought the Soviet Union any special advantage in either subsystem. Having few instrumentalities at its disposal, the Soviet Union turns periodically to the United Nations. This was the reason that Stalin raised the Greek question before the United Nations after World War Two. It was for this same reason too that the Soviet Union had recourse to the Security Council following the 1974 Cyprus conflict.[45]

Looking Inward at the Region

Soviet policy toward Greece in the years immediately after World War Two was 'simply the incoherent residuum' of Soviet security policy towards the major powers (the United Kingdom, France, Germany, the United States), minor powers in eastern Europe (Poland, Romania, Hungary, Czechoslovakia), and Greece's neighbours involved in Balkan conflicts (Albania, Yugoslavia, Bulgaria). '[P]atriotic Greeks could never appreciate [this fact], since they held it to be axiomatic that Greece was central to the foreign policy of every major power.'[46] Papandreou's foreign policy perhaps reflected such a conviction. His policy could be called neo-Gaullist, except that

Greece, unlike France, is not a former great power and does not have nuclear weapons. There was, therefore, no Greek analogue to de Gaulle's central doctrine of *tous azimuts*. Indeed Papandreou declared in the mid-1980s that the principal threat to Greece came from the east (that is from Turkey rather than from the Soviet Union).

The Turkish straits are too easily bottlenecked and therefore of little offensive use to the Soviets during military hostilities. It would be logistic folly for the Soviets to try to pass ships through them in time of war, but they have achieved *de facto* unhindered peacetime passage even for vessels prohibited by the Montreux Convention. Cyprus, not the straits, is the principal point of antagonism between, and indicator of the state relations between, the Soviet Union and Turkey today. Increasing Soviet estrangement from Turkey yields some disquiet in Moscow. Believing it still has insufficient means to further its interests in the Balkan/Asia Minor region, the Soviet Union will continue to use multilateral initiatives such as a Balkan nuclear-free zone and international instrumentalities such as the United Nations and the Non-Aligned Movement (of which latter, Cyprus is an increasingly prominent member) to heighten its influence in the region.[47]

One need not subscribe to Mackinder's famous theory about the Eurasian 'heartland' and its 'rimlands' (including Asia Minor) to see from a map that the territory occupied by the Turkish nation should be more important to any Russian state than that occupied by the Greek nation. But this insight needs to be modified in the light of the corollaries generated from the 'lessons of pre-Montreux history' by the post-1974 era. In particular, Corollaries 3(a) and 3(b) together produce the inference that Turkey's role in the region will continue to rise in the future. However, Corollaries 1, 2 and 4, taken together, yield the inferences (i) that Turkish–Soviet differences will remain prominent, (ii) that these will be managed but not fundamentally resolved and (iii) that Soviet policy in the region will increase its attention to Greece.

NOTES

1. For a discussion of this region's significance pertaining to the Central European theatre, see Michael McGwire, *Military Objectives in Soviet Foreign Policy* (Washington, DC: Brookings Institution, 1987) pp. 141–6.

2. For details, see Nicholas V. Gianaris, *Greece and Turkey: Economic and Geopolitical Perspectives* (New York: Praeger, 1988) p. 179.
3. Frederick L. Schuman, *International Politics: The Western State System in Transition* (New York: McGraw-Hill, 1941) p. 59.
4. World wars or other conflicts involving the major states of the system (Napoleonic Wars, wars of German unification, World War One, World War Two) separate the systems and define their terminus dates. An exception is the transition from the nuclear superpower system to multipolar interdependence. For this, the year 1979 was taken as terminus because it marks the first round of the international debt crisis. This crisis confirmed not only the significance of the Third World on the global (as opposed to regional) agenda, but also that of global finance. At one jump it controverted the two exclusive conceptual bases of the nuclear superpower system, under which bipolar strategic issues monopolised that agenda. Compare L. Carl Brown, *International Politics and the Middle East: Old Rules, Dangerous Game* (Princeton, NJ: Princeton University Press, 1984).
5. For felicity of expression, 'the Russian state' will be used as a generic term for the Russian Empire and the Soviet Union together, and 'the Turkish state' for the Ottoman Empire and the Turkish Republic together. When the reference is to one of these historical states in particular, then its proper name is used.
6. The noun 'lessons' takes on special significance in recent work in international-relations theory about learning and behaviour. The limits of this chapter do not allow integration of a theoretically based 'learning' perspective. Therefore, 'lessons' in this chapter refer to analytical inferences from the historical record generally, rather than to any principle learned by any particular countries or leaders.
7. No clearly defined successor system to the concert of Europe emerged before Prussian primacy consolidated the German state. The Crimean War is therefore treated as the *beginning* of the decline of the concert of Europe.
8. The British conceived the 1826 protocol which established a tributary vassal Greek state to be the first step in a protracted series of arrangements. However, the Russians, regarding it as a diplomatic victory, promptly made the text public. See Douglas Dakin, *The Greek Struggle for Independence, 1821–1833* (Berkeley and Los Angeles: University of California Press, 1973) pp. 173–81. The quotation comes from B. Kondis, 'Aspects of Anglo-Russian Rivalry during the Greek Revolution (1825–1829)', in *Les relations gréco-russes pendant la domination turque et la guerre d'indépandance grecque* (Thessaloniki: Institute for Balkan Studies, 1983) p. 118.
9. Serbe A. Gyalistras, *Hellinism and its Balkan Neighbors during Recent Years* (Athens: Hestia, 1945).
10. G. Astakhov, *Ot sultanata k demokraticheskoi Turtsii: Ocherki iz istorii kemalizma* [From the Sultanate to Democratic Turkey: Sketches from the History of Kemalism] (Moscow: Gosizdat, 1926), is an example of this tendency in the Soviet historiography, which also animated Soviet analyses of regional affairs at the time. For the latter, see B. Zherv

A. Petrov and E. Shvede, *Sredizemnoe mor'e: Politiko-strategicheskii ocherk* [The Mediterranean Sea: A Political-Strategic Essay] (Moscow: Voennyi Vestnik, 1927).

11. Still the best concise narrative, hitting all the salient points, is Max Beloff, *The Foreign Policy of Soviet Russia, 1929–1941*, vol. 2: *1936–1941* (London: Oxford University Press, 1949) pp. 39–48. For the early years, see Roderic H. Davison, 'Turkish Diplomacy from Mudros to Lausanne', in Gordon A. Craig and Felix A. Gilbert (eds), *The Diplomats* (Princeton, NJ: Princeton University Press, 1973) pp. 172–209.

12. Elizabeth Barker, *Macedonia: Its Place in Balkan Power Politics* (London: Royal Institute of International Affairs, 1950).

13. An incipient bipolar system followed World War Two, but it was not until 1948 that Czechoslovakia fell under communist control. One cannot begin to speak of a *nuclear superpower* system until after 1949, the year the Soviet Union exploded an atomic device. The question of delivery capability then remains, but the belief systems of mass publics, concerning the fact of a Manichean bipolarity, are by then fixed.

14. Van Coufoudakis, 'The United States, the United Nations, and the Greek Question, 1946–1952', in John O. Iatrides (ed.), *Greece in the 1940s: A Nation in Crisis* (Hanover, NH: University Press of New England, 1981) pp. 278–86; quotation at p. 290.

15. C. M. Woodhouse, *The Struggle for Greece, 1941–1949* (Brooklyn Heights, NY: Beekman/Esanu, 1976) pp. 179–83; quotation at p. 160.

16. Anthony R. Deluca, *Great Power Rivalry at the Turkish Straits: The Montreux Conference and Convention of 1936* (Boulder, Col.: East European Monographs, 1981), provides a detailed and useful diplomatic history.

17. This provision was similar to that of the Treaty of Unkiar Skelessi (1833), reversed by the subsequent Straits Protocol (1841). 'When forced to choose, [Russia] has in the past placed the exclusion of noncontiguous powers over her own right of naval transit.' Michael McGwire, 'The Mediterranean and Soviet Naval Interests', in Michael McGwire (ed.), *Soviet Naval Developments: Capability and Context* (New York: Praeger, 1973) pp. 348–9.

18. Christos L. Rozakis and Petros N. Stagos, *The Turkish Straits* (Dordrecht: Martinus Nijhoff, 1987) pp. 41–2; see pp. 101–26 for an excellent explication of the Convention's provisions.

19. P. P. Moiseev, 'CCCP i Turtsiia v gody vtoroi mirovoi voiny (1939–1945)' [The USSR and Turkey during the Second World War (1939–1945)], in *SSSR i Turtsiia, 1917–1979* [The USSR and Turkey, 1917–1979], edited by E. M. Zhukov *et al.* (Moscow: Nauka, Glavnaia redaktsiia vostochnoi literatury, 1981) pp. 184–6. Along the same lines, see Zehra Onder, *Die türkische Aussenpolitik in Zweiten Weltkrieg* (Munich: R. Oldenbourg, 1977); and Selim Deringil, *Turkish Foreign Policy during the Second World War: An 'Active' Neutrality* (Cambridge: Cambridge University Press, 1989).

20. Rozakis and Stagos, *The Turkish Straits*, p. 46. On the Turkish application of the Montreux Convention during World War Two, see the somewhat legalistic but still informative monograph of Ernst Tennstedt,

Die türkischen Meerengen unter der Konvention von Montreux im Zweiten Weltkrieg (Frankfurt: Alfred Metzner, 1981) esp. pp. 11–22, 33–40, 49–73.
21. Alvin Z. Rubinstein, *Soviet Policy toward Turkey, Iran, and Afghanistan: The Dynamics of Influence* (New York: Praeger, 1972) pp. 9–17.
22. The full diplomatic correspondence, including the frequently omitted British and American notes, is in Ferenc A. Váli, *The Turkish Straits and NATO* (Stanford, Calif.: Hoover Institution Press, 1972) pp. 246–97.
23. S. Belinkov and I. Vasil'ev, *O turetskom 'neitralitete' vo vremia Vtoroi mirovoi voiny* [On Turkish 'Neutrality' during the Second World War] (Moscow: Gospolitizdat, 1952) is a typical anti-Turkish polemic of the late Stalin years. Petr P. Moiseev and Iuri N. Rozal'ev, *K istorii sovetsko-turetskikh otnoshenii* [Toward the History of Soviet–Turkish Relations] (Moscow: Gospolitizdat, 1958) reflects the more amicable tendency that reappeared under Khrushchev.
24. Keith Allen, 'The Black Sea Fleet and Mediterranean Naval Operations', in Bruce W. Watson and Susan M. Watson (eds), *The Soviet Navy: Strengths and Liabilities* (Boulder, Col.: Westview, 1986) p. 217; McGwire, 'The Mediterranean and Soviet Naval Interests', pp. 352–3; Bruce W. Watson, *Red Navy at Sea: Soviet Naval Operations on the High Seas, 1956–1980* (Boulder, Col.: Westview, 1982) pp. 80–1, 87.
25. The Soviet Union apparently continues to observe a stipulation of the Montreux Convention that submarines of Black Sea powers must transit the straits in daytime on the surface. Under the Convention, submarines of non-Black Sea powers may not transit the straits.
26. Allen, 'The Black Sea Fleet and Mediterranean Naval Operations', pp 219–21; McGwire, 'The Mediterranean and Soviet Naval Interests', pp 346–7. For a discussion of longstanding logistic problems and Soviet attempts to meet them, see Gordon McCormick, 'Soviet Strategic Aims and Capabilities in the Mediterranean: Part II', Adelphi Papers no. 229 (Spring 1988) pp. 32–48.
27. Rubinstein, *Soviet Policy toward Turkey, Iran, and Afghanistan*, pp 26–7, 35–6.
28. Events in the years 1973–5 made the incipient decline of the bipolar nuclear superpower system obvious: the emergence of the European Community as an independent actor in world politics, the embargo by the Organisation of Petroleum Exporting Countries, and the conclusion of the Conference on Security and Co-operation in Europe (Helsinki Accords). It is convenient to mark beginning of the decline with 1974 the year the United Nations approved the Declaration on the Economic Rights and Duties of States. This document confirmed the introduction of normative debate over the distribution of the world economic product onto the agenda of international relations.
29. The next two paragraphs draw heavily on Robert M. Cutler, 'Domestic and Foreign Influences on Policy Making: The Soviet Union in the 1974 Cyprus Conflict', *Soviet Studies*, vol. 37 (January 1985) no. 1, pp. 60–89.
30. They seem to have been correct. Watson, *Red Navy at Sea*, p. 124.
31. For an interesting discussion of co-operation in the energy sector, see Judith Gurney, 'Energy Needs in the Balkans: A Source of Conflict or

Co-operation?', *The World Today*, vol. 34 (February 1978) no. 2, pp. 44–51.
32. For an authoritative statement, see Bulent Ecevit, 'Turkey's Security Policies', *Survival*, vol. 20 (September/October 1978) no. 5, pp. 203–8.
33. However, for antecedents in the early 1970s, see Kemal H. Karpat, 'Turkish–Soviet Relations', in Kemal H. Karpat (ed.), *Turkey's Foreign Policy in Transition, 1950–1974* (Leiden: E. J. Brill, 1975) pp. 105–7.
34. Apparently significant was the monograph by E. I. Ukrazova, *Turtsiia: Problemy finansirovaniia ekonomicheskogo razvitiia* [Turkey: Problems of Financing Economic Development] (Moscow: Nauka, 1974). Compare Anne O. Krueger, *Foreign Trade Regimes and Economic Development: Turkey* (New York: Columbia University Press, 1974).
35. Text in Basil Dmytryshyn and Frederick Cox (trans. and eds), *The Soviet Union and the Middle East: A Documentary Record of Afghanistan, Iran and Turkey, 1917–1985* (Princeton, NJ: Kingston Press, 1987) pp. 671–8.
36. This probably violated the Montreux Convention, to which the appended definitions exclude carriers from the category of 'capital ships' allowed to transit. Allen, 'The Black Sea Fleet and Mediterranean Naval Operations', p. 218; see also Rozakis and Stagos, *The Turkish Straits*, pp. 132–3, who note that the *Kiev* violated the Convention's provision on allowable tonnage.
37. B. M. Potskhveriia, *Vneshniaia politika Turtsii v 60-kh – nachale 80-kh godov XX v.* [Turkey's Foreign Policy from the 1960s to the Early 1980s] (Moscow: Nauka, Glavnaia redaktsiia vostochnoi literatury, 1986) p. 170.
38. A. K. Sverchevskaia, 'K razvitiiu dvukhstoronnikh otnoshenii Turtsii s evropeiskimi sotsialisticheskimi stranami' [Toward the Development of Turkey's Bilateral Relations with European Socialist Countries], in *Politika i ekonomika sovremennoi Turtsii* [Politics and Economics of Contemporary Turkey], ed. V. I. Danilov, P. P. Moiseev and A. M. Shamsutdinov (Moscow: Nauka, Glavnaia redaktsiia vostochnoi literatury, 1977) pp. 100–8.
39. L. S. Voronkov, 'Vneshniaia politika malykh zapadnoevropeiskikh stran i aktual' nye problemy mezhdunarodnykh otnoshenii' [The Foreign Policy of the Small West European Countries and Current Problems of International Relations], in *Vneshniaia politika kapitalisticheskikh stran* [The Foreign Policy of Capitalist Countries], ed. S. L. Tikhvinskii *et al.* (Moscow: Mezhdunarodnye otnosheniia, 1983) p. 242, citing *Le Monde*, 2 September 1982.
40. See General Secretary Gorbachev's letter to Prime Minister Papandreou, published in *To Pondiki* (Athens), 3 July 1987, p. 12, translated in Foreign Broadcast Information Service, *Soviet Union: Daily Report* (hereafter FBIS-SOV), 9 July 1987, pp. H/1–3.
41. Shevardnadze quoted by Tass in English, 10 June 1988, cited in FBIS-SOV, 10 June 1988, p. 4. See further Soviet Foreign Ministry spokesman Gennadii Gerasimov, reported by Tass in English, 23 August 1988, cited in ibid., 24 August 1988, p. 4; and Soviet Ambassador to Cyprus Iurii Fokin, interviewed by *Kharavyi* (Nicosia), 23 April 1989, translated in ibid., 24 April 1989, pp. 37–9.

42. Soviet experience with the Federal Republic of Germany in the late 1960s is the basis for this reasoning. It appears in many Soviet writings about East–West relations in the 1970s. A notable example is Sh. K. Sanakoev and N. I. Kapchenko, *O teorii vneshnei politiki sotsializma* [On the Theory of Socialism's Foreign Policy] (Moscow: Mezhdunarondye otnosheniia, 1977) pp. 162, 169, 202, 210, and esp. pp. 216–19; also R. I. Kosolapov, 'Mezhdunarodnye otnosheniia i sotsial'nyi progress' [International Relations and Social Progress], *Voprosy filosofii* (May) 1974 no. 5, pp. 3–18, esp. pp. 6–8.
43. Semih Vaner, 'Le rapprochement turco-soviétique et l'affaire chypriote', *Revue française d'études politiques méditerranées* (June–July 1976) no. 18–19, pp. 63–74.
44. For a frank criticism of Denktash, see also V. Potapov, 'Kiprskii reportazh' [Cypriot Reportage], *Pravda* (13 May 1989) p. 4.
45. Other than Cyprus, the only Greek–Turkish dispute implicating the Soviet Union is the demarcation of territorial waters in the Aegean Sea. Since a bilateral Greek–Soviet arrangement has become unlikely, the Soviets have argued that territorial claims must not impede the sea-lanes there.
46. Woodhouse, *The Struggle for Greece*, pp. 288–9.
47. See the Tass report of Foreign Minister Shevardnadze's meeting with President Vassiliou of Cyprus, cited in FBIS-SOV (10 June 1988) pp. 4–5.

14 The EC Factor in the Greece–Turkey–Cyprus Triangle
CONSTANTINE STEPHANOU and CHARALAMBOS TSARDANIDES

Throughout the last several years the Greek–Turkish dispute and the Cyprus problem have remained very complex and troubled issues and have affected the stability of the whole eastern Mediterranean region, the foreign policy of Greece, Turkey and Cyprus, their domestic politics, the relations of the superpowers and the defence of western Europe. After 1974, in particular, the two dispute areas have raised important questions about the role and influence of the European Community in this strategically important part of the world.

This chapter deals with the policy of the European Community towards these questions. Its purpose is to analyse critically the Community's attitudes and the factors that have affected their evolution. The chapter is divided in two parts: the first focuses on the Greek–Turkish conflict, while the second treats separately EC policies towards the Cyprus problem.

EC ATTITUDES TOWARD GREEK–TURKISH DISPUTES PRIOR TO GREEK MEMBERSHIP OF THE COMMUNITY

The Association Agreements

The European Community inaugurated its external relations by signing on 9 June 1961 and on 12 September 1963 respectively Association Agreements with Greece and Turkey.[1] Although economic considerations, such as access to the markets and labour of the two countries, had influenced Community policies, political considerations had played a determining role.

Thus, with respect to the Greek Association, a UK author has pointed out that the importance of Greece within NATO made the US particularly anxious that the Greek economy be strengthened. Throughout the negotiations the State Department encouraged the Community in its chosen course of action. For its part the Community was pleased to take a chance to consolidate the US's general support for it in its rivalry with EFTA.²

Turkey's Association counter-balanced the Greek Association. It was in line with NATO's even-handed policy towards the two allies. Although Greece's economy was far more developed than Turkey's the two countries obtained the same political status in their relations with the European Community. The two agreements provided for financial aid to the two associates but differed in respect of reciprocity in trade.

Greece had to implement two time schedules leading to customs union with the Community: a twenty-two-year schedule for free movement of so-called sentive goods (that is those with local substitutes), and a twelve-year schedule applying to goods that did not fall in this category. Under these circumstances customs union between Greece and the Community would have been established by 1984. During the period of Greek dictatorship (1967–74), Greece continued performing its obligations although, for political reasons, the Community froze financial aid to Greece and halted negotiations on agricultural policy harmonisation.

In the case of the EC–Turkey agreement, the latter was allowed to develop its industry under existing tariff protection, during the first stage of the Association, referred to as preparatory period, which in practice lasted until 1 January 1973. The next stage, referred to a transitional period in the Association Agreement, was defined in the Additional Protocol to this agreement, signed on 23 November 1970.³ This protocol laid down a twelve-year and a twenty-two-year schedule for achieving customs union.

EC Attitudes towards Greek Membership

The Greek application for full membership of the European Community, submitted by the government of Constantine Karamanlis on 12 June 1975, presented a formidable challenge to the Community. As a result of the Turkish invasion of the Republic of Cyprus in the summer of 1974, Greek–Turkish antagonism had reached its highest point since the Lausanne Treaty of 1923. The member-states of the

Community had criticised Turkey but had refrained from imposing sanctions.[4] On the other hand they could not reject an application for membership coming from a European state which had been the first to be associated to the Community and had re-established democratic rule with strong support from European governments and public opinion.

Although the international climate was favourable to Greece, the Community wanted to consider the Greek application for accession without disrupting the close relationship with Turkey. Thus, following the meeting of the EC Council of Ministers on 24 June 1975, the EC Presidency assured the Turkish government that the Greek application would not affect Turkey's rights.[5]

In its opinion on the Greek application, delivered within seven months to the Council of Ministers,[6] the European Commission did not limit itself to an economic assessment of Greek membership but went on to recommend a pre-accession period that would allow, among other things, for the settlement of the Greek–Turkish disputes. The Commission was clearly afraid that the Community would become involved in these disputes if they were not settled prior to Greek accession. Seen from the Greek side, the Commission's position was tantamount to granting to a non-member state the right to veto the accession of another state to the Community. After effective Greek lobbying the Commission's opinion was overruled by the Council of Ministers at its meeting of 9 February 1976.[7]

Turkish efforts aimed at preventing the launching of accession negotiations continued in the course of 1976. Turkey declined to accept Community offers of compensation (financial aid and so on) and refused to participate in the Association Council scheduled for mid-July 1976. It has been maintained that the purpose of the dispatching the Turkish survey ship *Sismik 1* to explore the east Aegean continental shelf in mid-July 1976 was to provoke a crisis in Greek–Turkish relations and make visible to the Community the dangers involved in accepting Greece as a member-state:[8] this explanation looks plausible, although no evidence of such intentions on behalf of Turkey has yet been found.

The meeting of the Association Council of 20 December 1976 was to be the last before 1980: at this meeting, although the EC side offered new concessions, the Turkish government announced its decision to freeze the Association Agreement and, by implication, arrangements on political consultations.

Accession negotiations with Greece lasted two years (1976–8).

However, following the submission of the accession applications of Spain and Portugal in the course of 1977, the Community made an attempt to handle the three applications as a package, a measure that would have made Greek accession less provocative to Turkey.

Subsequent Turkish policies aimed at minimising the political disadvantages that would arise from Greek membership, namely Greek participation in EPC and the right of Greece to oppose eventual Turkish accession to the community. As far as EPC is concerned, during his visit to European capitals in May 1978, the Turkish prime minister, Bulent Ecevit, asked for equal political status of Turkey in EPC and received open support from the United Kingdom.[9] The Nine were unable to accept the Turkish demand because participation in EPC is reserved for member-states of the Community. An agreement was reached, however, in 1980, providing for regular meetings between the EPC, represented by the so-called *troika*, and Turkey, for the purpose of exchanging and assessing information.

With respect to Greece's right to oppose eventual Turkish accession to European Community, the Community, represented by the Italian presidency, gave formal assurances to Turkey at the meeting of the EC–Turkey Association Council held on 5 February 1980: the EC representative declared that the Community wished to strengthen relations with Turkey and that Greece's accession to the Community would not affect the development of these relations.[10] Commenting on the policies of his government, a Turkish author wrote that 'the possible Greek veto became an overplayed card, by itself it could not raise enough favorable sentiment for Turkey's early application'.[11]

Community gestures towards Turkey culminated with the decisions reached at the meeting of the Association Council on 30 June–1 July 1980,[12] providing among other things for the phased dismantlement of remaining Community duties on Turkish agricultural products, technical assistance to Turkey and social security rights for Turkish migrant workers. The Community did not get in return any commitment regarding the implementation of customs union by Turkey.

Although Turkish demands went much further than what Turkey finally obtained from the Community and EPC, it can clearly be seen that after the signing of the Greek accession agreement on 28 May 1979 and before the effective accession of Greece on 1 January 1981, the Community adopted a flexible attitude towards Turkey. This attitude reflected willingness to compensate Turkey for the acceptance of Greece as a full member of the Community, as well as fear of possible Greek obstruction after the accession became effective.

IMPACT OF GREEK MEMBERSHIP OF THE COMMUNITY ON THE DEVELOPMENT OF EC–TURKISH RELATIONS

Looking at EC–Turkish relations in retrospect, one cannot fail to notice that the basic, if not exclusive, cause of their deterioration during the first three years of Greek membership of the Community was the domestic political situation in Turkey. Following the Turkish generals' coup of 12 September 1980 a consensus emerged in the EC Council of Ministers to freeze the development of EC–Turkish relations, including approval of the Fourth Financial Protocol, which provided for the disbursement of 600 million ECUs between 1982 and 1987. The Community's position, arising from its concern about human rights, although questionable from a legal viewpoint was in line with the position it had adopted *vis-à-vis* the Greek colonels in 1967.

It is interesting to note, however, that these negative developments for Turkey did not spill over to her relations with EPC, and, one might add, to her bilateral relations with most member-states. Thus, pursuant to the agreement implementing the 1970 undertakings on political consultations, the first meeting between the EPC *troika* and Turkey took place at ambassadorial level on 19 December 1980. These meetings continued during the period of military rule, some of them taking place at ministerial level; they focused on Turkey's timetable for return to democracy.[13] With respect to bilateral relations, it is indicative that the Federal Republic of Germany increased its aid to Turkey while the Community, as such, had frozen the Fourth Financial Protocol.

The Community would have adopted a more friendly attitude towards Turkey after the elections held in this country on 6 November 1983, had there not been the unilateral declaration of an independent TRNC in the occupied area of the Republic of Cyprus and the subsequent recognition of the secession by Turkey. Strong condemnations were issued by EPC ministers on 16 November 1983 and 27 March 1984.[14] Moreover, in the first statement EPC called upon the international community not to recognise the secessionist state and in the second statement it called upon Turkey to cease such recognition and to exert its influence on the Turkish Cypriots.

Although the international community refrained from recognising the secessionist state, abiding by Resolutions 541 and 550 of the UN Security Council, Turkey exchanged ambassadors with the pseudo-state, allowed elections to be held in 1985 and arranged for the visits of Prime Minister Ozal and President Evren in the occupied area, in the course of 1986–7. As a result of this sequence of events, Greece and other EC member-state opposed moves aimed at reactivating the Association Agreement.

Early in 1986, the Dutch presidency, together with the United Kingdom, which would take over the presidency in the second semester of 1986, and the Commission, agreed on a plan to reconvene the Association Council and reactivate the Association. Greece insisted on mentioning the Cyprus problem in the joint declaration of the Twelve to be made in the first Association Council. This Council was finally held in Brussels on 16 September 1986 but, prior to it, the Community had been unable to adopt a common position and thus nothing concrete came out of this meeting. The meeting of the Association Council scheduled to take place on 25 April 1988 was postponed, at the last moment, when the Turkish delegation was informed that the Community had included in its joint declaration a sentence stating that, in its view, the Cyprus issue affected relations between the Community and Turkey.[15]

The Community position received subsequent support from the European Parliament with the adoption, on May 20, of a strongly worded resolution.[16] Moreover, upon the initiative of the Greek presidency, a reference to the Cyprus problem was included in the conclusions issued by the European Council at the end of the Rhodes summit held on 2–3 December 1988.[17]

The conclusion that can be drawn from the above examination of EC and EPC practice is that it has led to a substantial upgrading of the Cyprus issue and, by implication, has hindered the development of EC–Turkish relations. The question that should be asked is how the Community institutions would have acted without Greek participation. The general feeling, is that the condemnation of the Turkish–Cypriot secession may have been expressed by EPC without Greek participation, bearing in mind the parallel condemnations by the UN Security Council.

Moreover, it should be underlined that Greece did not implicate the Community in the Greek–Turkish conflict as such (Aegean Sea disputes). Greece presented her views about the conflict at the European Council meeting in The Hague, in June 1986 but, later on, during the Greek–Turkish crisis of March 1987, Greece did not ask for a crisis meeting of EPC, as she had the right to do under the Single European Act. Greece probably assumed that she would not receive substantial support from her partners who were also NATO allies of Turkey. Support came, however, from the European Parliament, which passed a resolution (with no opposition), calling on the two parties to refer the question of the delimitation of the Aegean Sea continental shelf to the ICJ,[18] a move that Turkey has been unwilling to make.

EPC intergovernmental bodies have never discussed the Greek-Turkish disputes up to now. The question can be raised as to whether Greece could obtain EPC support if it brought the Greek-Turkish disputes to the attention of these bodies. Although a case for Community solidarity clearly exists, all the member-states except Ireland are NATO allies of Turkey and would be quite reluctant to adopt pro-Greek declarations in the framework of EPC or instruct the *troika* representatives to raise the issues of the disputes in the meetings between EPC and Turkey.

Moreover, Community solidarity is a two-way process and Greece under the Papandreou government failed to demonstrate its solidarity on a number of issues involving vital interests of member-states. However, under present circumstances, a consensus could be reached by Greece and its EPC partners, whereby, in exchange for adjustments to its policies, Greece would obtain EPC support in procedural aspects of Greek-Turkish disputes, such as the one dealt with in the aforementioned resolution of the European Parliament.

THE IMPACT OF THE TURKISH APPLICATION FOR MEMBERSHIP

The Background: Non-implementation of the Association Agreement

In 1976 Turkey stopped fulfilling its obligations towards the Community under the Additional Protocol of 1970. Thus, when the government of Turgut Ozal applied for membership of the Community on 14 April 1987, the Turkish economy was far more protected than the Greek one had been when Greece had applied for membership in 1975. After submitting its application, Turkey resumed the process of trade liberalisation but domestic production remained highly protected and exports heavily subsidised.[19]

For its part, the Community had eliminated on 1 January 1973 tariffs on Turkish industrial goods and on 1 January 1987 tariffs on Turkish agricultural goods. However, the Community applied quotas on Turkish steel exports and had obtained 'voluntary' restraints on Turkish textile exports, thus hindering the flow of those goods in which Turkey had a comparative advantage. On the other hand, some of the benefits resulting from the elimination of Community tariffs on Turkish agricultural goods had been eroded by the preferences granted to other Mediterranean countries and beneficiaries of the Lomé Convention. Moreover, the Community still applied some quotas on Turkish agricultural exports, as well as the Common Agricultural Policy, entailing entry prices and countervailing duties on low-priced Turkish exports.

Problems also arose in areas other than trade. The Community, just before the deadline of 1 December 1986 applying to the free movement of workers, made an offer to Turkey which postponed the full implementation by the Community of Article 12 of the Association Agreement and Article 36 of the Additional Protocol. Last but not least, Turkey had not been receiving financial assistance from the Community since 1981.

In view of the above, there was cause for dissatisfaction on both sides. Turkey could, however, have extracted substantial concessions from the Community if the Association Agreement was reactivated. It would have been possible, for example, to implement Article 33 of the Additional Protocol of 1970, which provides for the adjustment of Turkey's agricultural policy to that of the Community, which is less than the goal of harmonisation set forth in the 1961 Association Agreement with Greece but easier to implement. Following such an adjustment, the Community would have had to abolish non-tariff obstacles, such as quotas, entry prices and countervailing duties on Turkish agricultural goods.

Community dissatisfaction with the evolution of the Association relationship with Turkey focuses on the non-implementation, by the latter, of its obligations in the field of trade. Turkey did not resume trade liberalisation, even after the substantial concessions made by the Community in 1980. In view of this unhappy experience, there is great uncertainty as to whether Turkey would be in a position to fulfil the obligations that would arise immediately upon its accession to the Community or in the course of a transitional period.[20]

Although the full implementation of customs union is not a prerequisite for accession to the Community, it has been pointed out by a Turkish author that 'Greece found a major advantage during the membership negotiations through her previous achievement in the field of the customs union within the association.'[21]

Turkish Objectives

By submitting its application for membership of the Community,

Turkey demonstrated its pro-Western and pro-European feelings and its determination to participate in the process of European integration. The status of an applicant country entails political advantages; it upgrades the political dimension in the EC–Turkey relationship and puts pressure on the Community to be more accommodating to Turkish demands.

Moreover, accession to the Community, whenever it takes place, will earn Turkey the political benefits resulting from participation in the EC and EPC decision-making processes. Thus, Turkey can be expected to make every effort to participate in the respective institutions. Second-best solutions, such as an observer status or a right to prior consultation would, it seems, satisfy Turkey if they applied for a limited period of time, such as a pre-accession period.

Last but not least, Turkey could negotiate the immediate or phased dismantlement of non-tariff barriers to its exports and, if she had to accept a pre-accession period, she would claim and probably obtain substantial financial aid from the Community, to compensate for the non-implementation of the freedom of movement of workers.

The main arguments that Turkey is likely to use in order to launch and keep on track, the negotiation process are political in nature. As early as 1983 an influential Turkish author wrote that 'Turkey cannot remain indefinitely a security asset for Europe, without being integrated in other European structures: These include also consultations for political decision making which is inseparable from security.'[22] This position can be considered as a warning to those who would take for granted Turkey's attachment to the West. Another argument relates to the way Turkish membership of the Community may affect domestic stability in Turkey and, by implication, stability in Europe.[23]

EC Responses

The Turkish application has been transmitted to the Commission, which is expected to deliver an opinion in accordance with Article 237 of the Rome Treaty, before the European Parliament and the Council of Ministers decide on whether to launch the negotiation process.

At a preliminary stage the Commission will have to assess the implications of Turkish membership on the Community.[24] In its final opinion, the Commission may recommend to the member-states the acceptance of a long pre-accession period allowing for the gradual opening of the Turkish economy to international competition and for the achievement of some degree of convergence with the Community. Such a period would also give time to the Community to reform its financial system in a way that would enable it to respond to the challenges resulting from Turkish accession.

The preliminary opinion of the Commission on the Turkish accession, delivered in December 1988, was influenced by political factors. It was on the basis of Turkey's contribution to Western security that the Commission refrained from rejecting Turkish membership. However, Greek–Turkish disputes and the continuing occupation by Turkey of northern Cyprus emerged as serious obstacles to Turkish membership. The Commission pointed out that the Greek–Turkish conflict as well as the Cyprus problem could prove negative factors for Turkey's admission and reaffirmed the Community's support of the unity, independence, sovereignty and territorial integrity of the Republic of Cyprus. It is true that in the case of the Greek application the same recommendation made by the Commission was rejected by the member-states. However, if Turkey became a full member before the settlement of its disputes with Greece, the conflict between the two countries would be transferred to a Community context, affecting EC and EPC decision-making to a point that cannot be clearly foreseen.

Although the idea of a pre-accession period appears to solve many problems, the question remains as to whether such a period should be open-ended or not. Turkey is likely to insist on a definite date of accession. Alternatively, a mechanism allowing for guaranteed progression from one stage to the other and finally to full membership could be devised. Another question that has to be dealt with is what rights would Turkey have during the pre-accession period. A special status would have to be devised in the accession treaty.

However, it is by no means certain that a pre-accession period will make Turkish accession acceptable to the member-states of the European Community. The Turkish economy and society are so far behind Community standards and averages that even if Turkey continued its present rates of economic growth, salaries and living standards would remain very low in the foreseeable future, due to high population growth. Thus, accession to the Community would, under any present estimation, destabilise labour markets and create serious social and political problems for some member-states of the Community. These member-states would be relieved if it was Greece and not themselves that was seen to be opposing Turkish accession.

As things stand today, Greece is not opposing Turkey's accession against the will of the other member-states. Although some opinion-leaders in Greece are opposed to Turkish accession and others are tempted to ask for far-reaching concessions from Turkey, most policy-makers would consider the Turkish demand as an opportunity to achieve a breakthrough in Greek–Turkish relations: under present circumstances such a breakthrough depends on achieving a compromise solution in the negotiations between the two communities in Cyprus and referring the Aegean Sea continental shelf dispute to the ICJ.

Some sections of government and élites in Turkey are opposed, on principle, to making concessions on the above issues, whatever the cost for Turkish accession. It has been maintained, for example, that Turkish military presence in Cyprus deters Greece from extending its territorial sea to twelve miles.[25] Others appear to doubt the prospects of Turkish accession and believe that even if concessions were made to the Greek side, the other member-states would delay, *ad infinitum*, accession negotiations; moreover, other gains such as those that could result from limited participation in EC and EPC institutions and large financial transfers to Turkey during a pre-accession period may be considered not worth any concessions to Greece.

If the Turkish government believed that it could overcome the reservations to Turkish accession by member-states other than Greece and/or obtain substantial political and economic gains by embarking on accession negotiations, it could decide that some concessions are worth making in order to overcome Greek objections.

THE IMPACT OF THE EUROPEAN COMMUNITY ON GREEK–TURKISH ECONOMIC RELATIONS

Greek Participation in the EC–Turkey Association Agreement

Greece had refused to sign the protocol extending to its relations with Turkey, the EC/Turkey Association Agreement. Greece argued that Turkey was discriminating against Greek nationals domiciled in Istanbul by keeping in force secret decree no. 3801, issued in 1964, which sequestrated Greek properties; this decree had to be abolished so that, upon entry into force of the protocol, Greek nationals would be treated like the citizens of the other Community countries.

Following the Davos and Brussels meetings of the Greek and Turkish prime ministers, Turkey repealed the decree and Greece signed the protocol on 22 March 1988.

The above protocol can be regarded as an important contribution of the Community to the development of Greek–Turkish economic relations. Under this protocol the two sides are committed to granting the mutual preferential treatment provided for in the Association Agreement; in practice this entails that Turkish exports to Greece will be admitted free of any duties, whereas Greek exports to Turkey will be subjected to the special rates applicable to products originating from the Community, which have remained very high. Thus, the signing of the protocol implied much larger concessions on the Greek side.

Moreover, Greece, worried about the fact that discrimination continued after the abolition of the secret decree of 1964, discovered that the Turkish administration and justice were violating Article 58 of the additional protocol of 1970, by implementing secret decree no. 3706, issued also in 1964, restricting the rights of Greek nationals to acquire property by any means, including inheritance, in certain areas of Turkey, including Istanbul.[26] Greece felt that it had been deceived by Turkey, which only added to the difficulties encountered in the development of EC–Turkish relations.

Future Prospects

The EC/Turkey Association Agreement will remain for some time the framework of EC–Turkish relations. This agreement aims at gradually achieving full economic integration between the Community and Turkey and, therefore, between Greece and Turkey. Trade between the two countries was very limited under the pre-existing restrictive conditions[27] and a great potential lies ahead. What worries the Greek side, however, is that Turkey now ranks in third place among Greece's most important competitors in foreign markets[28] and further Community concessions to Turkey are likely to harm Greek exports.

The problem of the free movement of Turkish labour faced by the Community as such is also faced by Greece. In its proposals of November 1986 concerning this freedom, the Community accepted Greece's contention that it should be exempted from the liberalisation process for reasons of national security.

The development of Greek–Turkish economic relations depends, to a large extent, on the framework that will govern EC–Turkish relations in the future. The implementation of customs union between the Community and Turkey, entailing free trade between Greece and Turkey, can create some degree of interdependence between the two economies and, by implication, between the two countries; moreover, some bilateral issues, such as investment protection, could be solved by means of an EC–Turkey agreement. Thus, the development of EC–Turkish relations can have important implications for Greek–Turkish relations.

THE COMMUNITY'S ATTITUDE TOWARDS THE CYPRUS CONFLICT

The events in Cyprus in the summer of 1974 and the changes that followed in the wake of the crisis raised important questions about the role and influence of the European Community in this strategically sensitive area. However, the Community's ability, firstly to manage the crisis, and secondly to play an energetic and influential role in bringing the parties together, has proven to be limited. Once the Nine had decided to react, a diminishing scale of effectiveness became discernible.

The activity of the Community regarding the Cyprus question can be divided into three phases.

The phase of intensive intervention. This coincided with the period of the Cyprus crisis of July–August 1974. During this phase the Community tried to assume the role of an effective crisis-manager. In the name of the then nine member-states, France, then holding the presidency, took immediate diplomatic action both in Athens and Ankara to put an end to the hostilities.

The phase of reserved mediation: February 1975–November 1976. The duty of the Community during this phase, as perceived by the nine member-states, was to encourage negotiations between the Greek and Turkish Cypriots by contributing to the creation of conditions favourable to the pursuit of a dialogue. The Community, therefore, avoided presenting any concrete plan for mediation, thus giving the opportunity to the United States to resume a mediative role in the Cyprus dispute.[29]

The phase of detached concern from November 1977 on. During this phase the Community, following discussions within the EPC framework, tried to undertake an advisory role. The EPC's group of experts on Cyprus continued analysing the situation until its dissolution in 1980, attempting to work out proposals for the operational procedure of the Nine. However, the Community was of the opinion that the only means of arriving at a just and lasting solution to the problem in Cyprus was through direct negotiations between the parties concerned. Therefore, the Community aimed only to support the efforts of the UN Secretary-General who was working for a successful outcome of the intercommunal talks between Greek and Turkish Cypriots with the main objective of preventing any worsening of the situation.

The Cyprus problem was not discussed in the framework of the EPC during the period 1980-3, despite pressure by the Greek government. Meanwhile, EC-Cyprus relations entered a more complicated phase when the Turkish-Cypriot leader, R. Denktash, went ahead with the creation of the TRNC on 15 November 1983. The TRNC, recognised only by Turkey, was regarded by the EC member-states as a dangerous development impeding the solution of the Cyprus problem.[30] Since then, in the context of the EPC, the member-states have continued to condemn the unilateral Turkish and Turkish-Cypriot actions such as the exchange of ambassadors between Turkey and the pseudo-state, the so-called 'presidential' and 'legislative' elections held in the occupied areas of the island in 1985, and the visits of the Turkish prime minister and president in the course of 1986-7. But essentially the Community did not change its overall approach to the Cyprus problem, continuing to pledge support for the mediation efforts of the UN Secretary-General. This was the case on 2 January 1985 when the Community called on the Greek-Cypriot and Turkish-Cypriot leaders to resume reunification talks, following the breakdown, in New York, of the summit meeting between President Kyprianou and the Turkish-Cypriot leader Denktash, as well as on 3 December 1988, when the European Council expressed its satisfaction at the resumption of the intercommunal dialogue.

A question that needs answering is why the Community proved incapable of developing any effective operational position towards the Cyprus dispute and failed to advance its policies beyond declarations to positive action.

FACTORS AFFECTING THE COMMUNITY'S POLICY TOWARDS THE CYPRUS CONFLICT

It appears that the policy of the European Community was, and still is, dependent on the following three interrelated factors:

1. The extent to which a community of interests and attitudes existed between the member states.
2. The extent to which the common institutions and instruments of the Community were in a position to implement successfully EPC decisions and resolutions on the Cyprus problem.
3. The extent to which the disputants were willing to accept any mediation effort pursued by the Community.

The Member-states and their Attitudes towards the Cyprus Crisis

The views of the member-states ranged from the French inclination to pressure the Turks to the German preference for a more 'delicate' approach. Thus since September 1974, the Community's Cyprus policy has appeared to lack a certain degree of permanence and continuity, and in some instances even a common position. In 1976, for example, the Nine did not vote unanimously to adopt a UN General Assembly resolution concerning Cyprus. Some countries promoted their own national policies, and the optimism that had built up over the Community's handling of the crisis began to evaporate. The UK government was unwilling to intervene in the dispute more actively, without any advance support from the United States. For the United Kingdom therefore the main use of EPC was to provide an appearance of activity without making a substantial commitment enabling it to adopt a 'low profile policy'. France, after the second phase of the Turkish invasion, indicated its sympathies for Greece and openly condemned the unilateral resumption of military operations in Cyprus by Turkey.[31]

The attitudes of the other member-states towards the Cyprus conflict differed from that of France, with the exception of Ireland. They, particularly West Germany, adopted a more or less neutral position. The Federal Government found itself in the difficult position of maintaining a balance between its traditional friendship with Turkey and support for the new democratic regime in Greece. Thus, the German government, more anxious than France about the weakness of NATO's south-eastern flank, which was threatened by the dispute over Cyprus, encouraged both Athens and Ankara to hold discussions. However, Germany was unable to promote an effective EC initiative.[32]

The Effectiveness of the Community's Institutions and Instruments

The Community's degree of cohesion is the result of the member-states' will to act together, and of the institutions and instruments available to them. Up to 15 July 1974, the effectiveness of the EPC institutions had undergone only 'cold' testing. The Cyprus crisis of July–August 1974 meant that the Nine were, for the first time, seriously confronting the question of using their foreign policy consultation machinery for 'hot' crisis management. On the other hand, any attempt to explain the relative ineffectiveness of the EPC action during the Cyprus crisis must recognise that the Community was a peripheral actor in the crisis in which Turkey, Greece and Cyprus were the leading characters. It is clear that peripheral actors face several difficulties in intervening efficaciously even after the confrontation phase of a crisis becomes full-blown.

Another more serious difficulty was the fact that the Community lacked the necessary instruments to implement its decisions and make its advice heard. One could, of course, assert that there were numerous instruments available to individual member-states which could have been employed on behalf of the EPC. For example, there was the UK military presence on Cyprus and its legal obligation deriving from the Treaty of Guarantee of 1960. There was West Germany's special political and economic relationship with Turkey, and France's influence on Greece. But these national 'means' could not be converted successfully into a collective instrument as the above member-states were reluctant to use them. Another series of instruments, more suited to collective action, were those in the hands of the Community as a whole, such as EC economic relations with Greece, Turkey and particularly with Cyprus.

As far as the EC–Cyprus Association Agreement is concerned, the Community embraced the position that no real progress on the Agreement should be expected until the Cyprus dispute was approaching a settlement.[33] The Community adopted the policy that trade, and other arrangements flowing from it, should apply to the entire population of the island.

The EPC reports on the Cyprus issue influenced considerably both the attitudes of the member-states and the attitudes of the EC Commission. Accordingly, as the rounds of the intercommunal talks succeeded each other without any positive and encouraging results, the Community was determined not to proceed with the development of the Association Agreement despite the insistence of the Cypriot government.[34] As a consequence, it was only on 25 November 1985 that the Commission was given a mandate to negotiate the terms of transition to the second phase of the Association Agreement. The new protocol was signed on 19 October 1987. It provides for the establishment – in two stages lasting a total of fifteen years – of a customs union between the Community and Cyprus.[35]

The Community as a Mediator Acceptable to the Disputants

The Community's attempt to play a mediating role in Cyprus also depended on the willingness of the disputants to accept the Community as an 'honest broker'. From the beginning, Turkey took a negative attitude towards the Community's attempts to intervene in the conflict. On the contrary, Greece and Cyprus were eager to seek the EC mediation. The fact, however, that the Community's initiatives had not taken a concrete form, remaining only in the stage of exploring possibilities, disappointed the Cypriot government which sought the intervention of the United States: the latter stepped into the diplomatic arena from the beginning of 1977.

On the other hand, the Greek application for full membership of the Community, submitted in June 1975, not suprisingly had already neutralised any Community attempt at mediation. The Community had to view the Greek application for membership as a potential threat to the political balance between Athens and Ankara.

Since 1981 five new factors have influenced EC policy towards the Cyprus problem. They forged an attitude militating against any real active involvement of the Community in the Cyprus question.

First, Greece's accession to the Community. Greece saw its membership as a means to strengthen its security and as a deterrent against Turkey's further aggression. Greece's participation in the EPC framework intensified the Greek–Turkish problem in the view of EC members who did not want to be involved in the disputes over Cyprus and the Aegean.

The second factor was the EC policy of ignoring disputes between member-states concerning national matters. In the past, Community institutions have kept studiously aloof from political involvement in international disputes between members, such as those between the UK and Spain over Gibraltar, the UK and the Ireland over Ulster, and Spain and France over the Basque country. Turkey, of course is not a member-state but it is a full member of the NATO alliance. Moreover, the need to shore up Turkey's secular political élite against Islamic fundamentalism is a concern for those EC member-states who would bind the country to the West for security reasons.[36]

Third, developments in Iran, Afghanistan and the Iran–Iraq war, as well as the general trend towards increased political destabilisation in the Middle East, had left Turkey, at least until 1988, as the only country in the northern Middle East with a contractual arrangement with the West.[37]

Fourth, since 1981, Greek foreign policy had adopted, at least until 1985, positions contrary to those of the majority of EC member-states on crucial matters such as East–West relations, the Middle East crisis, and North–South relations. This differentiation was due partly to the Cyprus problem. 'In trying to obtain the backing of Third World countries, Greece had to align itself in many instances with them, often resulting in the disruption of Community cohesion particularly in the UN General Assembly.'[38] However, the Greek government's choice to differ from its Western allies has given some EC member-states an excuse to display unwillingness to support EC involvement in the Cyprus dispute.

Fifth, the support of the role of the UN Secretary-General and his efforts towards the resumption of the intercommunal talks since September 1988 has taken off the pressure felt by the Community to play an active role.

The Community may eventually revise its policy for several reasons. Some member-states are very interested in promoting a solution to the Cyprus problem. Four EC countries – the United Kingdom, France, Italy and West Germany – have already intervened, although outside the EPC framework, in order to avert a new deadlock of the intercommunal talks.

Furthermore, the Community's relationship with Cyprus has entered a new phase since the signing of a new protocol leading to a customs union with the island. The new protocol is undoubtedly of considerable political significance, because it would grant the Community a great opportunity to play a more positive and active role in the resolution of the Cyprus problem. For instance, as the Coste-Floret report points out, the Community could propose to the

Turkish-Cypriot side its direct participation in the EC–Cyprus Financial Protocol, which covers financial and technical co-operation, on the condition that the Turkish-Cypriot leadership would accept the eventual withdrawal of the Turkish occupying forces.[39] Also, it would seem quite reasonable for the Community to take a keen interest in the future constitutional settlement in Cyprus for two main reasons. (1) A confederation of two states or a loose federation unable to enforce the customs union would be unacceptable to the Community; moreover, the future state would not be in a position to become a member of the Community if it were to maintain restrictions on the freedom of movement and establishment of its citizens or the freedom to acquire property anywhere in the territory of the Republic. (2) In the case that a future federal Cyprus becomes a full member of the Community, the federation should have exclusive or, at least, concurrent jurisdiction in all areas affected or likely to be affected by Community legislation.[40] In view of Cyprus's wish to join the Community the definition on these areas is of the utmost importance.

Moreover, it is not certain that the UN Secretary-General's efforts for a successful outcome of the present intercommunal talks will succeed.

In addition, the Community is addressing the Turkish application for full membership, and thus the member-states finally may have some leverage to force Turkey to make substantial concessions on the Cyprus question and make Community policy towards Turkey dependent upon progress on the Cyprus issue. The Community adopted this position and linked the Cyprus problem with the development of EC–Turkish relationship by telling Turkey that the situation in Cyprus and human rights in Turkey itself were directly affecting Ankara's relations with the Community. As a consequence Turkey, as already discussed, refused to take part in a scheduled meeting of the EC/Turkey Association Council planned to take place in Luxembourg on 26 April 1988.

The European Parliament adopted, on 20 May 1988, a resolution calling upon EPC 'to put pressure on the Turkish government, which is linked to the EC by an association agreement and is an applicant for membership, to draw up a precise timetable for the withdrawal of its troops . . . and that of the Turkish settlers'.[41]

Finally, the European Council, at its meeting in Rhodes on 2–3 December 1988, reaffirmed the previous declarations of EPC on the Cyprus problem and added that 'while expressing its satisfaction at the resumption of the intercommunal dialogue, the European Council expressed the wish that this dialogue should progress and lead rapidly to a solution of the problem'.[42] The same position was reaffirmed by the European Council at its meeting in Strasbourg in December 1989.

Undoubtedly, this development was due more to Greek insistence and less to a rapid shift of the EC position. Greece is unlikely, as a Turkish-Cypriot observer has noticed, 'to accept Turkish membership until the Cyprus issue is resolved to its satisfaction, not to mention the question of the Aegean'.[43]

CONCLUDING REMARKS

Greek accession to the European Community has altered fundamentally the Greek–Turkish balance achieved under the association relationships. Greece, as a member of the Community, has become one of the key factors in the development of EC–Turkish relations.

Greece is not opposed, in principle, to the strengthening of EC ties with Turkey. It is in Greece's interest to have a moderate, European-oriented neighbour to the east and a potentially important market for its goods and services. Greece does not expect from Turkey anything more than other member-states of the Community would expect, that is implementation of international law principles and, in the context of the Cyprus conflict, of basic human rights embodied in international and European covenants and treaties.

The fact that Greece insists on these matters more than other member-states do results from its legal position as a guarantor of the Greek-Cypriot community. It is clear, however, that European public opinion as expressed in the European Parliament also cares about the Cyprus problem, as it cares about human rights in Turkey.

The Community's largely passive role in the Cyprus conflict as well as in the later Iran, Afghanistan and Falkland Islands crises demonstrates that its capacity to manage such local disputes is still limited. The Community's efforts have been primarily directed only towards damage limitation and the containment of such conflicts.

The Community cannot mediate in the Greek–Turkish conflict as such, since one party to the conflict is a member whereas the other is not. Theoretically, the Community could mediate only between Turkey and Cyprus, both non-members, or otherwise assist them in a settlement of their conflict. However, it would be wrong to assume that the Community, although it is increasingly catching up in Cypriot affairs, is ready to offer its good offices for mediation or is keen to replace the UN Secretary-General in his efforts to bring the opposing parties together. The Community has never proposed a concrete scheme for a peaceful solution of the Cyprus conflict and it had neither the ability nor the will to implement a policy of forcing the two conflicting parties to make more substantial concessions in the intercommunal talks. On the other hand, the Community has never been asked to mediate.

At any rate, if Cyprus requested EC mediation or assistance, it is unlikely that Turkey would give its consent, because of Greek membership of the Community. It should be possible, however, for individual member-states, interested in the development of Turkey's relations with the Community and in promoting the latter's role in the world, to contribute to the settlement of the Cyprus conflict.

NOTES

1. The agreement with Greece was published in the *Official Journal of the European Community* (hereafter abbreviated to *OJ*) (18 February 1963) pp. 293 ff. The agreement with Turkey was published in *OJ* (29 December 1964) pp. 3685 ff.
2. S. Hening, *External Relations of the European Community* (London: Chatham House, PEP, 1971) pp. 72–3.
3. The protocol was published in the *OJ* L293 (29 December 1972) p. 3.
4. It should be remembered that the US Congress had imposed an arms embargo to Turkey from 1975 to 1978.
5. *EC Bulletin*, 6/75, point 1209.
6. *EC Bulletin*, Supplement 2/76. N. Kohlase, 'The Greco-Turkish Conflict from a European Community Perspective', *World Today* (April 1981) p. 131, writes with regret that the Commission's opinion was 'the most disappointing example of attempted mediation'.
7. See J. Siotis, 'La Grèce sur le chemin de l'Europe', in *Melanoes Fernand Dehousse*, vol. 2 (Paris: Fernand Nathan; Brussels: Editions Labor, 1979) p. 81.
8. P. Tsakaloyannis, 'The European Community and the Greek–Turkish Disputes', *Journal of Common Market Studies*, vol. XIX (September 1989) no. 1, p. 47; S. Vaner, 'La Turquie, la Communauté Européenne elargie et la Mediterranée', in J. Touscoz (ed.), *La CEE elargie et la Mediterranée: quelle cooperation?* (Paris: PUF, coll. Travaux et recherches de l'Institut du droit de la paix et du devéloppement de l'Université de Nice, 1982) pp. 64–9.
9. See article by G. de Ionquières, 'Britain Calls for Closer EEC Links with

Turkey', *Financial Times* (22 May 1978); also M. Modiano, 'Greeks Annoyed Over British Recommendation', *The Times*, 23 May 1978.
10. *EC Bulletin*, 2/80, points 1.3.1.–1.3.5.
11. M. Hic, 'The Evolution of Turkish–EEC Relations and Prospects of an Early Application for Membership', *Foreign Policy* (Ankara), vol. IX (1982) p. 58.
12. *EC Bulletin*, 6/1980, points 1.4.1.–1.4.7.
13. See R. Bourguigno, *EPC–Turkey Relationship: Balance and Options* (Bonn: Institut für Europaische Politik) pp. 23–26.
14. See below, p. 220.
15. See the extensive coverage of this meeting in *Le Monde* (27 April 1988).
16. See below, p. 225.
17. Ibid.
18. The resolution was published in the *OJ*, C125 (11 May 1987) p. 136.
19. See the report drawn by Carlos Piments, European Parliament, Session Document A2-0350/89, at pp. 11–16.
20. See J. Bourrinet, 'La CEE confrontée a l'adhesion de la Turquie', *Revue du Marché Commun* (February 1989) no. 324, pp. 84–6.
21. J. Kamhi, *Turkey's Relations with the EEC* (unpublished paper, October 1986) p. 8.
22. S. Musto, *The Thirteenth Member of the European Community? Economic Problems and the Prospects of Possible Turkish Accession to the EC*, paper presented to the International Workshop of the Friedrich Naumann Stiftung on the Relations of the Eastern Mediterranean Bordering Countries to the EC after the Southern Enlargement and in view of the Turkish Accession Application, Brussels (24–7 May 1988) p. 16.
23. S. Tashan, 'Turkey and the European Community: A Political Appraisal', *Dis Politika*, vol. X (1983) nos. 1–2, p. 25.
24. The opinion of the Commission was published in Greek in the *Morning News* (Nicosia) on 21 December 1989.
25. See article by M. A. Birand in the Ankara daily *Millyet* of 4 July 1986 and extracts in the Athens weekly *To Vema* of 6 July 1986.
26. The Turkish government decided to repeal the decree before the meeting of the Greek and Turkish prime ministers scheduled for 30 May 1989, after the NATO summit in Brussels. Moreover, decision no. 89-32/1 of the Turkish Ministry of finance issued in August 1989 allows for the repatriation of the proceeds of investments, irrespective of the nationality of the investor.
27. Until the signing of the protocol, Greek–Turkish trade was governed by Regulation (EEC) no. 3555/80 of the Council. In 1986 the share of Greek exports to Turkey in the total exports of Greece was 1.5 per cent and the share of Turkish exports to Greece in the total exports of Turkey was 1 per cent.
28. According to calculations by the Centre of Export Research and Studies (KEEM) for the year 1986.
29. For this phase, see C. Tsardanidis, 'The European Community and the Cyprus Crisis of 1974', *Revue Héllénique de Droit International* (1984) pp. 185–207; and R. Rummel, *Zum Problem der Abstimmung in der*

Westlichen aus den Zypern Konflikt (Ebenhausen: Stiftung Wissenschaft und Politik, 1979).
30. The Community issued two condemnations: one on 16 November 1983 and another on 27 March 1984. In the first statement, the Community called upon the international community not to recognise the secessionist state and in the second statement it called upon Turkey to cease such recognition and to exert its influence on the Turkish Cypriots to revoke their unilateral declaration of independence.
31. C. Tsardanidis, 'The European Community and the Cyprus Problem since 1974', *Journal of Political and Military Sociology*, vol. 16 (Fall 1988) no. 2, p. 160.
32. R. Rummel, 'Bonn and European Political Cooperation', in W. Kohl and G. Basevi (eds), *West Germany: A European and Global Power* (Lexington, Ky: Lexington Books, 1980) pp. 79–80.
33. H. Gsanger, 'The EEC and Cyprus and Turkey', in P. Seers and C. Vaitsos (eds), *Integration and Unequal Development: The Experience of the EEC* (London: Macmillan, 1980) p. 288.
34. Only when there were hopes of a settlement during the first months of 1977, following the meeting between President Makarios and the Turkish-Cypriot leader R. Denktash, did the Community seriously examine the Cypriot demands and open negotiations for the definition of the second stage. See C. Tsardanidis, 'The EC–Cyprus Association Agreement: 1973–1983. A Decade of a Troubled Relationship', *Journal of Common Market Studies*, vol. 21 (June 1984) no. 4, p. 358. The protocol was published in *OJ*, L 393 (31 December 1987).
35. For an analysis of the EC–Cyprus Association Agreement evolution for the period 1972–87, see C. Tsardanidis, *The Politics of the EEC–Cyprus Association Agreement: 1972–1987* (Nicosia: Social Research Centre, 1988). For the most recent developments, see A. Antoniou, 'L'union douanière entre la CEE et Chypre: Une nouvelle experience en vue', *Revue du Marché Commun* (November 1987) no. 311, pp. 607–13.
36. R. McDonald, 'The Problem of Cyprus', Adelphi Papers no. 234 (Winter 1988/9) p. 71.
37. M. Cremasco, 'The Strategic Importance of Relations between Turkey and the European Community', *International Spectator* (January–June 1983) pp. 47–61.
38. T. Christodoulides, 'Greece and European Political Cooperation: The Intractable Partner', in N. Stavrou (ed.), *Greece under Socialism* (New Rochelle, NY: A. Caratzas, 1988) p. 283; and J. Loulis, *Greece under Papandreou: NATO's Ambivalent Partner* (London: Institute for European Defence and Strategic Studies, 1985) pp. 31–2.
39. European Parliament, Working Documents 1987–8 (26 February 1988) Doc. A2-317/87 by A. Coste-Floret, p. 23.
40. In a federally organised state, the implementation of Community directives, which have to be transformed into domestic law within a specified period of time, depends on the distribution of powers between the federation and its entities. See C. Stefanou, *Cyprus: Towards a Working Economic Union*, paper prepared for the Canadian Institute for

International Peace and Security, Fourth Workshop on Cyprus (29–30 June 1989).
41. The resolution was published in *OJ*, C 167/440 (27 June 1988).
42. *EC Bulletin*, 12/88, point 1.1.17.
43. Z. Necatigil, *The Cyprus Question and the Turkish Position in International Law* (Oxford: Oxford University Press, 1989) p. 301.

Appendices

APPENDIX 1 *Chronology of major events related to Greek–Turkish relations and the Cyprus question (July 1947–June 1988)*

Year	Government in Greece	Foreign-policy related event	Government in Turkey
1974	21 Apr. 1967–23 Jul. 1974 Military dictatorship 24 Jul.–21 Nov. Government of national unity under Karamanlis	15 Jul. President Makarios overthrown in coup led by Greek military regime 20 Jul. Turkey invades Cyprus 22 Jul. UN reports Cyprus ceasefire 16 Aug. Turkish forces reach 'Attila line' in Cyprus, proposed by Turkey as dividing line in 1965* 17 Aug. Greece withdraws from military structure of NATO protesting the alliance's failure to take any action in Cyprus 17 Aug. Karamanlis rejects US Secretary of State Kissinger's invitation to visit US to discuss the Cyprus crisis with President Ford	Social-Democratic and National Salvation parties had formed a coalition government under Ecevit since 20 Jan. 1974

(continued on page 232)

Appendix 1 continued

Year	Government in Greece	Foreign-policy related event	Government in Turkey
		19 Aug. US Secretary of Defense Schlesinger warns Turkey against using her military superiority to drive the new Greek government into a corner *19 Aug.* US ambassador to Cyprus R. P. Davies is shot dead during Greek-Cypriot demonstration at the American Embassy in Nicosia *22 Aug.* Turkish Cypriots declare 'autonomous administration' *23 Aug.* Soviet Union proposes international conference of the fifteen members of the UN Security Council as well as Cyprus, Greece and Turkey to deal with the situation in Cyprus *28 Aug.* Turkish foreign minister rejects Soviet proposal for an international conference on Cyprus	

18 Sep.
Ecevit government resigns

18 Sep.
US senators sponsor amendment urging President Ford to cut off military aid to Turkey for illegal use of US-supplied military equipment in the Cyprus invasion

1 Nov.
UN General Assembly adopts unanimously Resolution 3212 calling on Greek and Turkish Cypriots to negotiate a mutually acceptable political settlement as well as for the withdrawal of all foreign troops

11 Nov.
Interim coalition government under Irmak; fails to gain vote of confidence but remains in office in a caretaker capacity

21 Nov.
Conservative/moderate New Democracy Party under Karamanlis wins general election with 54.5% of the vote

(continued on page 234)

Appendix 1 *continued*

Year	Government in Greece	Foreign-policy related event	Government in Turkey
1975		*27 Jan.* Karamanlis, with the support of opposition parties, proposes that the continental shelf issue be referred to the ICJ *29 Jan.* Turkey accepts proposal on the condition that it will proceed with oil exploration activities scheduled for next month *5 Feb.* US Congress imposes arms embargo on Turkey *13 Feb.* Turkish Cypriots declare 'Turkish Federated State of Cyprus' *6 Apr.* Demirel government reverses its earlier ICJ proposal and suggests settlement of continental shelf issue through bilateral negotiations *31 May* Karamanlis and Demirel meet in Brussels; agree to resolve their conflicts peacefully; Turkish government concedes that dispute over continental shelf be submitted to ICJ and Cyprus issue settled through intercommunal talks that had already started in Vienna (28 Apr.) under UN auspices	*31 Mar.* Coalition government of the Nationalist Front (four parties: Justice, National Salvation, Republican Alliance, Nationalist Action) under Demirel

25 Jul.
Turkey shuts down US bases in retaliation for embargo
29 Jul.
Turkey announces the establishment of Fourth ('Aegean') Army, a force not assigned to NATO stationed along the western coast of Anatolia facing the Greek islands
24 Sep.
Soviet Foreign Minister Gromyko in UN speech advocates the withdrawal of foreign forces from Cyprus
21 Nov.
UN General Assembly approves (by 117–1) resolution calling for immediate withdrawal of Turkish invasion force from Cyprus, return of refugees to their homes and resumption of talks between the two communities – US abstains
29 Dec.
Soviet Union signs friendship and co-operation accord with Turkey

(continued on page 236)

Appendix 1 *continued*

Year	Government in Greece	Foreign-policy related event	Government in Turkey
1976		*27 Mar.* US signs a Defense Co-operation Agreement with Turkey *17 Apr.* Karamanlis proposes non-aggression pact with Turkey; the latter state's preference for a practical step-by-step normalisation of relations prior to a non-aggression pact, says settlement of continental shelf issue through ICJ no longer a proper course *24 Apr.* Turkish Government grants oil exploration licenses over contested region of the Aegean *23 Jul.* Turkish research vessel *Sismik 1* sent to prospect for oil in above region; threats by Demirel against any Greek attempt to interfere with the ship's mission *29 Jul.* Greek protests of *Sismik* exploration activity near the islands of Lemnos and Lesbos rejected by Turkey *9 Aug.* Greece asks for emergency meeting of UN Security Council and announces she plans to refer the issue unilaterally to ICJ *11 Aug.* Greece places her armed forces on alert while Turkey protests 'harassment' of her research vessel by Greek	

13 Aug.
Soviet government makes public her view that 'freedom of navigation should not be disturbed in that [Aegean] region' as a result of a future settlement of Greek–Turkish dispute; position widely perceived as favouring Turkey
25 Aug.
UN Security Council urges the two countries to seek peaceful solution to the Aegean dispute and consider taking the matter to the ICJ
31 Aug.
Nicos Sampson, who was appointed to replace Makarios after the 1974 coup, is sentenced to twenty years imprisonment by Cyprus courts
6–8 Sep.
Turkish vessel *Sismik 1* prospects for oil in disputed area
12 Sep.
ICJ rejects Greece's request for interim measures; finds that *Sismik* activities do not constitute a risk of irreparable prejudice to Greece's rights
2 Nov.
Greek–Turkish experts meet in Bern to discuss delimitation of continental shelf rights in the Aegean; agree to establish committee to study pertinent international rules and state practice; both countries should refrain during negotiations from 'initiatives or acts relating to the continental shelf of the Aegean which might prejudice the negotiations'

(continued on page 238)

Appendix 1 *continued*

Year	Government in Greece	Foreign-policy related event	Government in Turkey
1977		*4 Apr.* Talks resume in Geneva by representatives of the two Cyprus communities; end with no results after four days	*5 Jun.* Premature general election in which no party gains majority in the National Assembly; Demirel resigns
		18 Jul. Greece, on the invitation of ICJ, submits memorandum with her views on continental shelf dispute; Turkey refuses, claiming the court has no jurisdiction to try the case	*3 Jul.* Ecevit (Republican People's Party) fails to win vote of confidence for a minority government.
		3 Aug. Archbishop Makarios dies, Spyros Kyprianou chosen as successor	*21 Jul.* Demirel wins vote of confidence for a three-party government: Justice (pro-Islamic); National Salvation (ultra right-wing) and Nationalist Action
		14 Oct. Turkish minister of energy says in Brussels that Greece's admission as a full member of the European Community would not facilitate settlement of Cyprus or Aegean disputes	*31 Dec.* Demirel government loses vote of confidence and resigns
	28 Nov. New Democracy Party wins general election with 41.9%; socialist PASOK emerges as main opposition party with 29.3%		

1978

10–11 Mar.
Karamanlis and Ecevit meet in Montreux (Switzerland); communiqué says they will continue their talks at a later stage to obtain practical results

12 Mar.
Ecevit, continuing his strong criticism of Carter administration, threatens he will not submit proposals on Cyprus unless arms embargo is waived

2 Apr.
Carter administration in major policy shift decides to end embargo without waiting first for Turkish concessions on Cyprus issue

29 May
Karamanlis and Ecevit meet in Washington; Karamanlis repeats non-aggression pact proposal but gets inconclusive response from the Turkish premier

4 Jul.
As agreed in Montreux and Washington talks, general secretaries of foreign ministries of the two countries hold first-round talks in Ankara on the Aegean air-corridors issue; the talks continue in subsequent meetings in Athens (Sep. 1978) and in Ankara (Feb. 1979)

1 Jan.
Coalition government under Ecevit formed (RPP, Republican Reliance Party and Democratic Party)

(continued on page 240)

Appendix 1 *continued*

Year	Government in Greece	Foreign-policy related event	Government in Turkey
		26 Sep. President Carter formally ends three-year embargo on arms shipments to Turkey, declaring that Turkey is acting in good faith to achieve political settlement of Cyprus problem; lifting of embargo linked to periodic evidence of progress on Cyprus issue *9 Oct.* Turkey reopens four US military bases closed in 1975 because of embargo *19 Dec.* ICJ finds that it has no jurisdiction to try the Aegean continental shelf case, submitted only by one party to the dispute (Greece)	*15 Dec.* Martial law declared in thirteen Turkish provinces

1979	3 May	25 Apr.
	US and Greek diplomatic sources confirm that threat of Turkish veto is main obstacle to Greece's reintegrating into NATO alliance; Turkey demands extending area of operational responsibility up to the middle of the Aegean – a region under Greek operational control prior to 1974 – before Greece's readmission.	Martial law extended to cover the whole Kurdish region
	30 May	
	UN Secretary-General announces President Kyprianou and Turkish-Cypriot leader Denktash to resume intercommunal talks.	16 Oct.
	15 Jun.	Ecevit resigns following loss of his narrow majority in by-elections to National Assembly
	One more round of abortive intercommunal talks under UN auspices	25 Nov.
		Minority Justice Party government under Demirel

(continued on page 242)

Appendix 1 *continued*

Year	Government in Greece	Foreign-policy related event	Government in Turkey
1980		*20 Feb.* Turkey, putting into effect a 1976 bilateral agreement withdraws her 1974 NOTAM that had unilaterally extended Istanbul FIR to the middle of Aegean at the expense of Athens FIR; Greece announces next day withdrawal of her NOTAM that had declared the whole Aegean a 'dangerous zone'	
		29 Mar. US-Turkey DECA signed	
		5 May UN Special Envoy Javier Perez de Cuellar says that Turkish-Cypriot leaders have rejected UN initiative to resume talks on Cyprus	
	9 May Karamanlis elected president of the republic; G. Rallis succeeds him as premier and leader of the New Democracy Party	*28–9 Jun.* After NATO spring ministerial session Greece and Turkey announce agreement to resume bilateral negotiations in late 1980	
		10 Aug. Greek–Turkish Cypriot negotiators meet in Nicosia to resume UN-supervised talks	

21 Oct.
Greece returns to military wing of NATO after six years following acceptance of SACEUR General Rogers reintegration proposals by Turkey and other members of the alliance

10–11 Sep.
Military *coup d'état*: all major political leaders arrested; martial law extends to all of Turkey's sixty-seven provinces
21 Sep.
Cabinet of Army officers and civilians under Admiral B. Ulusu

(continued on page 244)

Appendix 1 *continued*

Year	Government in Greece	Foreign-policy related event	Government in Turkey
1981	21 Oct. Socialist PASOK under Papandreou wins an impressive victory in general elections with 48.1%; New Democracy gets 35.9%	8 May Greece protests NATO refusal to include Greek island of Lemnos in allied military manoeuvres thus acquiescing to Turkish position that the island is under an international demilitarisation regime 9 Dec. Papandreou blocks NATO joint communiqué in protest at refusal of the alliance to guarantee Greece's eastern frontiers against future Turkish aggression	
1982		29 Feb. Papandreou arrives in Nicosia; first visit by Greek premier to Cyprus	

1983

14 May
UN General Assembly resolution calls upon Turkey to pull her forces out of Cyprus

29 Sep.
Greece cancels a NATO landing exercise that had excluded island of Lemnos

15 Nov.
Turkish Cypriots proclaim the TRNC as an independent 'state'; Turkey extends immediate recognition; move condemned by UN Security Council Resolution 541 (submitted by the UK) adopted by 13 votes to 1 (Pakistan) with 1 abstention (Jordan)

23–9 Nov.
Final communiqué of the New Delhi meeting of the heads of government of British Commonwealth condemns the proclamation of TRNC

6 Nov.
Elections to the new 400-seat Grand National Assembly; victory for the Motherland Party of Ozal; state of martial law unaffected

13 Dec.
Ozal becomes prime minister of Turkey

(continued on page 246)

Appendix 1 *continued*

Year	Government in Greece	Foreign-policy related event	Government in Turkey
1984		*20 Jan.* Greece again cancels participation in NATO manoeuvres over the Lemnos issue	
		31 Mar. Ozal announces that visa restrictions for Greek citizens visiting Turkey will be abolished as a sign of goodwill	
		17 Apr. Turkey exchanges ambassadors with the TRNC	
		13 May UN Security Council Resolution 550 condemns move as a 'secessionist activity'; adopted by 13 votes to 1 (Pakistan) – US abstains	
		10 Sep. Kyprianou and Denktash meet in New York with UN Secretary-General; two weeks of talks end without apparent progress	
		15–26 Oct., 26 Nov.–12 Dec. Series of meetings of UN Secretary-General with Kyprianou and Denktash; main issues of disagreement are withdrawal of Turkish troops and third-state guarantees	
		23 Oct. Representatives of Greek and Turkish Ministries of Communication hold talks in Athens; first bilateral government contacts since Nov. 1983	

1985

29 Feb.
Greek officials list 421 violations of Greece's airspace by Turkey during 1984
29 Mar.
UN Secretary General submits proposals for Cyprus settlement; Turkish-Cypriot leader Denktash on 21 Apr. announces positive reply; President Kyprianou submits counter-proposals and on 10 Jun. gives a negative response claiming that the draft framework agreement was unbalanced and contained no specific deadline for withdrawal of foreign troops and Turkish settlers
5 Apr.
Lord Carrington, NATO's General Secretary suggests that the Lemnos issue might be approached from a legal rather than political angle, a shift of policy that would open the door for Greek participation in allied manoeuvres; statement causes upheaval in Turkey and is subsequently corrected
23 May
Ozal warns Greece that in the event of armed conflict she will find herself in 'a disadvantageous position'

(continued on page 248)

Appendix 1 *continued*

Year	Government in Greece	Foreign-policy related event	Government in Turkey
		2–4 Jul. Ozal visits the TRNC; second visit by a Turkish premier (first by Bulent Ulusu in May 1982); responding to international protests over the visit Denktash closes 'frontier crossings' to the rest of Cyprus from 4 to 12 Jul.	
		5 Dec. At a NATO defence ministers meeting in Brussels, Papandreou offers to assign Greek forces in Lemnos to NATO; move vetoed by Turkey whose own defence plan for 1985 is vetoed by Greece; as a result no Greek or Turkish forces are committed to NATO for 1986 and Greece announces she will not participate in any future NATO manoeuvres (having previously taken part in exercises outside the Aegean)	
26 Jul. Papandreou wins general election with 45.8%; New Democracy second with 40.8%			

1986

8 Jan.
Greek government Council for Foreign Policy and National Defence approves 'New Defence Doctrine': Turkey main threat to Greece's security; a similar Doctrine ('New Defence Concept') had been announced by Ecevit, then Turkish premier, in 1978

21 Jan.
Soviet proposals for a Cyprus settlement seek to preserve independence, unity and territorial integrity of the republic as well as the withdrawal of all foreign troops and closure of foreign bases; proposals are accepted by Greece and Cyprus but rejected by Turkish government

1 Feb.
Unofficial meeting of Papandreou and Ozal in Davos, Switzerland: no bilateral talks.

16 Sep.
Greece sets conditions for the reactivation of EC–Turkey Association Agreement suspended since the military coup of 1980

19 Dec.
Serious incident in the Evros (Thrace) frontier: three soldiers – two Turkish, one Greek – killed

(continued on page 250)

Appendix 1 *continued*

Year	Government in Greece	Foreign-policy related event	Government in Turkey
1987		*13 Feb.* Greece, Turkey veto again NATO's defence projects on each other's territory.	
		6 Mar. Greek government tables a bill to take control of Canadian-owned North Aegean Petroleum Company (NAPC) that exploited the Prinos oilfield off the Greek island of Thassos. NAPC had earlier made public plans to prospect for oil outside Greece's territorial waters; Turkey saw takeover as signifying Greece's intention to proceed with oil prospecting	
		25 Mar. Turkey issues permit to the state-owned Turkish Petroleum Corporation for oil exploration outside Turkey's territorial waters off the islands of Lesbos, Lemnos and Samothraki	
		27 Mar. Papandreou warns that Greek armed forces could 'teach the Turks a very hard lesson' if Turkey continued aggressive acts in the Aegean. At the same time announces intention to exercise a right granted by 1983 US–Greek DECA and suspend operation of a Greek-based American communications facility. Turkey's general staff threatens that any Greek attempt to harass Turkish survey vessel would meet with 'unhesitating retaliation' (crisis defused later the same	

day when Ozal, on a visit to London, said that research will be conducted within Turkey's territorial waters)

8 Apr.
Papandreou announces that his government is considering settling continental shelf issue through ICJ, in agreement with Turkey

14 Apr.
Turkey submits application for admission to the EC

22 May
EC and Cyprus initial a protocol on customs union after eighteen months of negotiations; the accord which came into effect on 1 Jan. 1988 covers the whole of Cyprus and recognises Cyprus government as the only representative of the whole island

2 Oct.
Papandreou and Ozal continue exchange of confidential messages over methods of settlement of bilateral disputes

16 Dec.
US Congress votes to preserve the 7:10 ratio

29 Nov.
Ozal's Motherland Party wins general election with 36% of the vote and 292 seats in the 450-seat Grand National Assembly

(*continued on page 252*)

Appendix 1 *continued*

Year	Government in Greece	Foreign-policy related event	Government in Turkey
1988		*30–1 Jan.* Papandreou and Ozal meet in Davos, Switzerland. Agree to establish committees that would promote co-operation in trade, tourism, communications, etc., and define problem areas *13–17 Jun.* Ozal arrives in Athens for talks with Papandreou; first official visit to Greece by a Turkish premier in thirty-six years; talks end without a breakthrough in any of the issues dividing the two countries but both premiers pledge to continue their efforts	

* Wilson, ibid., p. 120; D. A. Rustow, *Turkey: America's Forgotten Ally* (New York: Council of Foreign Relations, 1987) p. 93, fails to take that fact into account when he attributes the 14 Aug. offensive to 'the overcautious Turkish military [who] had fallen short of their operational goals'.

SOURCE Compiled by the editor. Data for this chronology were mostly drawn from *Keesing's Contemporary Archives*; *The New York Times Index*; and A. Wilson, 'The Aegean Dispute, Appendix 3: Greek–Turkish Relations 1973–1978', in J. Alford (ed.), *Greece and Turkey: Adversity in Alliance* (Aldershot: Gower, 1984) pp. 90–137, see esp. pp. 120–4.

APPENDIX 2 An agenda of Greek–Turkish disputes (up to 1988)

Issues and related legal rules	Greek position	Turkish position	Regime in effect since	Time that dispute arose
1 Bilateral issues *1.1 Delimitation of the continental shelf of the Aegean Sea* (a) Do islands have continental shelf? (b) Where should the delimitation line be drawn? *Rules* General customary international law Geneva Convention on the Continental Shelf (1958) arts. 1 and 6 1982 UNCLOS not yet ratified, arts. 15 and 121 ICJ decisions: North Sea Continental Shelf Case (1959); Tunisia v. Libya (1982); Gulf of Maine (Canada v. US, 1984); Libya v. Malta (1985)	(a) Islands are entitled to continental shelf exactly as any other state territory (b) Delimitation should take into account a median line, i.e., half the distance between the eastern coast of the islands and the western coast of Turkey	(a) Greek islands along the Turkish coast are an extension of the Anatolian peninsula (b) For coastal states applicable principle of delimitation is not equidistance but the method of applying equitable principles (c) Proximity of Greek islands to Turkey gives rise to a case of special circumstances (d) Given the semi-closed nature of the Aegean Sea, general international law is not applicable and	No delimitation in effect; Greece first exercised what still it deems as inalienable rights to the continental shelf of the islands in 1970	November 1973: Turkey awarded mineral exploitation rights to areas claimed by Greece

(continued on page 254)

APPENDIX 2 continued

Issues and related legal rules	Greek position	Turkish position	Regime in effect since	Time that dispute arose
1.2 Breadth of territorial sea zone Is Greece entitled to extend her current six-mile territorial sea zone to twelve miles?* *Rules* General customary international law Geneva Convention on the Territorial Sea Contiguous Zone (1958) 1982 UNCLOS, arts. 3, 122, 123 and 300	(a) A twelve-mile territorial sea zone is now almost universally accepted; even Turkey who has not ratified any of the main Law of the Sea conventions has contributed to the formulation of a rule of international customary law by enacting a twelve-mile zone in the Black Sea (1973) (b) The 1982 UNCLOS does not make the twelve-mile rule	the dispute should be settled through bilateral negotiations (a) Given the geography of the region, a twelve-mile Greek territorial sea zone would restrict freedom of navigation (b) A twelve-mile Greek territorial sea zone will automatically	Not applicable	Not applicable

conditional on the circumstances prevailing in different seas provided that there is enough space, i.e. a minimum of twenty-four nautical miles between opposite coasts, for the rule to apply

(c) Extension of Greece's territorial sea zone would not imperil freedom of navigation; foreign ships will have right of innocent passage and transit passage in the relevant straits

(d) As owner of the world's largest commercial fleet, Greece has no interest to limit freedom of navigation

extend Greece's seabed underneath that zone leaving little for future delimitation of the continental shelf between the two coastal states

(c) As a semi-closed sea, the Aegean is exempt from the delimitation rules of the 1982 UNCLOS which in any case prescribes only a maximum permitted breadth

(continued on page 256)

APPENDIX 2 continued

Issues and related legal rules	Greek position	Turkish position	Regime in effect since	Time that dispute arose
1.3 *Breadth of national air-space* Greece has a six-nautical-mile territorial sea covering all the usual functions of that zone and a ten-nautical mile territorial sea which only covers sovereign control of the air above the sea and amounts to a ten-nautical mile national airspace. Turkey recognises only a six-mile airspace and Turkish military aircraft are continuously violating Greece's airspace and are intercepted by Greek jets	(a) Greece's ten-mile national airspace zone, although broader than the territorial sea zone, does not exceed the twelve-mile maximum. Turkey raised no objections to that regime for more than forty years	(a) The breadth of national airspace should correspond to that of the territorial sea zone (b) Airspace beyond the outer limit of the territorial sea zone should either be international or belong to another state	1931 Greek laws no. 5017 of 3–13 Jun. 1931 – ten nautical miles and no. 330 of 17 Sep.–13 Oct. 1936 – six nautical miles	1975 The issue was placed on the agenda of Greek–Turkish disputes on 17–19 June 1975 by Ambassador Yuksel Soylemer during an Ankara meeting of Greek and Turkish government delegations

2 International institutional issues

2.1 Breadth of Athens FIR

The breadth of Athens FIR was set by the ICAO to a line corresponding to the outer limits of the territorial sea of the eastern Greek islands. Turkey requires extension of Istanbul FIR up to the middle of the Aegean at the expense of Athens FIR and refuses to submit flight plans or notify Greek authorities on military exercises in the region.

(a) For almost twenty-two years there have been no complaints from Turkey or other ICAO member-states as to the manner in which Greece has exercised her FIR responsibilities

(b) Complaints should, in any case, be addressed to the ICAO not to Greece who acts as a trustee of that organisation and changes should be effected through ICAO decisions not by unilateral acts of disobedience

Greece has abused her position as control authority in order to strengthen her alleged sovereign rights over most of the Aegean.

1952
ICAO, Regional Air Navigation Agreement: Europe Mediterranean 23 Jun. 1952

1974
Turkish NOTAM of 6 Aug. 1974 unilaterally placing part of Athens FIR under Turkish control

(continued on page 258)

APPENDIX 2 continued

Issues and related legal rules	Greek position	Turkish position	Regime in effect since	Time that dispute arose
2.2 *Operational responsibilities in the Aegean under NATO* Whether the 'Rogers' Agreement 16 Oct. 1980 (NATO SACEUR proposals concerning return of Greece to the integrated military structure of NATO) re-establishes Greek operational control over the same regions of the Aegean as prior to her withdrawal from NATO in 1974.	Greek operational responsibility zone in the Aegean had been determined by NATO's Military Committee Decision MC 38/4 of Jan. 1957 and SACEUR decision of 22 Feb. 1964 to more or less coincide with the outer limits of Athens FIR. The 'Rogers' Agreement provides that the responsibilities of the SEVENATAF, be established in Larissa, Greece under a Greek commander will extend into areas over which the 28th Tactical Airforce – the existing Greek Air Force Command – was responsible prior to Aug. 1974.	The correct interpretation of the 'Rogers' Agreement is that it leaves the area of responsibility of the SEVENATAF issue to be settled through negotiations between the Greek commander of SEVENATAF and the Turkish commander of SIXATAF situated in Smyrna, Turkey. Also, for the purposes of delimitation, Military Committee Decision (MC 66/1) of 1960 should be taken into account providing that the purposes of the alliance territorial sea and air zones are deemed as having equal breadth	1957 The Greek operational responsibility zone in the Aegean remained in effect since it was established by NATO decisions in 1957 and 1964. Following Greek withdrawal from NATO in 1974, the alliance under Turkish pressure placed under Turkish command the LANDSOUTHEAST and SIXATAF since only Turkish forces were then under NATO. However, the alliance rejected proposals by Turkey to entrust to SIXATAF, as in the past, operational responsibility over the whole Aegean and limited it to areas corresponding to Istanbul and Ankara FIRs	1974 From 1964 to 1974 Greece's area of control was challenged by Turkey only once, in 1967, during a Cyprus crisis when Turkish jets repeatedly violated the zone of Greek control

2.3 *Militarisation of Greek eastern and north-eastern Aegean islands*
General issue: has Greece the legal right to keep armed forces on the Greek islands along the coast of Turkey?
Related issue: is NATO entitled to include one of the most strategically located of the islands, Lemnos, in Allied manoeuvres in the Aegean? (Since 8 May 1980 NATO has treated Lemnos as a 'dispute' and excludes the island from Allied planning in the region. In protest Greece has refused to take part in NATO exercises.)

(continued on page 260)

APPENDIX 2 continued

Issues and related legal rules	Greek position	Turkish position	Regime in effect since	Time that dispute arose
2.3.1 *Greek islands of Lemnos and Samothrace; Turkish islands of Imvros, Tenedos and Lagoussa* **Rules** 1923 Lausanne Convention on the Straits of the Dardanelles and the Bosporus, art. 4(3) 1923 Treaty of Lausanne, arts. 12 and 13 1923 Montreux Convention on the Straits of the Dardanelles and the Bosporus, preamble and *travaux preparatoires*	(a) Art. 13 of the Treaty of Lausanne, specifying demilitarised territories, makes no reference to Lemnos or Samothrace. Reference to Lemnos and Samothrace in Art. 12 only intends to reconfirm Greek sovereignty over them. (b) The preamble of the Montreux Convention makes explicit the intention of the contracting parties to replace *in toto* the Lausanne Convention on the Straits	(a) The Montreux Convention makes no explicit reference to Lemnos and Samothrace while it does so for the Turkish islands concerned (b) Greece's demilitarisation servitude does not derive from the Lausanne Convention on the Straits but the Treaty of Lausanne (art. 12); this remains unaffected by the replacement of the former by the Montreux Convention	1936	1975 Turkey started raising objections to the fortification of Lemnos by Greece by middle 1975 but NATO's SACEUR general defence plan was not affected until J. Luns, then General Secretary of the alliance characterised the island in a 8 May 1980 report to SACEUR as a 'dispute area'

(c) As evidenced from the Record of the Turkish National Assembly of 31 Mar. 1936 the Turkish foreign minister expressly recognised that the Montreux Convention relieved Greece from her obligations to keep Lemnos and Samothrace demilitarised (*Record of the Turkish Grand National Assembly* vol. 12, p. 309, 5th Parliamentary Session, 61st Meeting)

(continued on page 262)

APPENDIX 2 *continued*

Issues and related legal rules	Greek position	Turkish position	Regime in effect since	Time that dispute arose
	(d) A confidential report by NATO's legal advisor B. A. E. Boyle (doc. 6100/SHCGU 509/78 of 2 Nov. 78) confirms that: 'there is no limitation to Greek national sovereignty over Lemnos', but advises SACEUR to stay clear of the issue and let Greece and Turkey settle it through negotiations			

2.3.2 Greek islands of Lesbos, Chios, Samos and Ikaria

The Treaty of Lausanne provides for the limited demilitarisation of these islands† and Greek forces stationed there allegedly exceed the limits set in the Treaty

Rules

1923 Treaty of Lausanne, art. 13
UN Charter, arts. 2(4) and 51

(a) The contractual obligations that Greece undertook in 1923 are still valid. However, given Turkey's resort to threat of force in her relations with Greece (in violation of art. 2(4) of the UN Charter) the latter has a right to defend her territory. The deployment of the powerful Turkish Fourth Army (Army of the Aegean) along the Turkish coast facing the Greek islands makes that point even clearer

(a) Greece is in clear violation of art. 13 of the Treaty of Lausanne

1923   1975

It appears that Greece observed her limited militarisation servitude well into the middle 1960s. However, following tense confrontation with Turkey over Cyprus, Greece gradually increased its military presence in the islands to levels beyond the Lausanne Treaty limits.

(continued on page 264)

APPENDIX 2 *continued*

Issues and related legal rules	Greek position	Turkish position	Regime in effect since	Time that dispute arose
	(b) There is broad consensus among legal scholars that the threat to use force makes defence measures legitimate provided that there is a balance between the threat and the preventive measures taken	(b) The UN Charter allows measures of self-defence only 'if an armed attacked occurs'.		

2.3.3 Dodecanese Islands (Greece)

The Dodecanese Islands were given to Greece after World War Two under a complete demilitarisation servitude with the exception of forces needed for internal security

Rules

1947 Peace Treaty of Paris between Italy and the Allied Powers, art. 14 and appendix XIII
UN Charter, arts. 2(4) and 51

(a) Self-defence (same as above)
(b) Turkey, who in World War Two remained an 'evasive neutral',[‡] is not a party to the Peace Treaty of Paris and consequently has no status under international law to raise the issue. None of the contracting parties to the Paris Treaty has objected to Greece's fortification of the islands after 1974

1947	
Greece has strengthened the *gendarmerie* in the islands to a point at which it is barely distinguishable from a regular armed force	

1975
The representative of Turkey to the UN in a letter to the Secretary-General of the organisation dated 12 Aug. 1975 pointed out the violation of the Treaty of Paris by Greece

(continued on page 266)

APPENDIX 2 continued

Issues and related legal rules	Greek position	Turkish position	Regime in effect since	Time that dispute arose
2.4 Protection of ethnic minorities Each country claims that the other has been acting in violation of the Treaty and Convention of Lausanne regarding protection of the Muslim minority in Greek western Trace and the Greek Orthodox minority in Istanbul and the Turkish islands of Imvros and Tenedos	Turkey since the death of Kemal Atatürk has engaged in a systematic prosecution of non-Muslim minorities: Jews, Armenians and especially Greeks.§ The 1955 anti-Greek riots organised by the Menderes government – a fact established during the trials of Menderes and high officials of his regime – destroyed 1000 houses, 4000 stores, 21 factories and 71 churches of the ancient Greek Orthodox community of Istanbul. After 1965 all Greek nationals (as distinct from the 'minority') were expelled from Turkey and strict financial and administrative controls	Practices of the Greek authorities have reduced the land area owned by Muslims in western Thrace from 60% to approximately 20%. In addition there is discrimination in the granting of driving licences and in admissions to Greek universities.**	1923	The issue has been raised periodically by both sides, most often by organisations officially unrelated to government. There has been an increase of such claims, especially from the Turkish side after 1974. It should be emphasised that since Greece (1985) and Turkey (1987) have accepted the procedure of individual petitions before the European Commission of Human Rights isolated cases of discrimination can now be settled without invoking the minority protection provisions of the Treaty of Lausanne

were imposed on Greek cultural foundations. As a result the Greek Orthodox minority of Istanbul was reduced from 110 000 in 1934 to less than 5000. ¶ Imvros had 8000 Greek inhabitants in 1922 and Tenedos 5320: today they have 600 and 200 respectively, in contrast to the Muslim community in western Thrace which has today 130 000, compared to 106 000 in 1934. ‖ These figures speak for themselves

* D. A. Rustow (see note to Appendix 1) p. 100, writes: 'The Athens Government . . . also proclaimed an extension of its territorial waters around Greece's islands from six to ten miles – which, if accepted, would close off Turkish passage from the Straits and its Aegean harbors to the Mediterranean – and protested Turkey's search for oil under the disputed waters.' The author not only confuses two distinct legal regimes: continental shelf versus territorial sea zone. He also has his facts wrong: Greek governments have repeatedly stated that Greece *has the right* to a twelve (not ten) mile territorial sea zone. This right will be exercised at a time deemed appropriate for such a move and, so far, Greek governments have refrained from doing so.
† Article 13 prohibits establishment of naval bases and construction of fortifications and stipulates that stationing of military forces should be

confined to persons locally recruited. A Turkish proposal during the preparation of the Treaty of Lausanne for complete demilitarisation was rejected. Wilson, 'The Aegean Dispute' (see source note to Appendix 1) p. 105.

‡ F. G. Weber, *The Evasive Neutral: Germany, Britain and the Quest for a Turkish Alliance in the Second World War* (London: University of Missouri Press, 1979).

§ Wilson, 'The Aegean Dispute', p. 106, writes: 'The good relations which had existed between the communities in the Atatürk years were marred in 1942 when Turkey imposed a capital tax, aimed nominally at those who had made profits from war conditions – the farmers (mainly Muslims) and the merchants (mainly Orthodox Christians, Jews and Armenians). For a majority of those, in the latter category, assessments were made arbitrarily by "special commissions". Payments were required in 15 days, no appeals were allowed, and thousands of defaulters were arrested and deported or sent to labor camps.' For an account of the effects of the tax written by a high-ranking Turkish official of that period, see Faik Okte, *The Tragedy of the Turkish Capital Tax* (London: Croom Helm, 1987).

¶ Wilson, 'The Aegean Dispute', p. 106.

‖ Ibid.

** Ibid., pp. 106–7.

SOURCE This agenda was compiled by the editor on the basis of unilateral claims that either side has occasionally made against the other in a bilateral or multilateral context since 1974. Inclusion of such a claim in this 'agenda' does not signify that the respective issue has officially been accepted, by both sides, as a legitimate 'dispute area' to be settled through negotiation, arbitration and adjudication. 'Legal rules' specified in each case mean provisions of treaty or customary international law and major ICJ cases that have been frequently cited by either side in order to sustain claims against the other or in defence against such claims. Reference to international law provisions for such purposes does not imply that the state concerned is interested in a judicial settlement of the dispute on account of such international law rules. The agenda does not include the 'Cyprus issue' which is characterised mainly by the Greek side as an 'international question' given the status of the Republic of Cyprus as a sovereign state, member of the UN and the latter's active role in the settlement of the dispute. Although technically a separate issue, the Cyprus question has since 1954 cast a heavy shadow on Greek–Turkish relations and continued to do so after 1974. For that reason the chronology of Greek–Turkish relations after 1974 (Appendix 1) takes into account Cyprus-related events. The data used in the agendas come from a variety of sources. Particularly useful were C. Rozakis's article, 'Greek–Turkish Relations: The Legal Dimension', in D. Constas and Ch. Tsardanides (eds), *Contemporary Greek Foreign Policy*, vol. II (Athens: Sakkoulas, 1989, in Greek) pp. 21–68; H. Pazarci's book, *La delimitation du plateau continental et les îles* (Ankara: Faculté des Sciences Politiques de l'Université d'Ankara, 1982); and finally, Andrew Wilson's balanced and comprehensive account, 'The Aegean Dispute', cited in Appendix 1.

Index

Page references in **bold** type indicate authorship of a chapter in this volume. Abbreviations used in the subheadings are listed on p. xi.

Acheson Plan, 158
Aegean Islands
 defensive restructuring, 146–7
 Greek fears, 53
 militarisation, 15–16, 21, 41, 61–2, 94, 99, 117, 146, 159
 Turkey's internationalisation of problem, 160
Aegean Sea disputes, 15–16
 and Greece's membership of EC, 212–13
 and Turkey's relations with West, 65
 armed forces operational control, 18
 dispute defined by Ozal, 78
 effect of force-reduction talks, 150
 Greece's perceptions of Turkey's aims, 42–3, 46
 Turkish diplomatic moves, 94
 US involvement in dispute, 161
 see also Airspace disputes; Continental shelf dispute; Oil exploration
Afghanistan, 112, 176, 194, 224
Airspace disputes, 15, 17, 20–1, 41, 43, 46–7, 53, 94
 Brussels meeting (1988), 82
 Davos meeting (1987), 34
 resolution, 17
 Turkey's infringements detailed, 18
Albania, 189
Ali Birand, Mehmet, 3–4, **27–39**
Alliances, *see* International organisations
Ankara Agreement (1964), 163
Ankara Convention (1930), 13, 22
Appeasement strategy, 104–5

Arab–Israeli conflict, 112
Armed conflict threats, 13–14, 16, 20, 27, 32, 45, 48, 54, 78, 119
 and offence–defence balance, 142–3
 avoidance, 123
 see also Deterrence strategy
Arms-limitation agreements, 130
 see also Conventional force reductions
Arms race, 130
Ataturk, Mustafa Kemal, 12, 40, 60, 64

Baku oilfields, 189
Balkan Conference, 113
Balkan Pact (1953), 13, 60, 189
Balkans, 9, 188
 and SEM strategy, 113
 post-1974 Greek policy, 194
 post-1974 Turkish policy, 194–5
 post-1979 Greek policy, 195
 strategic importance, 183
Batu, Inal, 21
Berne Declaration (1976), 17, 20
Bismarck, Otto, Prince von, 85–6
Black Sea, 183
 control of straits, 183, 189, 201
 submarines' transit through straits, 204n
'Boundary-crossing' events, 73–4
Boycotts, 130
Brussels meeting (1988), 34–6, 40, 49, 52, 82
Brzezinski, Zbigniew, 168
Bulgaria, 10, 11n, 49, 186
 Greece's non-aggression pact, 113
 Turkey's relations with, 28, 29, 113
 Turkish minority, 63

Bush, George, 174

Carter, Jimmy, 167–9, 176, 178
Casus belli, 101, 102–3, 120
CFE, *see* Conventional forces in Europe
CFR, *see* Conventional force reductions
Clogg, Richard, 3, 9, **12–23**
Concert of Europe, 185
Conference on Security and Co-operation in Europe (CSCE), 124
Confidence-building measures, 34–5
Constas, Dimitri, **1–11**, 5–6, **129–39**
Continental shelf dispute, 41, 43
   as national interest issue, 61
   leading to *rapprochement*, 50
   Turkey's explanation, 209
   Turkish exploitation as *casus belli*, 101
   Turkish rejection of ICJ offer, 44, 217
Conventional force reductions
   as forum for unilateral restructuring, 151–2
   background to CFE negotiations, 148
   case of Greek and Turkey, 149–50
   NATO–Warsaw Pact balance, 110–11, 118–19
   effect on Greek–Turkish disputes, 140
Conventional forces in Europe (CFE) negotiations, 110–11, 114
Coufoudakis, Van, 3, 4, **40–56**
Crimean War, 185
Cutler, Robert, 3, 5–6, **183–206**
Cyprus, 8
   anticipated effect of *rapprochement*, 50
   as federated state within EC, 225
   associate member of EC, 162
   attitudes to Papandreou's change of policy, 51
   bizonal federation proposed, 168
   breakdown of 1960 constitution, 13
   crisis in relations (1984), 19
   deepening levels of problem, 157
   distances from Greece and Turkey, 96
   EC as acceptable mediator, 223–6
   effect on EC 161–3, 219–20: effectiveness of institutions, 222–3; factors influencing, 221–6
   effect on Soviet–Turkish relations, 199–200
   effects of dispute in general, 41
   enosis, 13
   Greek attempts to involve NATO, 158
   Greek attitude to Turkish troops, 50–1
   Greek deterrent strategy, 101–2
   Greek-sponsored coup, 41
   imprisonment of Greek-Cypriots in TRNC, 83
   independent TRNC declared, 18–19, 48, 69, 162, 220: effect on EC–Turkey relations, 211
   interactions of Greece and Turkey with population, 8
   internationalisation of issue, 247–8
   left out of summit talks, 33, 34
   obstacle to *rapprochement*, 83–5
   obstacle to Turkey's EC membership, 216
   Papandreou's position on Turkish troops, 47
   place in Turkey's national interests, 69
   provocative Turkish actions, 220
   reaction to European changes, 182
   resolution of conflict, 124
   role in Turkish foreign policy, 64
   secret Greek–Turkish dialogue, 41
   settlement initiative (1978), 178
   Soviet view of problem, 193–4, 196
   strategic importance to West, 112
   treaties guaranteeing independence, 200

Turkey's association agreement with TRNC, 19
Turkish–Cypriot proposals (1989), 53
Turkish invasion (1974), 1, 12, 15, 41, 64, 84–5, 95, 122, 164, 193: as *casus belli*, 101; effect on Greece's policy decisions, 97–8; effect on NATO, 157, 158–60; effect on SEM strategy, 121–2; effect on US relations, 160–1
US contribution to UNFICYP, 136
US humanitarian involvement, 166
see also EC–Cyprus Association Agreement
Czechoslovakia, 144

Davos meeting (1987), 32–4, 40, 47, 49, 54, 178
agreements concluded, 16, 20, 82: effects, 21–2
as personal initiative by leaders, 78
first (1985) experiment, 31
following near-war situation, 80
future prospects, 123
importance, 38
in linkage politics, 78–85
Ozal's stance, 67
Papandreou's summing-up, 69
purposes, 119–20
reasons for lack of success, 36–8
spirit, 2, 7, 8, 27: decline of, 53
Defence and Economic Co-operation Agreement (DECA), 45, 47
Defence policies
'confidence-building' measures, 34–5
of weak states, 141–2
restructuring forces, 143–7: effect on Greek–Turkish conflict, 145–7; implementing defensive restructuring, 147–52; potential for unilateral restructuring, 150–2
Demirel, Suleyman, 37, 55n, 71n, 196
political method, 37–8
visits Moscow, 191
Denktash, Rauf, 8, 10–11n, 53, 120, 200, 220
Deterrence strategy
Greek, 99–104
stability and credibility, 104
Dole, Robert, 174, 180
Dountas, Mihalis, 52, 56n
Drossoyannis, Antonis, 95

East–West relations
changes affecting SEM, 109–11, 123
effect of improvements, 9, 10
effect of increasing multipolarity, 133–4
implementing defensive restructuring, 147–52
improvement in late 1980s, 140
influence on Greece and Turkey, 13
US policy, 175–7
Eastern Europe
improved relations with Greece and Turkey, 198
liberalisation, 124
political changes, 113, 122, 176
EC, *see* European Community
EC–Cyprus Association Agreement, 222–3
EC–Cyprus Financial Protocol, 224–5
EC–Turkey Association Agreement, 82, 83, 162, 210
future prospects, 218–19
Greek participation, 217–18
Ecevit, Bulent, 15, 55n
continuation of oil exploration, 16
meeting with Kosygin, 194–5
Montreux summit, 17, 79
Washington meeting with Karamanlis, 178
Economic Committee, 33, 34, 82
Economic co-operation potential, 67

Economic resources, Greece and
    Turkey compared, 96
Economies, *see* Trade
Enosis, 13
Esenbel, Melih, 93
Europe
    historical analysis of pressures on
        Greece and Turkey, 184–7
    inter-war league, 186
    see also Eastern Europe
European balance (1713–89), 184,
    185
European Community (EC)
    attitude to Cyprus conflict,
        219–20: as mediator, 223–6;
        calls on Turkey to withdraw
        troops, 225; variations
        between member states,
        221–2
    attitude to Greek–Turkish
        disputes, 2: before Greek
        membership, 207–10
    effect of Cyprus issue, 157, 161–3
    flexible attitude to Turkey's
        demands, 210
    impact on Greek–Turkish
        economic relations, 217–19
    increase in political power, 161
    non-involvement in members'
        disputes, 223–4
    problems posed by free
        movement of labour, 218
    see also Greece; Turkey
European Political Co-operation
    (EPC)
    advantages to Turkey of
        membership, 215
    Cyprus discussions, 220
    first meeting with Turkey, 211
    Greek participation, 210
    Greek–Turkish dispute
        discussions, 213
    ineffectiveness in Cyprus crisis,
        222
Evangelista, Matthew, 6, **140–54**
Evren, Kenan, 84, 172, 196
    visit to Cyprus, 211
Evros river incident, 19

Ford, Gerald, 166–7
Foreign policies
    and world-view of
        decision-making, 77
    Greek, 42, 46, 198–9
    objectives, 8
    Turkish, 59, 66, 199

Gorbachev, Mikhail S., 109–10,
    118–19, 140, 143, 145, 148,
    176, 196
Greece
    air defence problems, 96
    anti-terrorist measures
        inadequate, 171
    as 'weak state', 129–30
    Balkan policy in late 1970s, 194
    centres within range of Turkish
        artillery, 96
    chronology of events (1947–88),
        231–52
    defence doctrine cites Turkey as
        threat, 19
    defence policy, 75: high ratio of
        special forces, 98; military
        expenditure, 120, 121;
        increases, 100; navy and air
        force strengthened, 99; new
        policy announced (1985), 99;
        seeking autonomy, 98–9;
        total defence organisation, 99;
        weapons supply policy, 99
    defensive restructuring, 145–7;
        potential, 151
    deterrence strategy, 99–104:
        active, 103–4; value of
        Western presence, 101
    effect of 1989 election, 22
    emigrants returning from Soviet
        Union, 106n
    foreign and security policies, 46:
        in 1970s, 198–9; post-1974,
        42; contrary to other EC
        members, 224
    government attitude to Turkish
        policies, 43–5
    historical relations with Turkey,
        58–9

in EC: application for membership, 208–10; Association Agreement, 207–8; membership, 18, 45, 79, 162, 169; effect on EC mediation in Cyprus, 223; Greek–Turkish balance altered, 226; position during junta, 208

in NATO, 97: demands border guarantees, 159; leaves NATO, 17, 158, 167, 193; exercise boycotts, 18, 20, 21, 46; 'NATO plus' strategy, 98–9; refuses to approve missile deployment, 195; reintegration, 8, 41, 44, 53, 158–9, 169, 194

influences, up to Second World War, 184–7
liberation war, 12
military establishment for internal security, 97
military junta, 14: downfall, 15, 164, 193
need to encourage economy, 208
non-aggression stance, 51
nuclear weapons removed, 111
PASOK government, 18, 29, 46–9
perceived threats to security, 92
perceived vulnerability to communist influence, 176
population size as constraint, 95
power plays in 1760s, 185
pre-1974 security position, 97
quality of military potential, 100
refusal of Ozal's moves, 31
relations with Soviet Union, 187–8: pre-1939, 186; after Second World War, 190, 191, 200; after 1979, 195–6; importance to Soviet policy, 197; shipping repairs offer, 194, 195
relations with US, 114, 142, 164–81: anti-US bias, 75, 115, 166, 170–1; Bush administration, 174; improvements, 173; issues causing US concern, 181; military aid, *see* United States: military assistance; threat to US communications facilities, 49; US policy, 164–81
resumé of disputes (to 1988), 253–68
retaliation capability, 100–1
risk-taking capability, 103
security-independence trade-off, 97–8
sovereignty, 46
strategic importance to West, 112
strategic problems of geography, 96
territorial limits dispute, 14–15, 41, 43, 46, 94, 147
threatened by Turkish expansionism, 92–3
Turkish minority, 16, 63–4, 94
views of New Democracy Party, 52: on Davos process, 83
views on Turkish military deployment, 94–5
vulnerability to attack, 95
see also Strategic doctrine
Greek Orthodox Patriarchate, 120
Group of Twenty-three, 148

Haass, Richard, 172
Haig, Alexander, 169, 178
Haralampopoulos, Yannis, 18
Helsinki Conference (1986), 123
Historical background to conflict, 12–13
'Hot-line' established, 17, 20, 82

INF Treaty, 110
Inonu, Erdal, 37
Inonu, Ismet, 61
Internal balancing strategy, 98
International Court of Justice (ICJ) continental shelf dispute, 17, 38
Karamanlis's case to, 45

Index

International organisations
  anomaly of Greece's and Turkey's joint membership, 117
  concentration of military power, 130
  effect of *détente* on alliances, 141
  in linkagage politics, 75
  internal and external balancing, 141
  intra-bloc rivalry, 131–2
  system characteristics, 129
  see also European Community (EC); NATO; Warsaw Pact
International relations
  attitude to Turkish–Greek conflict, 2–3
  effect on Turkish–Greek conflict, 8–9
  see also East–West relations
Ioannidis, George, 14
Iran
  capture of US embassy, 175
  collapse of Shah's regime, 168, 169
  Turkey's relations with, 28
Iran–Iraq war, 66, 81, 111–12, 116, 224
Iraq, 28
Irmak, Sadi, 93
Isik, Hasan East, 93

Jivkov, Tudor, 113
Jordanian crisis (1970), 190

Kapsis, Yannis, 146
Karamanlis, Constantine, 15, 16, 38
  looks for non-aggression pact, 44, 45
  on Greek withdrawal from NATO, 158
  summit meetings, 55n:
    Montreux, 17, 79
  visits Balkans (1975), 194
  Washington meeting with Ecevit, 178
Kararname Decree (1964), 71n
Kerkuk–Iskenderun oil pipeline, 112
Kissinger, Henry, 161, 165, 166

Koskotas, George, 173
Kostopoulos, Sotiris, 21
Kramer, Heinz, 4, **57–72**
Kurdish issue, 9, 50, 60, 112, 172
Kyprianou, Spyros, 220
  refuses to sign draft UN agreement, 48
  support from PASOK government, 48

Laipson, Helen, 3, 6, **164–82**
Lausanne Treaty (1923), 16, 40, 41, 59, 61–2, 92, 146, 159, 186
Lebanon, 112, 116
Ledsky, Nelson, 174
Lemnos, *see* Aegean Islands
'Linkage politics', 73
  characteristics, 74–8
  Davos process, 78–85
  inner- and outer-directed, 74, 86
London Agreement (1959), 13

Macedonia, 186, 187–8
Makarios, Archbishop, 1, 14, 165, 193
Media
  influence on decision-makers, 77
  role in conflict, 70n
  role in *rapprochement*, 86
Mediterranean, 109–24
  effects of changes in East–West relations, 109–11
  Greece–Turkey–Cyprus interactions, 123
  Soviet build-up, 189–90
  strategic importance, 183
  views of Carter administration, 167–8
Meinardus, Ronald, 6, **157–8**
Mersin, 149
Middle East instability, 124
Military expenditure, 88
Military manoeuvres, 34–5
Military power, correlated with trade relations, 133
Minority rights, 16
Mitsotakis, C., 52
Mladenov, Petar, 113
Montreux Convention (1936), 16,

Index

40, 41, 62, 92, 146, 159, 184, 188, 201
Montreux summit meeting (1978), 17, 19
Moratorium agreed (1982), 47
Muslim minorities, 9, 52, 53, 54, 199
Mutual and Balanced Force Reductions (MBFR), 48

National identity issues, 58
National interests
  defining, 57
  Turkey, 59
Nationalist tension, 9
NATO (North Atlantic Treaty Organisation)
  advantages of Warsaw Pact restructuring, 145
  Brussels Declaration (1986), 148
  change in relations with Warsaw Pact, 114
  concentration of military power, 130
  Defence Review Committee disagreement, 21
  defensive restructuring, 143–4: US attitudes to, 147–8
  effect of Cyprus issue, 157, 158–60
  effect of Greek–Turkish disputes, 2
  favours negotiated settlements, 44
  Greece's role, see Greece: in NATO
  importance of SEM, 113–14, 117–19
  interest in avoiding Greek–Turkish war, 101
  lessening influence, 124
  membership of Greece and Turkey, 13
  naval superiority, 117–18
  position of Lemnos, 117
  role in Warsaw Pact attack, 97
  short-range nuclear weapons, 110, 111
  Turkey's policies linked to, 43
Naval forces
  exclusion from force-reduction mandate, 150
  Greece's offer to repair Soviet ships, 194, 195
  Montreux Convention terms, 190
  NATO and Warsaw Pact compared, 117–18
Nea Makri US base, 20
Non-aggression agreement (1978), 31
North Atlantic Treaty Organisation, see NATO
Nuclear weapons
  excluded from force-reduction mandate, 150
  INF Treaty, 110
  modernisation by NATO, 110, 111

Offence–defence balance, 142–3
Oil exploration, 2, 14–15, 16, 19–20, 32, 38, 49, 103–4
  mediation offers declined, 177
  Turkish moves, 93–94
Oil price increases, effects on international relations, 113, 134
Ottoman Empire, 185
  see also Turkey
Ozal, Turgut, 8, 19, 151, 196
  ability to make concessions doubted, 84
  accession to presidency, 8, 36–7
  actions to improve relations with Greece, 30–2
  Brussels meeting (1988), 34–6
  character, 28
  Davos meeting (1987), 2, 32–4: agreement, 20
  de-escalation of Aegean dispute, 78
  elected prime minister, 28: Papandreou's reactions, 29
  foreign policy, 66
  internal problems, 85
  international support, 28
  political style, 37, 67
  relations with Reagan administration, 170
  secret communications with Papandreou, 49

views on Greek–Turkish
    relations, 27, 29–30
  visit to Athens (1988), 34–5, 40,
    49, 51, 83–5
  visit to Cyprus, 211

Papadopoulis, Georgios, 14
Papaioannou, Ezekias, 199
Papandreou, Andreas, 8, 16
  actions taken against Turkey, 29
  attitude on Soviet relations, 195
  Brussels meeting (1988), 34–5
  Davos meeting (1987), 2, 31, 33:
    agreement, 20; pressures
    following, 84; summing-up,
    69
  decline of power, 85
  domestic concerns, 81–2
  dominance in policy-making, 78
  election, and relations with
    Reagan administration,
    170–1
  electoral defeat (1989), 21
  on Turkish troops in Cyprus, 47
  political problems, 35
  secret communications with Ozal,
    49
  seeks NATO border guarantees,
    18, 159
  suspension of American
    communications facilities, 20
  visit to Cyprus (1983), 48
  volte-face on Turkish troops in
    Cyprus, 51, 82
Papoulias, Karolos, 20, 49
Paris Treaty (1947), 16, 40, 41, 62,
    92
Penetrated systems, 74–5, 86
Perez de Cuellar, Javier, 48
Perle, Richard, 171, 172
Plastiras, Nikolaos, 13
Platias, Athanasios, 5, **91–108**
Political Committee, 33, 34, 82
Political relations, 20
Population exchanges, 12, 13
Power, balance of, 130
Pridham, Geoffrey, 4–5, **73–88**
Property rights of Greeks in
    Turkey, 16, 21, 31, 42, 53,
    217–18

Public opinion, effect on
    rapprochement, 84–5
Public relations failures, 36

Rachid, Mohammed, 173
Reagan, Ronald, 169–73, 175,
    178–9
Regime fragmentation, 76
Rogers, Bernard, 129, 178
Rogers' Agreement (1980), 34, 46,
    53, 117, 159
Romania, 144
Russian Empire, 185
  Balkans policy, 185–6
  see also Soviet Union

Saadabad Pact, 60
Search-and-rescue operations, 21, 53
Serbos, Dimitrios, 52, 56n
Sezer, Duygus, 5, **109–25**
Sirkhov, Todor, 20
Six Day War (1967), 190
Sovereignty claims, 1
  Greek, 93–4
Soviet Union, 9
  advantages of *détente*, 198
  Black Sea naval dominance, 118
  complaint against UK to UN, 188
  concentration of military power,
    130
  importance of SEM, 114
  interest in non-provocative
    defence, 143
  Mediterranean naval strength,
    118, 189–90
  overall effect of *détente*, 50
  preceived threat to Turkey, 81
  relations with Greece, 187–8:
    pre-1939, 186; post-World
    War Two, 190, 191, 200;
    post-1979, 195–6; shipping
    repairs, 194, 195
  relations with Turkey, 28, 60,
    138n, 188–9: pre-1939, 186;
    post-World War Two, 190–1;
    post-1979, 196
  strategic interests, 44
  suggests Cyprus conference, 48
  support for Cyprus
    independence, 196

Turkey's response to Gorbachev, 110
withdrawal from Afghanistan, 112
see also Superpowers
Stephanou, Constantine, 7, **207–30**
Stoforopoulos, Efthimios, 52, 56n
Strategic comparisons, 119–22
Strategic doctrine
definition, 91
development, 92
factors involved, 91–2
functions, 91
small states' problems, 105
Summit meetings, 55n
proposal, 47
see also Brussels meeting; Davos meeting; Montreux summit meeting
Superpowers
avoidance of provocation, 131
decline of system since 1974, 193
détente: effects on regional conflicts, 179; effect on relations with weak states, 141
development, 189–91
effect of international debt crisis, 202n
effect on intra-alliance conflict, 140, 141
effect on weak states, 131
interaction, 130–1
see also Soviet Union; United States
Syria, Turkey's relations with, 28, 66
Systems approach to linkage, 76

Third parties, 86
involvement in disputes, 157–63
reasons for involvement, 157
Third-world countries, trade with, 134
Tourism policy, 67
Trade
Davis meeting, 33, 81
Greek–Soviet Union, 196
Greek–Turkish, 217–18
relations, 20
Turkish policy, 30

Turkish–Soviet, 191
Turkish–United States, 172
see also European Community
Treaty of Friendship and Co-operation (1933), 60
Truman Doctrine, 189
Tsardanides, Charalambos, 7, **207–30**
Turkes, Colonel, 71n
Turkey
abolition of visas for Greek tourists, 21, 30, 66
advantages of *détente* with Greece, 67
allied bases, 116
anti-Greek riots (1955), 13
armed forces: Aegean Army, 94–5, 120; deployment, 94–5; size, 95
balance of power, 180
Balkans policy in late 1970s, 194–5
bipolycentrism, 133
chronology of events (1947–88), 231–52
defence spending, 120, 121
defensive restructuring: effect, 145–7; potential, 150–1
defining role within Europe, 124
economic problems, 28
effect of 1989 election, 22
elections (1983), 28
foreign policy, 59, 66, 199
Greek minority, 14, 16, 63, 71n; property rights, 16, 21, 31, 42, 53, 217–18
historical relations with Greece, 58–9
influences up to World War Two, 184–7
international strength compared with Soviet Union, 192
invasion of Cyprus, see Cyprus: Turkish invasion
liberalisation, 138n
limits to use of force, 60: see also Armed conflict threats
minorities in neighboring states, 62–3
Motherland Party prospects, 36–7

Turkey – *cont.*
  nationals as 'guestworkers' in Europe, 63
  need for dialogue with Greece, 68–9
  nuclear arsenal, 111
  origin of republic, 12: preserving legal base, 65–2
  perceived vulnerability to communist influence, 176
  perception of Aegean claims, 42–3
  political coalitions, 7
  population size, 95
  probable policy shifts, 37
  recognition of independent TRNC, 18–19
  relations with EC, 10, 213–14: after generals' coup, 211; attitude to mediation on Cyprus, 223; EC Association Agreement, 21, 207–8, 213–14; effect of TRNC's UDI, 211; impact of Greek membership, 209–10, 211–13; membership application, 10, 41, 54, 65, 68, 80, 122–4, 162, 213–15; responses from members, 215–17; objectives, 214–15; pre-accession period, 215–16
  relations with Soviet Union, 28, 60, 138n, 188–9: pre-1939, 186; post-World War Two, 190–1; post-1979, 196; Soviet intolerance of increasing autonomy, 197
  relations with Syria, 28, 66
  relations with the United States, 67–8: arms embargo, 160, 165–6, 167, 168; 227n; bases, 169; Bush administration, 174; effect of Reagan's election, 169–70; issues causing US concern, 181; military aid, 161, 171; missiles withdrawn, 190; policy of US, 164–81
  response to Gorbachev, 110
  resumé of disputes (to 1988), 253–68
  sovereignty issues, 60
  strategic importance, 112, 183
  territorial integrity, 60, 61
  territory excluded from force-reduction talks, 149–50
  threats perceived by Greece, 93
  treaty of friendship with Germany, 189
  vetoes Greece's re-entry into NATO, 158–9
  westernisation, 64–5
  see also EC–Turkey Association Agreement
Turkish dissidents in Greece, 42
Turkiye Petrolleri Anonim Ortakligi, 14
Turkmen, Ilter, 18

Ulusu, Bulent, 18
United Nations
  Declaration of the Economic Rights and Duties of States (1974), 204n
  Greece seeks sanctions against Turkey, 135
  growth in membership, 135
  introduces new negotiating procedures, 50
  law of the sea conferences, 62
  reduction in US contributions, 135–6
  Secretary-General's talks on Cyprus, 224, 225, 227
  Security Council: continental shelf dispute, 16–17; Karamanlis takes case to, 45
  Soviet use of, on Cyprus question, 193–4
United States
  as penetrating agent, 75
  bases: changing views on needs, 114–15; in Greece, 81; withdrawal of missiles from Turkey, 137–8n
  'Camp David' approach, 45

concentration of military power, 130
Congress/Executive policy disagreements, 169–81
DECA negotiations, 47
dominant foreign-policy issues, 175
effect of Cyprus issue, 160–1, 165–6
end of trade hegemony, 133
ethnic interest in Greek–Turkish disputes, 164
humanitarian involvement in Cyprus, 166
implications of NATO restructuring, 145
in favour of negotiated settlements, 44
involvement in Aegean disputes, 161
military assistance to Greece and Turkey, 13, 41, 45, 68, 115–16, 161, 168–9, 180: amounts, 180; calls for cuts, 116; embargo on arms to Turkey, 165–6, 167–8, 180
overall effect of *détente*, 50
policy on regional conflicts, 117–9
probable reduced presence in Europe, 177
protectionist influences, 173
receptiveness to Gorbachev's reforms, 140
reduction in UN contributions, 135–6
relations with Greece, *see* Greece: relations with United States
relations with Turkey; *see* Turkey: relations with United States
role in attack by Warsaw Pact, 97
Special Cyprus Co-ordinator appointed, 174
'unilateralist' foreign policy, 135
see also Superpowers
Utrecht, Treaty of (1713), 184

Varlik Vergisi, 13
Vassiliou, George, 11n, 53, 120, 196, 199
election, 50
Venizelos, Eleftherios, 13, 22, 40, 60
Vienna Conference (1989), 123

Warsaw Pact
Budapest Communiqué (1986), 148
change in relations with NATO, 114
concentration of military power, 130
defensive restructuring, 143–4: implications, 144–5
importance of SEM, 114, 117–19
lessening power, 124
Weak states, 129
importance of strong external forces, 129
Weapons
modernisation, 119
offence–defence balance, 143

Yom Kippur War (1973), 190
Yugoslavia, 144

Zurich Agreement (1959), 13